John L. Liechty
Integrated Financial Planning Solutions
1403 Ashton Court
Goshen, IN 46526

MAY 2010

Praise for

The RIA's Compliance Solution Book
Answers for the Critical Questions
by Elayne Robertson Demby, JD

"A great book. It's extremely valuable to both the experienced and soon-to-be adviser. If I'd had it when I was setting up my RIA firm, it would have saved me hundreds of dollars in legal fees. Now, as an experienced adviser, *The RIA's Compliance Solution Book* can save me thousands in fees. Demby's book is an important tool to preventing many compliance problems and heading off potential noncompliance fines. I learned a lot while reading it. The Q&A format is great and very easy to read. Overall, a very useful, all-in-one guide book."

JEFFREY B. BROADHURST, MBA, CFA
Financial Advisor and President of Broadhurst Financial Advisors, Inc.

"If someone could define all those murky terms regulators like to use and put them in one place with a clear outline of all the regulatory issues advisers must address along with a roadmap for getting all the answers into an ADV, that resource would look a lot like *The RIA's Compliance Solution Book*."

DAVID J. DRUCKER, MBA, CFP
President, Drucker Knowledge Systems
Coauthor, *Virtual-Office Tools for a High-Margin Practice*

"This book isn't just for RIAs—every business journalist should have a copy! It's really helping me understand Form ADV."

RICHARD J. KORETO
Editor in Chief
Wealth Manager and *Advising Boomers* magazines

The RIA's Compliance Solution Book

Also available from Bloomberg Press

Building a High-End Financial Services Practice
by Cliff Oberlin and Jill Powers

The Financial Services Marketing Handbook
by Evelyn Ehrlich and Duke Fanelli

Practice Made Perfect
by Mark C. Tibergien and Rebecca Pomering

Virtual-Office Tools for a High-Margin Practice
by David J. Drucker and Joel P. Bruckenstein

The New Fiduciary Standard
by Tim Hatton, CFP, CIMA, AIF
In cooperation with the Foundation for Fiduciary Studies

Making Referral Relationships Pay
by Thomas Grady

Deena Katz on Practice Management
by Deena B. Katz

Deena Katz's Tools and Templates for Your Practice
by Deena B. Katz

*Getting Started as a Financial Planner:
Revised and Updated Edition*
by Jeffrey H. Rattiner

———

A complete list of our titles is available at
www.bloomberg.com/books

The RIA's Compliance Solution Book

Answers for the Critical Questions

Elayne Robertson Demby, JD

BLOOMBERG PRESS

NEW YORK

First edition published 2006
1 3 5 7 9 10 8 6 4 2

Library of Congress Cataloging-in-Publication Data

Demby, Elayne Robertson
    The RIA's compliance solution book : answers for the critical questions / Elayne Robertson Demby. -- 1st ed.
        p. cm.
    Summary: "A handbook for registered investment advisers that not only explains how regulations affect their firms, but also provides step by step directions on what they need to do to comply with them"--Provided by publisher.
    Includes index.
    ISBN 1-57660-192-7 (alk. paper)
    1. Investment advisors--Legal status, laws, etc.--United States. 2. Investment advisors--Licenses--United States. 3. Investments--Law and legislation--United States. I. Title

KF1072.D46 2006
346.73'0926--dc22   2006009549

Acquired by Jared Kieling
Edited by Mary Ann McGuigan

To Glenn, Evan, and Charlotte

Contents

ACKNOWLEDGMENTS   ix

INTRODUCTION   xi

1 Terms and Acronyms   1

2 Federal and State Laws and Other Regulations   19

3 RIA Registration: What It Means, How It's Done   27

4 The Nuts and Bolts of Form ADV   37

5 How to Complete Form ADV Part 1   51

6 How to Complete Form ADV Part 2   65

7 RIA Compliance Programs and Codes of Ethics   73

8 Investment Recommendations and Fiduciary Obligations   83

9 Advisory Contracts and Fees   89

10 Custody of Customer Accounts   95

11 Selecting Brokers and Executing Trades   101

12 Personal Securities Trading and Reporting   109

13 Voting Client Proxies   117

14 Record-Keeping Requirements   123

15 Advertising and Client Communications   129

16 Referrals   139

17 ERISA Plans   147

18 Soft Dollars   161

19 Protecting Clients' Privacy   171

20 Money Laundering   185

21 Supervising Employees   191

22 SEC Examinations and Enforcement Actions   195

APPENDIX A: Contact Information for the SEC and
Securities Regulators   205

APPENDIX B: Form ADV   216

APPENDIX C: Adviser Designation Requirements   262

CONTINUING EDUCATION EXAM for
CFP Continuing Education Credit and PACE Recertification Credit   281

INDEX   289

Acknowledgments

I WOULD LIKE TO THANK Bloomberg Press for giving me the opportunity to write this book. In particular, my thanks go to Robert Casey for recommending me for the project. Thanks also to Jared Kieling for his enthusiasm for and support of my vision and concept for the work and to Mary Ann McGuigan and Tracy Tait for guiding me through the publishing and editorial processes.

I thank my husband, Glenn Demby, for his encouragement and my parents, Marion and Charles Robertson, for sacrificing for years to send me to college, graduate school, and law school. My children, Charlotte and Evan Demby, also deserve a thank you for being good when Mommy had to work, as does Sayuri Aguillon for entertaining Charlotte and Evan so that I could work.

Introduction

IN THE PAST DECADE, the Securities and Exchange Commission has measurably increased the breadth and scope of investment adviser compliance requirements. Mushrooming federal rules and regulations have made it increasingly difficult for investment advisers to keep their practices in compliance. New SEC rules put in place since 2001 include requiring registered investment advisers to have written compliance procedures and written rules of ethics. The SEC also imposed new rules on personal securities trading by firm personnel who are access persons.

Layering on new rules and regulations increases the complexity of compliance and places a burden on investment advisers to stay informed about what they must do or not do to avoid running afoul of the rules. For example, if an investment adviser wants to send a quick e-mail to several clients, the adviser must ascertain whether or not the content of the e-mail would violate the advertising rules set out in the Investment Advisers Act of 1940. Even trading a stock for an adviser's personal account is now subject to a myriad of new rules.

The RIA's Compliance Solution Book fills the adviser's need for a convenient desk reference, addressing the rules and regulations under the Investment Advisers Act of 1940. This book explains in plain English the federal securities laws, rules, and regulations for investment advisers who are registered with the SEC. It is a hands-on reference manual for investment advisers working with individual clients. It includes instructions on how to fill out Form ADV and how to comply with federal rules when advertising, executing trades, voting proxies, or any other task the adviser may encounter in the day-to-day management of the firm. Issues relating to retirement and ERISA plan issues are also discussed in the context of working with individual clients.

The RIA's Compliance Solution Book is designed to help registered investment advisers comply with their legal obligations under the Investment Advisers Act of 1940 when they work with individual clients. The book provides only general guidance, however, to serve as a reference. No book can take the place of qualified legal advice from an attorney experienced in securities law compliance. More complex issues may need to be referred to a competent attorney.

Information is presented in a question-and-answer format, and individual questions can be accessed easily. Related information is cross-referenced to help direct advisers to the complete answers for their questions.

The RIA's Compliance Solution Book

1 | Terms and Acronyms

- ◆ Terms Defined in the Investment Advisers Act
- ◆ Defining an Investment Adviser
- ◆ Terms Used on Form ADV
- ◆ Acronyms

1

The regulation of investment advisers is a complex topic. To make sense of it, advisers will find it helpful to become familiar with a number of standardized terms and acronyms. For example, the Investment Advisers Act of 1940—the main statute regulating investment advisers—defines twenty-seven words and phrases, and many of the rules promulgated under the act employ terms of their own. Working with Form ADV and its accompanying schedules and disclosure reporting pages, which investment advisers must use in filling out or revising their forms, involves no fewer than thirty-five defined words and phrases.

Gathered and defined here for convenient reference are all the terms and acronyms that are used throughout the book. Terms

---

FIGURE 1.1 **Directory of Defined Terms**

adviser	**1.3**	employee	**1.20**
Advisers Act of 1940	**1.4**	enjoined	**1.20**
advisory affiliate	**1.20**	Employee Retirement Income	
annual updating amendment	**1.20**	Security Act of 1974 (ERISA)	**1.21**
bank	**1.17**	felony	**1.20**
certified financial planner (CFP)	**1.21**	foreign financial regulatory	
certified public accountant (CPA)	**1.21**	authority	**1.20**
charged	**1.20**	Form ADV	**3.14**
chartered financial analyst (CFA)	**1.21**	found	**1.20**
chartered financial consultant (ChFC)		government entity	**1.20**
	1.21	high-net-worth individual	**1.20**
chartered life underwriter (CLU)	**1.21**	home state	**1.20**
chief compliance officer (CCO)	**1.21**	impersonal investment advice	**1.20**
client	**1.20**	in the business of providing advice	
compensation	**1.15**	or of issuing analysis or reports	
control	**1.20**	on securities	**1.13**
custody	**1.20**	investment adviser	**1.6**
discretionary authority	**1.20**		

defined specifically as they apply in this book are defined first, followed by terms and definitions under the Investment Advisers Act and terms and definitions used on Form ADV. Terms that are used in only one chapter are defined in that chapter and, where necessary, cross-referenced. The meanings of various acronyms are given in question 1.21.

Defined Terms

The terms in figure 1.1 are used throughout this book and defined here in chapter 1.

Investment Adviser Registration Depository system (IARD)	**1.21**	principal place of business	**1.20**
investment related	**1.20**	proceedings	**1.20**
involved	**1.20**	registered financial consultant (RFC)	**1.21**
management persons	**1.20**	registered investment adviser (RIA)	**1.1; 1.21**
managing agent	**1.20**	related person	**1.20**
minor rule violation	**1.20**	Securities Industry Association (SIA)	**1.21**
misdemeanor	**1.20**	security	**1.18**
National Association of Securities Dealers (NASD) CRD	**1.20; 1.21**	self-regulatory organization	**1.20**
		solely incidental	**1.8**
New York Stock Exchange (NYSE)	**1.21**	sponsor	**1.20**
nonresident	**1.20**	state securities authorities	**1.20**
North American Securities Administrators Association (NASAA)	**1.21**	supervised person	**1.19**
		United States Securities and Exchange Commission (SEC)	**1.2**
notice filing	**1.20**	wrap fee program	**1.20**
order	**1.20**		
performance-based fee	**1.20**		
person	**1.20**		

Key Terms in This Book

1.1   What is a registered investment adviser?

A registered investment adviser (RIA) is an investment adviser as defined under the Investment Advisers Act of 1940 (see question 1.6 and figure 1.1), who is registered with the SEC (see question 1.2) or a state securities regulatory authority (see question 1.20).

1.2   What is the Securities and Exchange Commission (SEC)?

The Securities and Exchange Commission (SEC) is the federal body in charge of registering, examining, and regulating investment advisers. The primary mission of the SEC is to protect investors and maintain the integrity of the securities markets.

1.3   What is an adviser?

An adviser is a "registered investment adviser" (see question 1.1) who provides investment advice and may be either an individual adviser or an advisory firm. For the purposes of this book, an adviser specifically refers to a registered investment adviser who is registered with the SEC.

1.4   What is the Advisers Act?

The Advisers Act is the Investment Advisers Act of 1940 as described in question 2.2.

Terms Defined in the Investment Advisers Act

1.5   Are there any terms in the Investment Advisers Act of which advisers need to be aware?

The Investment Advisers Act of 1940 defines twenty-seven terms. Not all are relevant to the scope of this book. The terms included here from the Advisers Act are used throughout this book.

Definition of Investment Adviser

1.6   How does the Advisers Act define investment adviser?

An investment adviser is any person who engages in the business

---

FIGURE 1.2   **Defining an Investment Adviser**

PRACTITIONERS ARE investment advisers if they advise others regarding the purchase or sale of securities or issue reports and analysis on securities, and are not

- teachers, lawyers, accountants, or engineers whose advice is given only occasionally and is solely incidental to their profession
- brokers or dealers and the investment advice they provide is solely incidental to their profession
- registered representatives of a broker-dealer, acting within the scope of their employment with the brokerage firm and do not have an independent financial-planning practice
- publishers of a bona fide newspaper, news magazine, or business or financial publication of general and regular circulation
- persons who give investment advice only on U.S. government obligations
- banks

---

of advising others for compensation, either directly or through publications or writings, as to the value of securities or as to the advisability of investing in, purchasing, or selling securities, or who, for compensation and as part of a regular business, issues or promulgates analyses or reports concerning securities.

1.7   Are lawyers, accountants, engineers, or teachers investment advisers?

Lawyers, accountants, engineers, or teachers who occasionally give advice "solely incidental" to the practice of their professions are not investment advisers (see question 1.8). However, lawyers, accountants, engineers, or teachers who give advice through an independent business are investment advisers.

To avoid being considered investment advisers, teachers must teach courses on investment advisory methods at accredited schools as part of a curriculum or with a content that demonstrates that the course's purpose is education. In other words, the purpose cannot be to provide investment advice for a fee under the guise of education.

1.8   When is advice "solely incidental" to the normal professional activities of a lawyer, accountant, engineer, or teacher?

According to the SEC, advice is solely incidental to normal professional activities if

a. the professionals do not hold themselves out to the public as providing investment advice

b. the investment advisory services are connected with and reasonably related to the provision of primary professional services

c. any fee charged for investment advisory services is based on the same factors as those used to develop fees for primary professional services

1.9   Are brokers, dealers, or registered representatives investment advisers?

Brokers or dealers whose provision of investment advice is solely incidental to their businesses as brokers or dealers and who receive no special compensation for investment advice are not investment advisers.

Under certain circumstances, a broker-dealer's registered representatives are also excluded from the definition of investment adviser. To be excluded from the definition, registered representatives providing advisory services must be acting within the scope of their employment with the brokerage firm, with the knowledge and consent of the firm, and fully subject to its control. Registered representatives with independent financial planning or other advisory businesses that are not subject to the brokerage firm's control cannot rely on the broker-dealer exclusion and are investment advisers.

The SEC staff takes the position that investment advice offered as part of an overall financial plan for a client is not solely incidental to the brokerage business. However, investment advice on individual securities is considered to be solely incidental to the business.

1.10 Are publishers investment advisers?

Publishers of bona fide newspapers, news magazines, or business or financial publications of general and regular circulation are not investment advisers.

1.11 Are persons who give advice with respect to U.S. government obligations investment advisers?

Persons whose advice, analyses, or reports relate to no securities other than securities that are direct obligations of or obligations guaranteed as to principal or interest by the United States or securities issued or guaranteed by corporations in which the United States has a direct or indirect interest and which are designated by the Secretary of the Treasury are not investment advisers.

1.12 Are banks investment advisers?

Banks or bank holding companies as defined in the Bank Holding Company Act of 1956 that are not investment companies are excluded from the definition of investment adviser. However, to the extent that it acts as an investment adviser to a registered investment company, any bank or bank holding company is an investment adviser. If the bank or bank holding company provides advisory services only through a separately identifiable department or division, then that department or division is an investment adviser but the bank as a whole is not.

1.13 How does an adviser determine whether he is "in the business of providing advice or of issuing analysis or reports on securities"?

According to the SEC, the giving of investment advice need not be the person's principal business for that person to be considered an investment adviser; nor is the frequency of giving advice a determination. If, however, giving investment advice constitutes a business activity occurring with some regularity, then one is "in the business." People who hold themselves out as investment advisers or as being in the business of providing investment advice and who receive separate compensation for such investment advice are "in the business."

1.14   When is an adviser considered to be providing advice?

Generally, anytime advisers make comments regarding clients' investments and savings, they are giving advice, even if that advice does not relate to a specific course of investment or investment strategy.

1.15   When is the advice, analysis, or report considered to be "for compensation"?

Anytime advisers receive any economic benefit from any source, they are compensated. Receiving commissions or fees from the sales of securities, insurance products, or any other investment product constitutes "compensation," as does receiving separate fees for financial planning.

1.16   Does the definition of investment adviser differ under state securities laws?

Securities laws in most states define investment adviser generally the same way the Advisers Act does. However, variations do exist. For example, a state might exclude from the definition an adviser who only services financial or institutional investors. Likewise, a state's definition of investment adviser may be broad enough to include a financial planner who may not meet the definition of investment adviser under the Advisers Act. Advisers should consult the state laws of every state in which they conduct business.

Other Advisers Act Definitions

1.17   How does the Advisers Act define a bank?

A bank is
   a. any banking institution organized under U.S. law;
   b. a member bank of the Federal Reserve System;
   c. any other banking institution or trust company, whether or not incorporated, doing business under the laws of any state or the United States, for which a substantial portion of the business consists of receiving deposits or exercising fiduciary powers similar to those of national banks, and which is supervised and examined by state or federal authorities having supervision over banks;

d. a receiver, conservator, or other liquidating agent of any of the institutions listed in (a.), (b.), or (c.).

1.18 What is a security under the Advisers Act?

A security is any

    a. note;

    b. stock;

    c. Treasury stock;

    d. security future;

    e. bond;

    f. debenture;

    g. evidence of indebtedness;

    h. certificate of interest or participation in any profit-sharing agreement;

    i. collateral-trust certificate;

    j. preorganization certificate or subscription;

    k. transferable share;

    l. investment contract;

    m. voting-trust certificate;

    n. certificate of deposit for a security;

    o. fractional undivided interest in oil, gas, or other mineral rights;

    p. any put, call, straddle, option, or privilege entered into on a national securities exchange relating to foreign currency;

    q. in general, any interest or instrument commonly known as a "security," or any certificate of interest or participation in, temporary or interim certificate for, receipt for, guaranty of, or warrant or right to subscribe to or purchase any of the foregoing.

1.19 What is a supervised person?

A supervised person is any partner, officer, director (or other person occupying a similar status or performing similar functions), or employee of an investment adviser, or other person who provides investment advice on behalf of the investment adviser and is subject to the supervision and control of the investment adviser.

Terms Used on Form ADV

1.20 Are there any definitions an adviser needs to know when filling out or amending Form ADV?
Form ADV defines thirty-five terms. These definitions are used when filling out Form ADV Parts 1 and 2 and all accompanying schedules and disclosure reporting pages. Form ADV definitions are used primarily in chapters 4, 5, and 6.

Advisory affiliate: Advisory affiliates are an adviser's or an advisory firm's (a) officers, partners, or directors (or any person performing similar functions); (b) all persons directly or indirectly "controlling" or "controlled" by the adviser; and (c) all of the adviser's current "employees" other than employees performing only clerical, administrative, support or similar functions.

If the adviser is a "separately identifiable department or division" of a bank, advisory affiliates are (a) all of the bank's employees who perform investment advisory activities (other than clerical or administrative employees); (b) all persons designated by the bank's board of directors as responsible for day-to-day conduct of the investment advisory activities (including supervising "employees" who perform investment advisory services); (c) all persons who directly or indirectly control the bank, and all persons whom the adviser controls in connection with the investment advisory activities; and (d) all other persons who directly manage any of the adviser's investment advisory activities (including directing, supervising, or performing advisory activities), and all persons whom the advisor controls in connection with those management functions.

Annual updating amendment: Within 90 days after a firm's fiscal year ends, the adviser must file an annual updating amendment, which is an amendment to the firm's Form ADV, reaffirming the eligibility information of Item 2, Part 1A of Form ADV and updating responses to any other items on which the information is no longer accurate. The term "annual updating amendment" is used in the general instructions to Form ADV, the Part 1A instructions, and in the introductory text of Item 2.

Charged: When an adviser is charged, it means he is accused of a crime in a formal complaint, information, or indictment (or the equivalent of a formal charge). The term "charged" is used in Part 1A, Item 11, and in the disclosure reporting pages (see question 5.42).

Client: Client means a firm's investment advisory client. This group includes clients from which the firm receives no compensation, such as family members. If the firm provides other services, such as accounting, then clients who do not receive investment advisory services are excluded from the term "client." The term client is used throughout Form ADV and Form ADV-W.

Control: Control means the power, directly or indirectly, to direct the management or policies of a person, whether through ownership of securities, by contract, or otherwise. Firm officers, partners, or directors who exercise executive responsibility (or persons having similar status or functions) are presumed to control the firm. A person is presumed to control a corporation if the person (a) directly or indirectly has the right to vote 25 percent or more of a class of the corporation's voting securities; or (b) has the power to sell or direct the sale of 25 percent or more of a class of the corporation's voting securities.

A person is presumed to control a partnership if the person has the right to receive upon dissolution, or has contributed 25 percent or more of the capital of the partnership.

A person is presumed to control a limited liability company (LLC) if the person (a) directly or indirectly has the right to vote 25 percent or more of a class of the interests of the LLC; (b) has the right to receive upon dissolution or has contributed 25 percent or more of the capital of the LLC; or (c) is an elected manager of the LLC. A person is presumed to control a trust if the person is a trustee or "managing agent" of the trust.

The term "control" is used in the general instructions to Form ADV, the Part 1A instructions; Items 2, 7, 10, 11, 12; Schedules A, B, C, D; and the disclosure reporting pages (see question 5.42).

Custody: A firm has custody of client funds or securities if it directly or indirectly holds them, has authority to obtain possession of them, or has the ability to appropriate them. A firm has custody if it has a general power of attorney over a client's account or has signatory power over a client's checking account. The term "custody" is used in Part 1A, Item 9 and in Part 1B, Item 2.

Discretionary authority: A firm has discretionary authority if it has the authority to decide which securities to purchase and sell on behalf of a client. A firm also has discretionary authority if it has the authority to decide which investment advisers to retain on behalf of the client. The term "discretionary authority" is used in the Part 1A instructions and in Items 1, 5, 7, and 11.

Employee: An employee is anyone working for the firm including independent contractors who perform advisory functions for the firm. The term "employee" is used in the Part 1A instructions and in Items 1, 5, 7, and 11.

Enjoined: An adviser is enjoined when the firm, its employees, or its advisory affiliates are subjected to a mandatory injunction, prohibitory injunction, preliminary injunction, or a temporary restraining order. The term "enjoined" is used in Part 1A, Item 11, and in the disclosure reporting pages (see question 5.42).

Felony: If a jurisdiction does not differentiate between a felony and a misdemeanor, a felony is an offense punishable by a sentence of at least 1 year imprisonment and/or a fine of at least $1,000. The term "felony" is used in Part 1A, Item 11, and in the disclosure reporting pages (see question 5.42).

Foreign financial regulatory authority: A foreign financial regulatory authority is either

a. a foreign securities authority;

b. another governmental body or foreign equivalent of a self-regulatory organization empowered by a foreign government to administer or enforce its laws relating to the regulation of investment-related activities; or

c. a foreign membership organization, a function of which is to regulate the participation of its members in the activities listed above.

The term "foreign financial regulatory authority" is used in Part 1A, Items 1 and 11, and in the disclosure reporting pages (see question 5.42).

Found: Adverse final actions, including consent decrees in which the respondent has neither admitted nor denied the finds, but does not include agreements, deficiency letters, examination reports, memoranda of understanding, letters of caution, admonishments, and similar informal resolutions of matters. The term "found" is used in Part 1A, Item 11 and in Part 1B, Item 2.

Government entity: A government entity is any state or political subdivision of a state, including

   a. any agency, authority, or instrumentality of the state or political subdivision;

   b. a plan or pool of assets controlled by the state or political subdivision or any agency, authority, or instrumentality thereof; and

   c. any officer, agent, or employee of the state or political subdivision or any agency, authority, or instrumentality thereof, acting in their official capacity.

The term "government entity" is used in Part 1A, Item 5.

High-net-worth individual: A high-net-worth individual is an individual with at least $750,000 in assets managed by the adviser, or whose net worth the adviser's firm reasonably believes exceeds $1.5 million, or who is a qualified purchaser, as defined in Section 2(a)(51)(a) of the Investment Company Act of 1940. The net worth of an individual includes assets held jointly with a spouse. The term "high-net-worth individual" is used in Part 1A, Item 5.

Home state: An adviser's home state is the state where a state-registered firm maintains its principal office and place of business. The term "home state" is used in the Part 1B instructions.

Impersonal investment advice: Impersonal investment advice is an investment advisory service that does not purport to meet the objectives or needs of specific individuals or accounts. The term "impersonal investment advice" is used in Part 1A.

Investment related: Something is investment related if it is an activity that pertains to securities, commodities, banking, insurance, or real estate (including but not limited to acting as or being associated with an investment adviser, broker-dealer, municipal securities dealer, government securities broker or dealer, issuer, investment company, futures sponsor, bank, or savings association). The term "investment related" is used in Part 1A, Item 11; the disclosure reporting pages (see question 5.42); and Part 1B, Item 2.

Involved: Someone is involved if he is engaging in any act or omission, aiding, abetting, counseling, commanding, inducing, conspiring with, or failing reasonably to supervise another in doing an act. The term "involved" is used in Part 1A, Item 11.

Management persons: A management person is anyone with the power to exercise, directly or indirectly, a controlling influence over the firm's management or policies, or to determine the general investment advice given to the firm's clients. Generally, the following are management persons:

a. The firm's principal executive officers, such as the chief executive officer, chief financial officer, chief operations officer, chief legal officer, and chief compliance officer, directors, general partners, trustees, and other individuals with similar status or performing similar functions;

b. Members of the firm's investment committee or group that determines general investment advice given to clients; and

c. If the firm does not have an investment committee, the individuals who determine general investment advice provided to clients, provided that if there are more than five people, the firm can limit this to supervisors.

The term "management persons" is used in Part 1B, Item 2.

Managing agent: An investment adviser's managing agent is any person, including a trustee, who directs or manages, or participates in directing or managing the affairs of any unincorporated organization or association that is not a partnership. The term "managing agent" is used in the general instructions to Form ADV and on Form ADV-NR.

Minor rule violation: A minor rule violation is a violation of a self-regulatory organization's rule that has been designated as minor by the SEC. Generally, rules are designated as minor if the imposed sanction is $2,500 or less and if the sanctioned person does not contest. The term "minor rule violation" is used in Part 1A, Item 11.

Misdemeanor: In jurisdictions that do not differentiate between a felony and a misdemeanor, a misdemeanor is an offense punishable by a sentence of less than 1 year imprisonment and/or a fine of less than $1,000. Special court martial is also a misdemeanor. The term "misdemeanor" is used in the general instructions to Form ADV, Part 1A, Item 11, and in the disclosure reporting pages (see question 5.42).

NASD CRD or CRD: These are abbreviations for the Web Central Registration Depository system operated by the NASD for the registration of broker-dealers and broker-dealer representatives. These acronyms are used in Part 1A, Item 1, and Form ADV-W, Item 1.

Nonresident: A nonresident is

a. an individual who resides in any place not subject to the jurisdiction of the United States

b. a corporation incorporated in and having its principal office and place of business in any place not subject to the jurisdiction of the United States

c. a partnership or other unincorporated organization or association that has its principal office and place of business in any place not subject to the jurisdiction of the United States

The term "nonresident" is used in the general instructions to Form ADV and on Form ADV-NR.

Notice filing: If required by state securities authorities, a notice filing is a filing with a state securities authority wherein SEC-registered advisers provide to these authorities copies of documents filed with the SEC. The term "notice filing" is used in the general instructions to Form ADV and on Form ADV-NR.

Order: An order is a written directive issued pursuant to statutory authority and procedures, including an order of denial exemption, suspension, or revocation. Unless included in an order, the order does not include special stipulations, undertakings, or agreements relating to payments, limitations on activity, or other restrictions. The term "order" is used in Part 1A, Items 2 and 11; Schedule D; and the disclosure reporting pages (see question 5.42).

Performance-based fee: A performance-based fee is an investment advisory fee which is based on a share of capital gains on, or capital appreciation of, client assets. A fee that is based on a percentage of assets managed is not a performance-based fee. The term "performance-based fee" is used in Part 1A, Item 5.

Person: A person is

a. a natural person, that is, an individual; or

b. a company, including any partnership, corporation, trust, limited liability company, limited liability partnership, or other organization.

The term "person" is used throughout Form ADV and Form ADV-W.

Principal place of business: An adviser's principal place of business or principal office and place of business is the firm's executive office from which officers, partners, or managers direct, control, and coordinate the firm's activities. The term "principal place of business" or "principal office and place of business" is used in the Part 1A instructions and Items 1 and 2; Schedule D; and Form ADV-W, Item 1.

Proceedings: Proceedings are

a. a formal administrative or civil action initiated by a governmental agency, self-regulatory organization, or foreign financial regulatory authority;

b. a felony criminal indictment or information, or the equivalent formal charge; or

c. a misdemeanor, criminal information, or equivalent formal charge.

A proceeding does not include other civil litigation, investigations, arrests, or similar charges effected in the absence of a formal criminal indictment or information, or equivalent formal charge. The term "proceedings" is used in Part 1A, Item 11; the disclosure reporting pages (see question 5.42); and Part 1B, Item 2.

Related person: A related person is any advisory affiliate or any person that is under common control with an advisory firm. The term "related person" is used in Part 1A, Items 7, 8, and 9; Schedule D; and Form ADV-W, Item 3.

Self-regulatory organization: A self-regulatory organization (SRO) is any national securities or commodities exchange, registered securities association, or registered clearing agency, including the Chicago Board of Trade, NASD, and the New York Stock Exchange. The term "self-regulatory organization" is used in Part 1A, Item 11; the disclosure reporting pages (see question 5.42); and Part 1B, Item 2.

Sponsor: A sponsor is a sponsor of a wrap fee program who sponsors, organizes, or administers the program or selects or provides advice to clients regarding the selection of other investment advisers in the program. The term "sponsor" is used in Part 1A, Item 5, and Schedule D.

State securities authority: A state securities authority is the securities commission or any agency or office performing similar functions in any state, the District of Columbia, Puerto Rico, Virgin Islands, or other possession of the United States. The term "state securities authority" is used throughout Form ADV.

Wrap fee program: A wrap fee program is any advisory program under which a specified fee or fees not based directly upon transactions in a client's account is charged for investment advisory services, which may include portfolio management, advice concerning the selection of other investment advisers, and the execution of client transactions. The term "wrap fee program" is used in Part 1, Item 5.

Acronyms

1.21 What acronyms are commonly used in the advisory profession?

The financial-services industry is rife with acronyms. The following acronyms are encountered most often.

CCO: chief compliance officer. See chapter 7.

CFA: chartered financial analyst. This is a designation awarded by the CFA Institute.

CFP: certified financial planner. This designation is awarded by the CFP Board.

ChFC: chartered financial consultant. This educational designation is granted by the American College in Bryn Mawr, PA.

CLU: chartered life underwriter. This educational designation is granted by the American College in Bryn Mawr, PA.

CPA: certified public accountant. This is a designation awarded to accountants after finishing a prescribed course of study and experience.

ERISA: Employee Retirement Income Security Act of 1974. This federal statute regulates employee benefit plans. See chapter 17.

IARD: Investment Adviser Registration Depository system. Administered by the NASD, the IARD is responsible for the electronic filing of Form ADV. See chapter 4.

NASAA: North American Securities Administrators Association. This organization of the fifty state securities agencies is responsible for investor protection. It promotes model codes and guidelines for individual states.

NASD: National Association of Securities Dealers. Subject to SEC oversight, NASD is a self-regulatory organization with responsibility for the Nasdaq Stock Market and the over-the-counter securities market.

NYSE: New York Stock Exchange

RFC: registered financial consultant. This designation is awarded by the International Association of Registered Financial Consultants.

RIA: registered investment adviser, who is registered with the SEC or with a state

SEC: United States Securities and Exchange Commission. This federal regulatory agency has responsibility for administering federal securities laws. The SEC also regulates firms engaged in the purchase or sale of securities, people who provide investment advice, and investment companies.

SIA: Securities Industry Association, a trade association of member securities firms

---

Note: See appendix C for a detailed chart of adviser designations and requirements.

2 | Federal and State Laws and Other Regulations

- ◆ Investment Advisers Act of 1940
- ◆ 1933 Securities and Exchange Act
- ◆ Securities and Exchange Act of 1934
- ◆ Investment Company Act of 1940
- ◆ Sarbanes-Oxley Act of 2002
- ◆ Employee Retirement Income Security Act of 1974 (ERISA)
- ◆ State Laws
- ◆ SEC Registration

The primary federal law regulating investment advisers is the Investment Advisers Act of 1940. Other federal laws that advisers need to be cognizant of in the course of their practice include the 1933 Securities and Exchange Act, the Securities and Exchange Act of 1934, and the Investment Company Act of 1940.

Additionally, even advisers registered with the SEC have to comply with a number of state laws and regulations. States, the District of Columbia, Puerto Rico, and Guam regulate securities through "blue sky laws." These laws are administered by state securities departments. State statutes and common-law principles governing contracts, trusts, and agency may apply as well.

All investment advisers, including those registered with the SEC, should contact state securities regulatory authorities in every state they do business in to discuss registration, licensing, bonding, notice, and other requirements. Advisers should contact the North American Securities Administrators Association (www.nasaa.org) for a list of contacts of state securities regulators.

Laws Governing Advisers

2.1   What are the relevant laws an adviser should know about in an advisory practice?
Investment advisers are regulated under a number of state and federal laws as well as through rules and regulations of self-regulatory organizations and private associations.

Federal Laws
2.2   What is the Investment Advisers Act of 1940?
Also known as the Advisers Act, the Investment Advisers Act of 1940 regulates advisers in a number of substantive areas, including the following:

   a. **Registration requirements.** Unless exempted from doing so, investment advisers must register either with a state securities regulatory agency or with the SEC. Larger investment advisers register with the SEC, smaller investment advisers with the states.

b. Disclosure requirements. Investment advisers are required to disclose certain information to clients and prospective clients. For example, investment advisers must disclose to clients all potential conflicts of interest.

c. Restrictions on investment adviser business practices. The Advisers Act specifically restricts certain types of business practices—such as charging performance fees or entering into contracts without a nonassignment clause—and certain types of trading transactions.

d. Antifraud provisions. Section 206 of the Advisers Act holds advisers to certain fiduciary standards when dealing with clients and prospective clients.

e. Inspections and enforcement. The Advisers Act empowers the SEC to conduct inspections and to enforce the act to prevent misconduct or fraud. The Investment Advisers Act of 1940 is the central piece of legislation regulating registered investment advisers who work with individual clients.

2.3   What is the 1933 Securities and Exchange Act?

Often referred to as the "truth in securities" law or the "'33 Act," the 1933 Securities and Exchange Act

  a. requires that securities sold in the United States be registered;
  b. requires that investors receive financial and other significant information concerning securities being offered for public sale;
  c. prohibits deceit, misrepresentations, and other fraud in the sale of securities.

2.4   What is the Securities and Exchange Act of 1934?

Also known as the "'34 Act," this law created the Securities and Exchange Commission and empowered it with broad authority over the securities industry. Under the '34 Act, the SEC has the power to register, regulate, and oversee brokerage firms, transfer agents, and clearing agencies as well as self-regulatory organizations such as the New York Stock Exchange, the American Stock

Exchange, and the National Association of Securities Dealers.

The '34 Act also prohibits a number of activities in the markets and empowers the SEC with disciplinary powers over regulated entities and persons associated with them. Additionally, the '34 Act requires companies with publicly traded securities to do periodic reporting to the SEC.

2.5   What is the Investment Company Act of 1940?

The Investment Company Act of 1940 regulates both investment companies and investment advisers to investment companies. Specifically, the Investment Company Act of 1940 regulates the organization of companies, including mutual funds, that engage primarily in investing, reinvesting, and trading in securities and whose own securities are offered to the investing public. These companies are required to disclose their financial condition and investment policies to investors when stock is initially sold and at regular intervals thereafter. The focus is on disclosure to the investing public of information about the fund and its investment objectives, as well as the investment company structure and operations.

Regarding investment advisers to investment companies, the Investment Company Act of 1940 contains provisions requiring that investment advisers have a written advisory contract. The written contract must

    a. precisely describe all compensation

    b. allow the fund to terminate it at any time without penalty on 60 days' written notice

    c. provide for automatic termination if assigned

If the contract term is for more than 2 years, then continuance hinges on annual approval by the majority of the board of directors or shareholders.

The Investment Company Act also imposes a fiduciary duty on investment advisers as to the compensation the investment adviser receives from the company and its shareholders. If this duty is breached, the SEC and/or shareholders may bring an action against the investment adviser for breach of this fiduciary duty.

2.6 What is the Sarbanes-Oxley Act of 2002?

The Sarbanes-Oxley Act of 2002 mandated a number of reforms to enhance corporate responsibility, enhance financial disclosures, and combat corporate and accounting fraud, and created the Public Company Accounting Oversight Board (PCAOB) to oversee the activities of the auditing profession.

2.7 What is ERISA?

ERISA is the Employee Retirement Income Security Act of 1974. ERISA is a federal statute governing retirement and other types of employee benefit plans. The requirements imposed by ERISA on advisers are explained in chapter 17. Generally, ERISA imposes a number of fiduciary duties and requirements on investment advisers who are dealing with plan assets.

State Laws

2.8 How do advisers determine which states' laws apply to their practice?

Advisers may be required to register or provide notice in any state in which they conduct business. The Advisers Act and most states do exempt advisers from registration requirements if they have a limited number of clients in a state. See question 2.9.

Generally, state-registered advisers are required to follow only the record-keeping, net capital, and bonding requirements of the state in which they maintain their principal place of business. An advisory firm's principal place of business is usually the state in which executive offices are located and from which officers, partners, or managers direct, control, and coordinate the firm's activities.

The Advisers Act provides that no state may enforce upon an adviser additional record-keeping, net capital, and bonding requirements beyond those required under the laws of the state where the investment adviser maintains its principal place of business. For this exception to apply, however, the investment adviser must be in compliance with its home state's requirements. A state may require that an investment adviser certify that it is in compliance with its home state's requirement.

2.9   Suppose a state-registered adviser's principal place of business is in one state—as are most of the firm's clients—but it has two clients in a neighboring state. Does the adviser need to register in a state where it has no office and only two clients?

Generally, advisers are required to register in each state where it transacts business. However, the Advisers Act provides that advisers are required to register in a state only if the adviser has a place of business in that state or if during the preceding 12 months it has had more than five clients who are residents of that state. Additionally, states can require that the firm have a greater number of clients before mandating state registration. For example, New York State provides that advisers with fewer than forty clients are exempt from registering in New York. To find out the registration and/or notice filing requirements for their business, advisers should contact the state regulatory authorities in every state in which they do business or have clients.

2.10   How does an adviser register with a state and what records must be kept to comply with state law?

To register, most states require advisers to file a Form ADV along with a Form U-4 for each advisory representative, show evidence of each representative having satisfied applicable exam requirements, and pay any applicable fee. Advisers should contact the state securities regulatory authority in every state in which they do business to discuss registration procedures and record-keeping requirements.

2.11   If an adviser is registered with the SEC, does it still have to comply with state laws?

SEC-registered advisers are exempt from having to comply with state laws regarding registration. However, states retain some regulatory authority over some activities of SEC-registered advisers. For example, states may require SEC advisers to file any information, such as their Form ADV, with the state—so-called notice requirements—and pay fees for practicing in the state. States can also require the licensing, registration, or qualification of an investment adviser representative of a SEC-registered adviser that has a place of business in the state. Thus, states can require advisory personnel who have a place of business in the state to obtain a license from the state to do business.

State securities commissions also have the authority to investigate and/or bring enforcement actions against any SEC-registered adviser for fraudulent or deceitful actions committed by the adviser or its associated persons. Investment advisers registered with the SEC should contact the state securities regulatory agencies in every state in which they do business to discuss notice filing requirements and other state securities laws that require their compliance. Appendix A offers a complete list of state securities regulator contacts.

3 | RIA Registration: What It Means, How It's Done

- ◆ **SEC vs State Registration**
- ◆ **SEC RIA Registration Rules**
- ◆ **Registration and Assets Under Management**
- ◆ **Registration Exemptions**
- ◆ **Registration Procedures and Changes**
- ◆ **Form ADV**

Advisers who meet the definition of investment adviser in chapter 1 and who are not otherwise exempted from doing so must register either with the SEC or with state securities regulatory bodies (see chapter 2). Investment advisers must first determine whether they are required to register with the SEC or the state. Thereafter, they must annually determine if they are required to switch registration from state to SEC or SEC to state. Generally, smaller investment advisers are required to register with the state, while larger investment advisers must register with the SEC. There are, of course, exceptions.

SEC vs State Registration

3.1   How does an adviser determine whether to register with the SEC or the state?

Investment advisers must determine whether they need to register with the SEC or a state. Generally, investment advisers with at least $30 million in assets under management (see question 3.9) as reported in Item 2A of Part 1A of Form ADV must register with the SEC unless they are otherwise exempt or prohibited from registration; those with less than $25 million in assets under management must register with a state.

FIGURE 3.1   **SEC RIA Registration Rules**

Under what circumstances does an adviser qualify to register with the SEC?

Advisers may register with the SEC if:

1. They are investment advisers, as defined in question 3.2, and have more than $30 million in assets under management

2. They have less than $25 million in assets under management but

  a. do business in a state that has no securities regulatory body;

  b. have a national or multistate practice, which would require them to register in thirty or more states;

  c. they advise clients exclusively via the Internet.

3.2   May an adviser simply choose to register with the SEC?

Advisers must register with the SEC if they meet the Advisers Act definition of investment adviser (see question 1.6), but they are not otherwise prohibited from registering with the SEC. Investment advisers that are generally required to register with the SEC include

a. advisers with at least $30 million in assets under management (see question 3.9);

b. advisers to an investment company registered under the Investment Company Act of 1940;

c. an adviser that is not regulated or required to be regulated in the state in which it maintains its principal office and place of business (see question 3.4);

d. advisers that, although not otherwise eligible to register with the SEC, are exempted from the prohibition against registering with the SEC by an order or rule from the SEC commissioner (see question 3.6).

3.3   May an adviser choose not to register with the SEC but register with the state instead?

An adviser does not have to register with the SEC if

a. its principal place of business is in one state and it give no advice regarding securities on a listed national exchange

b. its clients are limited to insurance companies

c. it had fewer than 15 clients in the preceding 12 months and does not hold itself out as an investment adviser

d. it had more than $30 million in assets under management but it is excluded from the definition of investment adviser because it is a bank, lawyer, accountant, teacher, someone whose advice about securities is incidental to his business, or qualifies as a certain type of publisher (see question 1.6).

3.4   If an adviser has less than $25 million in assets under management but does business in a state that has no securities regulatory body, what are its registration requirements?

The adviser should register with the SEC. The SEC retains regulatory responsibility for investment advisers with a principal office and place of business in states that have not enacted investment adviser statutes. Furthermore, the adviser should register with the SEC if its principal office and place of business is in a state that has an investment adviser statute, but the adviser is not required to be registered and has not registered under that state statute. Advisers who are exempted from registering with both the state and the SEC are, of course, exempted from registering with either.

3.5   May an adviser register with both the SEC and the state?

No, advisers may register with either the SEC or the state (or states) but not with both. However, advisers registered with the SEC may have to file notice filings with states in which they have principal offices and/or do business (see chapter 2).

3.6   Who is prohibited from registering with the SEC?

Generally, investment advisers who have less than $25 million in assets under management are prohibited from registering with the SEC. However, the SEC has adopted rules and orders that require certain investment advisers with less than $25 million in assets under management to register with the SEC.

3.7   If an adviser works with clients in several states but has less than $25 million in assets under management, may it choose to register with the SEC rather than the states?

That depends on the number of states in which it does business. Investment advisers who have less than $25 million in assets under management but have a national or multistate practice and conduct advisory activities requiring them to register in thirty or more states are required to register with the SEC.

3.8   If an adviser has less than $25 million in assets under management but advises clients exclusively over the Internet, may it choose to register with the SEC?

Yes, the SEC has adopted a rule that exempts investment advisers that provide advisory services through interactive websites on the Internet from the prohibition on SEC registration. They must register with the SEC. The rule requires that the adviser provide advisory services exclusively through a website. However, the adviser may provide advice to fifteen or fewer clients through other means in the preceding 12 months and still qualify for this exclusion.

Assets Under Management

3.9 What are assets under management?

Assets under management are securities portfolios (see question 3.10) with respect to which an investment adviser provides continuous and regular supervisory or management services (see question 3.11).

3.10 When does an account qualify as a securities portfolio?

An account is a securities portfolio if at least 50 percent of the total value of the account consists of securities (see question 1.18). Cash and cash equivalents may be included in determining whether the 50 percent threshold is met. However, real estate, commodities, and collectables are not securities for this purpose and should be excluded.

3.11 When do an adviser's services to an account constitute continuous and regular supervisory or management services?

Unfortunately, there is no clear-cut answer to this question. However, Form ADV states that an adviser provides "continuous and regular supervisory or management services" if the adviser either

a. has discretionary authority (see question 1.20) over and provides ongoing supervisory or management services with respect to the account; or

b. does not have discretionary authority over the account but has an ongoing responsibility to select or make recommendations, based on the needs of the clients, as to specific securities or other investments the account may purchase or sell and, if such recommendations are accepted by the client, is responsible for effecting the purchase or sale.

The SEC states on Form ADV that advisers also should consider

a. the terms of the advisory contract

b. the form of compensation received

c. the management practices of the adviser

Registration Exemptions

3.12   Is anyone exempt from registration with either the state or the SEC?

Lawyers, accountants, engineers, teachers, publishers, and authors who are excluded from the definition of investment adviser in question 1.6 are not required to register. However, simply being a lawyer, accountant, engineer, teacher, publisher, or author is not enough to exclude a person from registering if the person is indeed in the business of investment advising. For example, accountants do not qualify for the accountant exclusion simply by having a CPA designation or being employed by an accounting firm if they are, in fact, providing investment advice that is not solely incidental to their business.

Broker-dealers and their registered representatives are also excluded from the definition of investment adviser, and thus not required to register, provided that the advisory services they provide are solely incidental to the conduct of their business as a broker or dealer and that they receive no special compensation for advisory services.

Registered representatives do not qualify for the broker exclusion simply by being a registered representative of a broker. Registered representatives who do financial planning and market themselves under the broker name can use the broker exclusion if the broker supervises their plans and collects fees. Registered representatives with independent financial planning or other advisory businesses that are not subject to the brokerage firm's control cannot rely on the broker-dealer exclusion.

Investment advisers whose clients are all residents of the state within which the adviser maintains its place of business are exempt from registering provided that the adviser does not furnish advice or issue reports with respect to securities listed or admitted to unlisted trading privileges on any national securities exchange.

Investment advisers whose only clients are insurance companies are also exempted from registration requirements.

Private investment advisers who generally do not hold themselves to the public as advisers, do not act as an investment adviser for any registered investment company or business development company, and who had fewer than fifteen clients in the preceding 12 months are also exempt from the registration requirements.

FIGURE 3.2 **Persons Exempt From Registering With Either the SEC or the State**

Advisers do not have to register with either the SEC or the state if

1. They are lawyers, accountants, engineers, teachers, publishers, or authors who are excluded from the definition of investment adviser as described in question 3.1;

2. They are broker-dealers or registered representatives that provide advisory services that are solely incidental to their business as a broker or dealer and they receive no special compensation for advisory services;

3. All their clients are residents of the state where they maintain their place of business and they do not furnish advice or issue reports on securities listed or admitted to unlisted trading privileges on any national securities exchange;

4. Their only clients are insurance companies exempt from registering;

5. They are private investment advisers who had fewer than fifteen clients in the preceding 12 months.

Registration Procedures and Changes

3.13 How does an adviser register with the SEC?

To register with the SEC, an adviser files Form ADV with the SEC (see chapters 4, 5, and 6).

3.14 What is Form ADV?

Form ADV is the form advisers must use to register with SEC, with one or more state securities authorities, or to amend those registrations. (See chapters 4, 5, and 6.)

3.15   How does an adviser determine which state(s) to register in?
See questions 2.8 and 2.10.

3.16   How does an adviser register with the state?
To register with the state, an adviser files Form ADV. (See questions 2.8, 2.10, and chapters 4, 5, and 6.)

3.17   If an adviser is registered with the state but now has more than $25 million in assets under management, what must be done?
Advisers whose assets under management (see question 3.9) increase to $25 million or more but remain less than $30 million may, but are not required to, register with the SEC, unless, of course, they are otherwise required to register with the SEC. Advisers who report on their annual updating amendment (see questions 1.20 and 4.21) that assets under management have increased to $30 million or more must register with the SEC within 90 days after that annual updating amendment is filed.

3.18   If an adviser is registered with the SEC but its assets under management (see question 3.9) have dropped below $25 million, may it maintain SEC registration?
Advisers who report on their annual updating amendment (see questions 1.20 and 4.21) that they have assets under management of less than $25 million and are not otherwise eligible to register with the SEC must withdraw from SEC registration within 180 days after the end of their fiscal year by filing Form ADV-W through the IARD system and register with the appropriate state authorities.

3.19   If a solo practitioner registered with the SEC adds an associate to the practice who will also register with the SEC, does the firm then need to register with the SEC?
A registered investment adviser's registration applies to all employees and other persons the adviser controls as long as the employees'

advisory activities are made on behalf of the investment adviser. However, Form ADV may need to be amended since the Advisers Act requires disclosure of the education and business background of certain employees of the investment adviser firm.

Although there is no need for employees of SEC-registered investment advisers to register separately, individuals associated with a state-registered investment adviser, such as employees, may have to register separately or provide notice requirements in the states in which the investment adviser does business. Many states also require individuals who solicit business for investment advisers to register separately, even if they're not employees of the investment adviser.

3.20 Are there any penalties for failing to register?
Advisers can be fined up to $10,000 and be imprisoned up to 5 years per case for failing to register. States also impose penalties and jail time for failing to register.

4 | The Nuts and Bolts of Form ADV

- ◆ Form ADV Parts 1 and 2
- ◆ Form ADV Definitions
- ◆ Filing Form ADV
- ◆ The IARD System
- ◆ The CRD Account
- ◆ Exemptions
- ◆ Form ADV-NR
- ◆ Signing Form ADV
- ◆ Notice Filings
- ◆ Annual Updating Amendments
- ◆ Form ADV Cross-Referenced Questions

Form ADV is used by investment advisers to register with the SEC, register or provide notification with state securities authorities, and to amend previous registrations and notices. Both the SEC and most state securities regulators require investment advisers to fill out and file Form ADV.

All investment advisers registering with the SEC or any of the state securities authorities must complete and file Part 1A and any pertinent schedules. Part 1B asks additional questions required by state securities authorities. Advisers registering only with the SEC do not have to complete Part 1B.

Part 2 of Form ADV is an investment adviser's brochure, which must be delivered to prospective clients at least 2 days prior to entering into an agreement and be offered, in writing, to current clients annually. Advisers registering with the SEC do not have to file Part 2 with the SEC. Advisers registering with a state, however, may have to file Part 2 with the state, and SEC-registered advisers may also have to file Part 2 as part of their state notice filing requirement.

Items on Part 1 and Part 2 are often cross-referenced. Advisers should make sure that answers to cross-referenced items are the same. Furthermore, if amending cross-referenced items, advisers should make sure that they amend both Part 1 and the corresponding item in Part 2. (For a list of cross-referenced questions, see Figure 4.3 at the end of this chapter.)

Advisers should be aware that Form ADV is a public document. Anyone can go online to the SEC's website at www.sec.gov and view any adviser's Form ADV. Furthermore, advisers should be aware that it is unlawful under the Advisers Act to make any statement that is an "untrue statement of material fact" on Form ADV. Form ADV uses thirty-five terms, and those terms are defined in question 1.20.

Filing Form ADV

4.1 Which parts of the form does an adviser file with the SEC and how are they filed?

Part 1A asks advisers a number of questions about their firms,

FIGURE 4.1 **Form ADV Definitions**

Form ADV defines the following thirty-five words and phrases.

1. Advisory affiliate	**19.** Management persons
2. Annual updating amendment	**20.** Managing agent
3. Charged	**21.** Minor rule violation
4. Client	**22.** Misdemeanor
5. Control	**23.** NASD CRD or CRD
6. Custody	**24.** Nonresident
7. Discretionary authority	**25.** Notice filing
8. Employee	**26.** Order
9. Enjoined	**27.** Performance-based fee
10. Felony	**28.** Person
11. Foreign financial regulatory authority	**29.** Principal place of business or principal office and place of business
12. Found	
13. Government entity	**30.** Proceedings
14. High-net-worth individual	**31.** Related person
15. Home state	**32.** Self-regulatory organization (SRO)
16. Impersonal investment advice	**33.** Sponsor
17. Investment related	**34.** State securities authority
18. Involved	**35.** Wrap fee program

Question 1.20 defines these words and phrases and indicates where they are used on Form ADV.

business practices, persons (see question 1.20) who own and control (see question 1.20) the firm, and persons who provide investment advice on behalf of the firm. Advisers that are registered or applying for registration with the SEC must file Part 1 with the SEC electronically unless a hardship exemption is obtained to file it manually in hard copy. Advisers registering with states must check with state securities authorities (see question 1.20) in the states in which they are filing to determine whether they can or must file Form ADV electronically. Information about state laws and rules and how to contact state securities authorities can be found at http://www.nasaa.org.

4.2 How does an adviser file Form ADV electronically?

Electronic filing is handled through the Investment Adviser Registration Depository (IARD) system, which is administered by the National Association of Securities Dealers (NASD). Advisers first must get an entitlement package from the IARD at www.IARD.com and request access to the IARD system for the firm by completing and submitting the IARD Entitlement Package. The IARD Entitlement Package must be submitted on paper. Mail forms to IARD Entitlement Requests, NASD, PO Box 9495, Gaithersburg, MD 20898-9495. Once advisers get CRD numbers, user ID codes, and passwords, and have funded their CRD account, they may begin filing their ADV electronically.

4.3 What is a CRD number and how does an adviser get an ID code and password for the IARD system?

CRD stands for central registration depository, which is part of the IARD system run by the NASD. An adviser's CRD number is an identification number for the advisory firm. After the NASD receives the adviser's entitlement package, it will assign the adviser a CRD number, which is an identification number for the firm, along with a user ID code and password for use on the IARD system. Advisory firms can request ID codes and passwords for more than one individual.

4.4 When an adviser files electronically, must the entire Form ADV be filled out in one sitting?

No, advisers can store unfinished draft filings of Form ADV in the IARD system. IARD allows advisers to store draft Form ADVs for up to 120 days. To retrieve a draft filing, advisers should click on "pending."

4.5 Can an adviser access past filings to review them?

Yes. Go to the IARD's website, log in, and click on "historical."

4.6 Are there any filing fees and how does an adviser fund a CRD account?

There are filing fees both for initial registration and for annual amendments. When the NASD receives an adviser's entitlement package, it creates a financial account for that adviser from which the IARD will deduct filing fees and any state fees it is required to pay. However, the SEC approved a one-year waiver of IARD filing fees for advisers registered with the SEC. SEC-registered investment advisers will not have to pay the fee associated with their annual amendments filed from November 1, 2005, through October 31, 2006. The annual system renewal fee of $100 for each state-registered investment adviser and the $45 fee for each investment adviser representative were also waived for this time period. Updates on fees for filing and renewal can be found at www.sec.gov/iard.

4.7 May an adviser file on paper rather than electronically?

Investment advisers are required to file Form ADV through the IARD system. If an adviser cannot file electronically through the IARD system, it may apply for a hardship exemption from the electronic filing requirements.

Exemptions

4.8 Does a temporary hardship exemption allow an adviser to file on paper rather than electronically?

A temporary hardship exemption, unlike a continuing hardship exemption (see question 4.9), does not allow advisers to file a paper Form ADV. A temporary hardship exemption merely extends the deadline for filing an electronic filing for 7 business days. It is available to advisers who experience temporary, unexpected problems, such as a computer malfunction or electrical outage. (See question 4.22 for the rules on filing a temporary hardship exemption.)

4.9 What is a continuing hardship exemption?

Small firms that can demonstrate that filing electronically would impose an undue hardship can file for a continuing hardship exemption from the electronic filing requirement. To qualify for this exemption, an adviser must demonstrate that it is a "small business." (See question 4.10.)

4.10 When does an adviser qualify as a small business for purposes of a continuing hardship exemption?

To qualify as a small business needing a continuing hardship exemption (see question 4.9), advisers must answer "no" to every question in Item 12 of Part 1A of Form ADV, which means

a. the adviser's total assets (not assets under management) were less than $5 million on the last day of your most recent fiscal year;

b. the adviser does not control (see question 1.20) another investment adviser that had assets under management (see question 3.9) of $25 million or more on the last day of its most recent fiscal year;

c. the adviser does not control another corporation, partnership, trust, limited liability company, limited liability partnership, or other organization that had total assets of $5 million or more on the last day of its most recent fiscal year;

d. the adviser is not controlled by or under common control (see question 1.20) with another investment adviser that had assets under management of $25 million or more on the last day of its most recent fiscal year;

e. the adviser is not controlled by or under common control (see question 1.20) with another corporation, partnership, trust, limited liability company, limited liability partnership, or other organization that had total assets of $5 million or more on the last day of its most recent fiscal year.

4.11 How does an adviser submit a paper filing of Form ADV once it qualifies for a continuing hardship exemption?

Paper submissions of Form ADV must be submitted to the IARD

Document Processing, NASD, PO Box 9495, Gaithersburg, MD 20898-9495. When making the paper submissions, advisers must send one original signed copy of Form ADV and one copy. Originals and copies of paper Form ADV may also have to be submitted to appropriate state securities regulatory agencies. Advisers should check with state securities authorities in every state in which they do business to find out whether paper filings of Form ADV are permitted.

When making a paper filing, the following steps must be completed:
   a. All responses must be typed.
   b. Names must be as given in Item 1A of Part 1A and the date typed on every page.
   c. If amending Form ADV:
      i. Complete page 1, circling the number of any item for which responses are being changed must be included.
      ii. The adviser's SEC 801 number and CRD number (if applicable) must be typed on every page of the amendment.
      iii. Advisers must complete the amended item in full and circle the number of the item for which they are changing the response.
      iv. If an adviser is amending any information on Schedules A or B, Schedule C must also be submitted.

Form ADV Part 2

4.12   What is Form ADV Part 2?

Form ADV Part 2 is also known as the brochure. Investment advisers may fill in the actual Form ADV Part 2 and give it to clients, or they may substitute an alternative brochure that contains all the information required in Form ADV Part 2.

As of the end of 2005, advisers were required to keep only Form ADV Part 2 (including Schedule F) complete and up-to-date in their files. Advisers are not required to file Form ADV Part 2 with the SEC, although they may have to file Part 2 with any state in which they do business as part of their notice requirements. Advisers should contact all state securities regulators in states in which they do business to find out filing requirements.

Form ADV Part 2 or a written brochure must be filed in the adviser's office, delivered to prospective clients, and offered to current clients annually. Part 2 must be offered at least 2 days before entering into any agreement with any new client. Form ADV Part 2 may also be given to new clients at the time the agreement is entered into, provided that the client may cancel the agreement within 5 days without penalty. Thereafter, the adviser must offer all current clients Part 2 at least once annually. The offer must be made in writing, although the ~~offer to~~ deliver Form ADV Part 2 may be made at the bottom of a client statement.

NOTE: OFFER ONLY

Even though not filed with the SEC, Part 2 still needs to be continually updated whenever there are changes to the adviser's business. Part 2 must be amended annually within 90 days after the end of an adviser's fiscal year to accurately reflect any changes to the adviser's business practices or conflicts.

The SEC has proposed to amend Part 2 of Form ADV. If and when these proposed changes are adopted, advisers who are registered with the SEC may have to file their initial Part 2 as well as any amendments with the SEC.

4.13 What happens if there are changes to an advisory business?

Advisers must amend Form ADV annually by filing an annual updating amendment within 90 days after the end of the fiscal year (see question 4.21). Advisers also must file amendments to ADV Part 1A promptly

a. if information to certain in Items 1, 3, 9, or 11 of Part 1A responses becomes inaccurate in any way; or

b. if responses provided in Items 4, 8, or 10 of Part 1A become materially inaccurate.

Advisers also must amend any information in Part 2 if it becomes materially inaccurate, or if other responses or the brochure become materially inaccurate, although amendments to Part 2 do not have to be filed with the SEC.

FIGURE 4.2 **Interim Amendments to Form ADV**

ADVISERS MUST FILE additional interim amendments to Form ADV before the annual updating amendment is due if responses to certain items in the form are no longer accurate.

Advisers must promptly file interim amendments if the following items become inaccurate in any way:

ADV Part 1A Section	Item Description
Item 1	Identifying Information
Item 3	Form of Organization
Item 9	Custody
Item 11	Disclosure Information

Advisers must promptly file interim amendments if the following items become materially inaccurate in any way:

ADV Part 1A Section	Item Description
Item 4	Successions
Item 8	Participation or Interest in Client Transactions
Item 10	Control Persons

Form ADV Part 2 must be promptly amended whenever any item becomes materially inaccurate.

4.14 Does an adviser that's registering with the SEC or amending a SEC registration need to make notice filings with state securities authorities?

Advisers should check with the state securities regulatory authorities in every state in which they do business (see chapter 2). If advisers must make notice filings (see question 2.11), they can do so electronically through the IARD system. The NASD will electronically send notice filings to any state that advisers check on Item 2B of Part 1A of Form ADV. If granted a hardship exemption to file Form ADV on paper, the NASD will enter an adviser's ADV filing into the IARD system and send state notice filings electronically to the states checked on Item 2B of Part 1A of Form ADV.

Form ADV-NR

4.15   What is Form ADV-NR and who is required to file it?
Nonresident partners and the managing agent of all SEC-registered advisers must file Form ADV-NR with that adviser's initial registration. A general partner or managing agent of a registered investment adviser who becomes a nonresident after the adviser's initial application has been submitted must file Form ADV-NR within 30 days. Form ADV-NR cannot be filed electronically and must be filed on paper to the SEC at Securities and Exchange Commission, 450 5th Street, NW Mail Stop A-2, Washington, DC 20549, Attn: Branch of Registrations and Examinations.

Signing Form ADV

4.16   How does an adviser sign Form ADV?
There are three execution pages at the end of Form ADV. Advisers do not have to file all three execution pages. Advisers applying for or amending their SEC registrations must sign and submit either

    a. a domestic investment adviser execution page if the adviser is a resident of the United States; or

    b. a nonresident investment adviser execution page if the adviser is not a resident of the United States.

Advisers registering or amending their ADV with a state securities authority must sign and submit the state-registered investment adviser execution page.

4.17   How does an adviser sign the execution page?

Advisers do not have to actually manually sign the execution pages. The official signature is typed on the electronic filing.

4.18   Does the signature on the execution page have to be notarized?

No. The signature does not have to be notarized.

4.19   Who should sign Form ADV?

The individual who signs the execution page would be

a. the sole proprietor if the adviser is a sole proprietorship

b. a general partner if the adviser is a partnership

c. an authorized principal officer if the adviser is a corporation

d. a principal officer directly engaged in the management or direction or supervision of investment advisory activities if the adviser is a separately identifiable department or division of a bank

e. an authorized individual who participates in managing or directing the adviser's affairs for all other organizations

Notice Filings

4.20   How does an adviser make notice filings with state securities authorities?

If an adviser is either initially applying for registration with the SEC or amending an SEC registration, state securities regulatory authorities may require the adviser to provide them with copies of SEC filings including Form ADV. When using the IARD system to file Form ADV, advisers can send any state securities regulatory authorities the required notice filings by checking any states in Item 2B or Part 1A of Form ADV. If any state is checked, Form ADV will be automatically sent to such states, and fees for that filing deducted from the adviser's CRD account.

Annual Updating Amendments

4.21   What is an annual updating amendment?

An annual updating amendment (see question 1.20) must be filed annually within 90 days after the close of an adviser's fiscal year. The annual updating amendment reaffirms the eligibility information in Item 2 of Part 1A and updates the responses to any other item for which the information is no longer accurate.

In the past, advisers received no notification or reminder that the annual updating amendment was due and required to be filed. However, on October 31, 2005, the IARD system was enhanced to add an e-mail alert and reminder function. SEC-registered investment advisers who supply an e-mail address of a contact employee in Part 1A, Item 1J of Form ADV will receive e-mail reminders of certain filing deadlines as well as e-mail notices of SEC regulatory and compliance information. The e-mail function sends each active SEC registrant a "contact e-mail verification" e-mail at the contact employee's e-mail address, asking the contact employee to authenticate the e-mail address through the IARD website using an authentication key. Contact employees must visit a web URL beginning with the prefix https://www.webiard.com. An investment advisory firm will not receive e-mail alerts and reminders unless it

    a. supplies an accurate e-mail address in Item 1J

    b. authenticates the e-mail address through the contact e-mail verification notice sent to that address by the system.

Once authentication is done, the e-mail system will notify firms of

    a. changes to registration status

    b. annual amendment filing deadlines

    c. deadlines to update SEC registration eligibility for new registrants relying on Rule 203A-2(d) for 120 days

    d. announcements by the SEC of regulatory and compliance information

Advisers must know their filing deadlines. If the 90th day after the close of the fiscal year falls on either a Sunday or a holiday, the filing deadline is not extended. The adviser must file the annual updating amendment earlier.

4.22 What should an adviser do if the firm's computer crashes on the day the annual updating amendment is due?

The adviser may file for a temporary hardship exemption from the electronic filing requirements. (See question 4.8.) To file a temporary hardship exemption, fill out and mail Form ADV-H to the U.S. Securities and Exchange Commission, Office of

---

FIGURE 4.3 Form ADV Cross-Referenced Questions

ADVISERS ARE ASKED to answer a number of identical or similar questions on Form ADV Parts 1 and 2. When initially registering, advisers should answer corresponding items the same way; when amending the forms, advisers should check that they've amended the corresponding items.

ADV Part 1	Corresponds to ADV Part 2
Item 5D Clients	Item 2
Item 5E Compensation Arrangements and	
Item 5G Advisory Activities	Item 1B
Item 5E Compensation Arrangements	Item 1C
Item 5G Advisory Activities	Item 1A
Item 6 Other Business Activities	Item 7
Item 6A Other Business Activities and	
Item 7A Financial Industry Affiliations	Item 8A
Item 7A Financial Industry Affiliations	
and Activities	Item 8C
Item 7B Financial Industry Affiliations	
and Activities	Item 8D
Item 8A Proprietary Interest in Client	
Transactions	Item 9
Item 8B Sales Interest in Client Transactions	Item 9D
Item 8C Investment or Brokerage Discretion	Item 12A
Item 8D Investment or Brokerage Discretion	Item 12B
Item 8E Investment or Brokerage Discretion	Items 12B and 13A
Item 8F Investment or Brokerage Discretion	Item 13B

Registrations and Examinations, Mail Stop 0-25, 450 5th Street, NW, Washington, DC 20549. To obtain a copy of Form ADV-H, call SEC Publications at 202-942-4040. Filing Form ADV-H extends an adviser's electronic filing deadline for 7 business days.

4.23 Are there filing fees for filing Form ADV and any state notice requirements?

Yes, IARD charges filing fees, as do various states for filing registration and notification filings. IARD filing fees are due when Form ADV is initially filed and subsequently for each annual updating amendment (see question 1.20) filed. There are no filing fees for filing Form ADV-W. Advisers who qualify for a hardship exemption to file a paper Form ADV are also required to pay an additional filing fee. IARD filing fee schedules can be found at www.sec.gov/iard, www.nasaa.org, or www.iard.com.

4.24 How can an adviser make certain that the Form ADV and/or any amendments have been successfully filed?

An adviser can check the filing history on the IARD website to ensure that filings have been successfully filed.

4.25 If an adviser fills in something incorrectly, how may the mistake be corrected?

Once a filing has been submitted through IARD, the adviser cannot delete it. The proper procedure is to amend the filing if it has already been submitted. If, however, the filing has not been submitted through IARD but is pending, the adviser may delete the pending filing and start over.

5 | How to Complete Form ADV Part 1

FORM ADV PART 1A ITEMS 1–4

- ◆ Owners, Controllers, Investment Advisers
- ◆ Legal Name of the Firm
- ◆ Firms With Multiple Offices
- ◆ Websites
- ◆ Books and Records
- ◆ State Registration

FORM ADV PART 1A ITEMS 5 AND 6

- ◆ Business Description
- ◆ Services to Friends or Relatives
- ◆ Portfolio Manager Wrap Fees

FORM ADV PART 1A ITEM 7

- ◆ Financial Industry Affiliations
- ◆ Related Investment Advisers

- Private Funds
- Related Persons
- Investment-Related Limited Partnerships
- General Partners

FORM ADV PART 1A ITEMS 8–12

- Client Transactions
- Conflicts of Interest
- Employee Compensation
- Custody
- Direct and Indirect Owners of the Firm
- Judicial or Regulatory Action
- Arbitration Claims

FORM ADV PART 1A SCHEDULES A–D

- Disclosure Reporting
- Foreign Nationals
- Joint Ownership
- Trusts
- Indirect Owners
- Private Funds

DISCLOSURE REPORTING PAGES

- Disciplinary Events

Part 1 of Form ADV is principally for the use of state and federal regulators. Advisers registering with the SEC need to complete and file only Part 1A of Form ADV. Part 1B is for advisers registering with state securities authorities. The term "you," as used in Form ADV, refers to the investment advisory firm, unless the filer is a sole proprietor. Form ADV defines thirty-five terms and phrases, which are defined in question 1.20. For a list of terms used in Form ADV, see page 39.

5.1   How does an adviser fill in Part 1A of Form ADV?

Form ADV, Part 1A asks questions about persons who own and control the advisory firm and persons who provide investment advice.

Form ADV Part 1A Items 1–4

5.2   How does an adviser fill in Items 1 through 4?

Items 1 through 4 ask advisers for identifying and background information. Items 1, 2, and 3 are self-explanatory. Item 4 asks advisers whether they are taking over the business of another adviser or if their previous corporate structure or legal status has changed. For example, if a partnership incorporates, Item 4 should be answered "yes."

5.3   Item 1B asks if an adviser conducts business under a different name. If the adviser's legal name is the same as the name under which the adviser conducts business, how should the adviser respond to this question?

The IARD system will automatically list your legal name in both Item 1A and Item 1B unless you change it.

5.4   How should a firm with, say, ten offices answer Item 1F?

Investment advisers registering with the SEC need to list only their five largest offices in terms of total employees on Schedule D. A separate Schedule D must be completed for each location.

5.5   What's the correct way to answer Item 1, about websites?

If an adviser maintains a website, this question should be answered "yes" and the website address should be disclosed on Schedule D. Investment advisers should answer this question "No" if the adviser's firm appears on an association's website and the adviser does not have its own independently maintained website.

5.6   If an adviser keeps duplicate sets of books and records at an off-site location, should the adviser list that off-site location in Item 1K?

As long as a complete set of books and records is kept at the principal office, then only the principal office need be listed in Item 1K. However, to the extent that all books and records are not kept in a central location, then each of the main locations, besides the firm's principal place of business, where the firm's records are located must be listed on Schedule D.

5.7   If an adviser is registering with a state, what's the correct way to respond to Item 2?

Item 2 is filled out only by advisers registering with the SEC or those filing their annual updating amendment (see question 1.20). The purpose of the questions in Item 2 is to determine whether an adviser is eligible to register with the SEC.

Form ADV Part 1A Items 5 and 6

5.8   What's the correct way to answer Items 5 and 6?

Items 5 and 6 require advisers to describe their business, including the number and type of employees (see question 1.20) and the number and type of clients (see question 1.20), compensation arrangements, assets under management, and types of services provided. Item 6 asks advisers to describe what other business activities they engage in beyond advisory services.

Parts of Item 5 of Part 1 correspond to responses to Item 1 of Part 2. Advisers should make sure that they respond to corresponding questions with the same answers. Specifically, Items 5E and 5G of Part 1 correspond to Item 1B, Part 2. Item 5E of Part 1 corresponds to Item 1C, Part 2. Finally, Item 5D, Part

1 corresponds to Item 2, Part 2. Item 6, Part 1 corresponds to Item 7, Part 2.

5.9   If an adviser provides services at no charge to some relatives and friends, do they count as clients?

When counting the number of clients (see question 1.20), advisers must count all clients, even those who do not compensate the adviser. Thus, family members, relatives, and friends are counted as clients if the investment adviser provides services, even if no fees are charged.

5.10   If an adviser serves as portfolio manager under a wrap fee and it also provides wealth management for a number of families, how should it count the number of clients for the purposes of Item 5C?

Each wrap fee program (see question 1.20) participant to whom the adviser provides investment advisory services should be counted as a client. If the firm treats multiple members of one family or a family trust as a single client, then the firm should count that family as a single client. Conversely, if the firm treats multiple members of the same family or family trust as separate clients, then the adviser should count each family member as a separate client when answering Item 5C.

Form ADV Part 1A Item 7

5.11   What's the correct way to answer Item 7?

Item 7 is primarily intended for advisers to disclose all financial industry affiliations and activities. The purpose of these questions is to help the SEC identify potential conflicts of interest. Advisers should not check Items 7A(1) and 7A(3) if they have an employee (see question 1.20) that is a registered representative of a broker-dealer or investment adviser. That disclosure should actually be made in Item 5B(1) and 5B(2).

Item 7B asks advisers if they or a related person (see question 1.20) are a general partner in an investment-related limited partnership or a manager of an investment-related limited liability company. It also asks if the adviser advises any other private fund.

Item 7A of Part 1 corresponds to Item 8A of Part 2, and Item 7B of Part 1 corresponds to Items 8A and 8D of Part 2. Advisers should make sure that answers to these corresponding sections are the same.

5.12 If an advisory firm is part of a larger organization with hundreds of related investment advisers with whom it has no interactions, does the adviser need to list all of them on Section 7A of Schedule D?

No, the SEC says that a firm can omit related investment advisers if
  a. the firm has had no business dealings with them;
  b. the firm does not conduct joint operations with them;
  c. the firm does not provide advice that is formulated, in whole or in part, by them; and
  d. the related adviser does not present any potential for a conflict of interest with the firm's clients.

However, the SEC also states that if a firm omits related advisers in Section 7A of Schedule D, it should state in the Miscellaneous Section of Schedule D that it has a supplementary list of related investment advisers not listed and provide a statement of why they were not listed. The adviser should also state that a copy of that list will be provided upon request.

5.13 Does an adviser have to list in Item 7A employees who perform investment advisory services or who are registered representatives of a broker-dealer?

No. However, advisers do have to disclose in Item 5B (1) employees (see question 1.20) who perform investment advisory functions, and disclose in Item 5B(2) employees who are registered representatives of a broker-dealer.

5.14 What is a private fund for the purposes of Item 7B?

Although the definition is complicated, a private fund is essentially any hedge fund or investment pool that allows investors to redeem their interests within 2 years of purchase. In answering Item 7B, advisers are not required to "look through" clients that are insurance companies, broker-dealers, and banks, but are required to look through many types of pooled investment vehicles investing in securities, including hedge funds. Because the definition of private fund is so complicated, advisers who provide advice to or who are general partners or managers, or who are related to a person who provides advice to or is a general partner or manager of any unregistered investment pool should consult with an attorney to determine whether it is a private fund.

5.15   Related persons (see question 1.20) are general partners of family limited partnerships that were established for tax- and estate-planning purposes. Do these family limited partnerships have to be listed on Section 7B of Schedule D?
The SEC says that family limited partnerships do not have to be listed on Section 7B of Schedule D provided that in the Miscellaneous Section of Schedule D it is stated that the firm does have related persons who are general partners of family limited partnerships that are not listed on Section 7B of Schedule D. The firm may have to provide a list of these family limited partnerships to the SEC or other regulatory agency upon request.

5.16   Suppose an adviser is the general partner of several investment-related limited partnerships that are employees' securities companies as defined in Section 2(a)(13) of the Investment Company Act of 1940. Suppose further that the adviser is the general partner of several investment-related limited partnerships that are employees' securities companies for a number of related entities. Does that adviser have to list these employees' securities companies on Section 7B of Schedule D?
The SEC says the employees' securities companies do not have to be listed in Item 7B. However, if employees' securities companies are omitted from 7B, there must be a statement in the Miscellaneous Section of Schedule D that the firm has employees' securities companies organized as limited partnerships/limited liability companies that are not listed on Section 7B of Schedule

D. If requested by the SEC or other regulatory agency, the adviser must provide a list of all employees' securities companies.

5.17 Suppose an adviser has a related person (see question 1.20) who is a general partner in several investment-related limited partnerships. The limited partnerships are not employees' securities companies or family limited partnerships. No firm clients are invested in or have been solicited to invest in the limited partnership. Does the adviser have to list these limited partnerships on Section 7B of Schedule D?
Yes.

5.18 Suppose the firm has several related persons (see question 1.20) who are not SEC registered investment advisers but who are general partners in investment-related limited partnerships or managers of limited liability companies. Must these limited partnerships and limited liability companies be listed on Section 7B of Schedule D?
Yes.

Form ADV Part 1A Items 8–12

5.19 What is the correct way to answer Item 8?
Item 8 requests information about the adviser's participation in client (see question 1.20) transactions. It is used to identify whether the adviser or advisory firm can benefit in any way from client transactions and whether there are any potential conflicts of interest. The purpose of Item 8D is to determine if an adviser is meeting its obligation of best education. Item 8E asks advisers about their soft-dollar arrangements (see chapter 18), and Item 8F asks advisers to disclose their solicitor arrangements (see chapter 16). Item 8 on Part 1 corresponds with Items 9, 12, 12B, 13A, and 13B on Part 2, and advisers should take care that the responses to both are the same.

5.20 If the firm compensates its employees for bringing in clients, should Item 8F be answered "yes"?

Yes. If an employee receives compensation that is specifically linked to bringing clients (see question 1.20) into the firm, for example, cash or noncash compensation in addition to the employee's normal salary, then Item 8F should be answered "yes."

5.21 How should an adviser answer Item 9 of Part 1A of the form?

Item 9 is used to determine if an adviser has custody (see question 1.20) of client assets (see chapter 10 for a full discussion of the custody rules). Advisers who are registering or are registered with the SEC who deduct fees directly from clients' accounts but otherwise do not have custody of clients' funds or securities may answer "no" to both Items 9A(1) and 9A(2).

5.22 Item 9C asks if a related person (see question 1.20) who has custody of client assets is a registered broker-dealer. In a case where related persons do have custody of advisory clients' cash and securities and some of these related persons are broker-dealers registered under Section 15 of the Securities Exchange Act of 1934 while others are not registered broker-dealers, what should be the response to Item 9C?

The SEC states that if any related person who is a registered broker-dealer has custody of clients' assets, the response to Item 9C should be "yes." Item 9C should be marked "no" only if none of them is a registered broker-dealer.

5.23 How should an adviser answer Item 10?

Item 10 asks advisers to identify every person (see question 1.20) that directly or indirectly controls it (see question 1.20). Essentially, if the firm is owned either directly or indirectly by any person not named in Item 1A or on Schedules A, B, or C, this item should be answered "yes."

Advisers who are filing their initial Form ADV must list direct owners and executive officers on Schedule A (see question 5.29) and list indirect owners on Schedule B (see question 5.34). Updates to Schedules A and B are done on Schedule C. If a person not named in Item 1A or on Schedules A, B, or C directly or indirectly controls an adviser's management or policies, that person must be designated on Section 10 of Schedule D.

5.24   What's the correct way to answer Item 11 of Part 1A?

In Item 11 advisers are required to answer questions about their disciplinary history. Specifically, Item 11 asks if the adviser or any advisory affiliate (see question 1.20) of the adviser within the past 10 years has been the subject of a judicial or regulatory action involving a crime, financial misconduct, or insolvency.

5.25   Are SEC-registered advisers required to report arbitration claims in Item 11?

No. However, state-registered advisers filing Part 1B of Form ADV are required by state law to report arbitration claims and complete corresponding disclosure reporting pages (see question 5.42).

5.26   Are events that occurred more than 10 years ago required to be disclosed in Item 11?

SEC registered investment advisers can limit Item 11 disclosures of events to 10 years following the date of the event. Advisers, however, may have a continuing antifraud obligation to disclose to clients (see question 1.20) and prospective clients information about an event that occurred more than 10 years ago. State-registered advisers must report events that occurred more than 10 years earlier.

5.27   How should Item 12 of Part 1A be answered?

Advisers are required to fill in Item 12 only if they are registering or are registered with the SEC and have assets under management of less than $25 million.

Form ADV Part 1A Schedules A–D

5.28   What schedules accompany Part 1A?

Schedules A, B, C, and D accompany Form ADV Part 1A. Additionally, disclosure reporting pages (DRPs) must also be filed with Form ADV Part 1A.

Schedule A

5.29 What is the correct way to fill out Schedule A?

Schedule A asks for information about a firm's direct owners and executive officers. If Schedule A needs to be amended, file Schedule C. Specifically, Schedule A asks advisers for

- **a.** a full legal name
- **b.** whether the listed person or entity as an owner is a domestic or foreign entity
- **c.** the title and status of the person
- **d.** how much that person or entity owns of the adviser

5.30 If a foreign national on Schedule A does not have a CRD number or a Social Security number, how should he be listed? How would a foreign entity that does not have an IRS tax number or employer ID number be listed?

An adviser can call NASDR's Gateway Call Center at 240-386-4848 to have a CRD number assigned to a foreign national. Advisers can type "foreign entity" into the box that asks for the IRS tax number or employer ID number, and the response will be accepted.

5.31 How does an adviser report a percentage of ownership when people jointly own part of an advisory firm?

According to the SEC, because maximum ownership must be reported, joint owners would be listed as owning the entire share jointly owned. For example, if two people jointly own 30 percent of an advisory firm partnership, then each would be listed as owning 30 percent. If each of these individuals owns part of the adviser in his own right, then that percentage ownership would be added to the jointly owned share. For example, if each individually owned 25 percent of the adviser, each would be reported as owning 55 percent of the adviser. Thus, ownership Code D, indicating ownership greater than 50 percent but less than 75 percent, would be inserted in the appropriate box.

5.32 If part of the adviser is owned by a trust that has two trustees, how should the ownership percentage of the trust be reported?

The SEC says that both the trust and all trustees must be listed on Schedule A along with the appropriate ownership code. If a trust with two trustees owns 35 percent of the adviser, then the trust and each of the trustees must be listed and ownership Code C—designating an ownership interest of greater than 25 percent but less than 50 percent—inserted in the appropriate box.

5.33 How should an adviser list executive officers who have had a number of different titles through the years?

Advisers may either make multiple entries for the executives, listing their officers' titles, and the dates the titles were acquired, or they may list each executive officer once, using only current titles, and the date the officers first acquired a title requiring that they be listed on Schedule A.

Schedule B

5.34 What is the correct way to fill in Schedule B?

Schedule B is filed only by advisers submitting their initial application and is thereafter amended by Schedule C. Schedule B asks for information about an adviser's indirect owners.

5.35 What is an indirect owner?

An indirect owner is a person (see question 1.20) that does not directly own the adviser but owns the adviser indirectly through either a direct owner or another indirect owner.

Essentially, anyone who indirectly owns 25 percent or more of the adviser is an indirect owner that must be listed on Schedule B. The SEC says that in determining which indirect owners must be listed on Schedule B, an adviser must first look at any person that owns 25 percent or more of a direct owner. Next, any person that owns 25 percent or more of any direct owners must be listed, then continue up the chain of ownership, and at each level determine if there are any 25 percent or more owners that are not public companies.

5.36   How does an adviser list a foreign national on Schedule B who does not have a CRD number or a Social Security number, and how should the adviser list a foreign entity that does not have an IRS tax number or employer ID number?
The adviser can call NASDR's Gateway Call Center at 240-386-4848 to have a CRD number assigned to a foreign national. You can type "foreign entity" in the box asking for the IRS tax number or employer ID number, and the response will be accepted.

Schedule C
5.37   What is Schedule C?
Schedule C is used by paper filers to update information required by Schedules A and B.

Schedule D
5.38   What is Schedule D?
Schedule D is used to provide additional information for certain items in Part 1A.

5.39   Section 7B asks whether a pooled investment vehicle is a private fund. What is a private fund?
Essentially, a private fund is a hedge fund, although the definition of private fund can include investment pools that sponsors do not consider hedge funds. If a pooled investment fund permits owners to redeem any portion of their ownership interest within 2 years of purchase, the adviser should consult with an expert to determine if it is considered a private fund.

5.40   Section 7B asks what percentage of an adviser's clients have invested in a limited partnership, limited liability company, or other private fund for which the adviser or a related person is a general partner, manager of a limited liability company, or other private fund it advises. Suppose a firm is a general partner in a limited partnership and although the firm has a management agreement with the limited partnership, the firm does not have a separate management agreement or

advisory client relationship with any of the limited partners. How would the adviser answer the question "Approximately what percentage of your clients have invested in the limited partnership?"

The answer in that case would be 0 percent because no advisory clients are invested in the limited partnership.

5.41 What is the purpose of the Miscellaneous Section of Schedule D?

An adviser can use the Miscellaneous Section to provide explanatory information about its responses to any item in Form ADV, not just information previously discussed in Schedule D.

Disclosure Reporting Pages

5.42 What are the Disclosure Reporting Pages and how are they filled out?

Disclosure Reporting Pages (DRPs) are for reporting details about disciplinary events involving the adviser or persons affiliated with the adviser.

5.43 Can a DRP ever be removed from a Form ADV?

DRPs can be removed from a current Form ADV in certain circumstances. The DRP, however, will not be removed from historical filings. Specifically, a DRP can be removed from an adviser's current Form ADV if

   a. the DRP was filed for an affiliate that is no longer associated with the adviser
   b. the adviser is registered with the SEC and the event or proceeding described in the DRP is move than 10 years old
   c. the event or proceeding was resolved in the adviser's favor.

   If one of these three situations exists, the DRP can be removed from an adviser's Form ADV through the IARD system. If a DRP is removed, the adviser also must change the response to Item 11 on Form ADV by filing an amendment.

6 How to Complete Form ADV Part 2

FORM ADV PART 2 ITEMS 1–14

◆ Investment Supervisory Services

◆ Client Base

◆ Investment Recommendations

◆ Investment Adviser Qualifications

◆ Disclosure of Brokerage Discretion

◆ Client Minimums

◆ Soft-Dollar Practices

FORM ADV PART 2 SCHEDULES F AND G

◆ Explanations

◆ Balance Sheet

Part 2 of Form ADV is a written disclosure statement, on paper, that provides clients (see question 1.20) with information about an investment adviser's business practices, fees, and possible conflicts of interest. The primary purpose of Part 2 is to provide clients and prospective clients with information about an adviser's firm, and it must be completed and delivered to prospective clients and offered annually to current clients.

Advisers are required to continually update Part 2 so that it accurately reflects a firm's business practices and conflicts, and they must amend Part 2 annually within 90 days after the end of their fiscal year. As an alternative to filling out the paper form, advisers can supply clients with a written narrative brochure, which must contain the same information required on Form ADV Part 2.

Disclosures on Part 2 of Form ADV must exactly align with actual business practices. Incorrect information on Part 2 can have financial consequences. For example, if fees actually charged to clients are not the same as described in Part 2, an adviser may have to refund fees to clients. Inaccuracies on Part 2 are also technically actionable under the Advisers Act if the SEC seeks enforcement. However, unless actual fraud is involved, the SEC generally issues a deficiency letter requesting correction of Form ADV to reflect actual business practices.

The SEC has proposed to amend Part 2 of Form ADV. However, as of late 2005, the changes had not been adopted. Until the SEC adopts these new rules for Part 2, the current rules remain in effect, and advisers are not required to file Part 2 with the SEC. Although advisers are not required to file with the SEC, many state securities authorities do require that Form ADV Part 2 be filed with them as part of their notice requirements (see question 4.12).

Form ADV defines thirty-five words and phrases, and those terms are listed and defined in question 1.20.

Form ADV Part 2 Items 1–14

6.1 What is the correct way to answer each item on Form ADV Part 2?

ITEM 1

In Item 1, advisers are asked to identify the services they provide and the time they allocate to each type of service. Advisers should check only the boxes for services actually provided. Conditions to providing services should be disclosed on Schedule F. For example, if clients are required to have a minimum asset value in a managed account, that should be noted on Schedule F.

Advisers should note that the SEC's definition of the term "investment supervisory services" in Item 1A(1) differs from industry usage of the term. The SEC defines investment supervisory services as continuous, ongoing, daily monitoring of portfolios. If these services are provided under another name, such as an "asset management account," advisers should check 1A(1) and note on Schedule F that supervisory services are provided but are referred to as "asset management accounts."

Advisers are also required to disclose their basic fee schedule and to state whether or not fees are negotiable. Advisers need to take care that fees disclosed in Item 1 of Part 2 are the actual fees charged. If there are any changes to the fee schedule, Part 2 should be amended immediately.

Parts of Item 1 of Part 2 correspond to Item 5 of Part 1, and advisers should ensure that answers correspond. Item 1B corresponds to Items 5E and 5G of Part 1. Item 1C corresponds to Item 5E of Part 1.

ITEM 2

Advisers are required to describe their client base in Item 2. For example, does the adviser service only individual clients, or are institutional investors represented as well? If there are conditions on what type of clients the adviser will take, they should be noted. For example, if the adviser will work only with clients with a minimum net worth of $1 million, that should be noted on Schedule F.

ITEM 3

Item 3 asks investment advisers to indicate what types of investments and financial instruments they recommend to clients.

Advisers should check only the type of investments they actually offer to clients. They should not check the box of any item they do not actually recommend to clients or provide advice on.

ITEM 4

Item 4 requires advisers to check off and describe
   a. the methods of analysis they use in recommending investments to clients
   b. the main sources of information they use
   c. the investment strategies they used to implement any investment advice given to clients

Once again, in filling out Item 4, advisers should check off only the boxes for methods of analysis that they actually currently use. If advisers use methods of analysis, sources of information, or investment strategies that are not indicated, they should check the "other" box and explain on Schedule F.

On Schedule F, advisers should disclose the frequency and level of reviews of client accounts, who reviews the accounts, what instructions the reviewers receive, and the number of accounts each reviewer reviews.

ITEM 5

Item 5 asks advisers if there are any educational or business experience requirements for their employees (see question 1.20) who determine or give investment advice to clients. If the answer is yes, advisers must disclose those requirements on Schedule F. For example, an adviser can state that its portfolio managers must have, at a minimum, a Master's degree in finance and a CFP or CFA designation.

Note that if an adviser does list minimum standards in Item 5, it must adhere to the standards disclosed on Schedule F. If an employee is hired to determine or give investment advice to clients and does not meet those standards, the adviser must revise its response to Item 5 on Schedule F.

ITEM 6

Item 6 asks advisers to identify the educational and business background of all individuals who provide investment advice. Include the name, year of birth, formal education, and business background of each individual who provides investment advice for your firm.

ITEM 7

Item 7 asks advisers if they engage in business activities other than giving investment advice. The purpose of this question is to determine if the adviser has any potential conflicts of interest. If the adviser receives any economic benefit from a person who is not a client, then the adviser must describe on Schedule F what the activities are and time spent performing them.

Item 7 of Part 2 corresponds to Item 6 on Part 1. Advisers should take care that these two sections are answered the same way.

ITEM 8

Item 8 requires the adviser to disclose whether it is registered in another capacity as a financial intermediary or whether it has a material relationship with another firm. Item 8A of Part 2 should correspond to Items 6A and 7A of Part 1. Item 8D should correspond to Item 7B and Part 1. Advisers should make sure that these questions are answered the same way.

ITEM 9

Item 9 requires advisers to disclose the nature of their investment or brokerage discretion with respect to client accounts. If the adviser has brokerage discretion or recommends brokers to clients, the adviser must disclose what factors it considers in selecting which brokers to use and how it determines that commissions are reasonable in Item 9 on Schedule F.

Although Form ADV does not specifically request it, the SEC expects the investment advisers' code of ethics summary to be explained in Item 9E (see chapter 7) along with personal securities transaction policies (see chapter 12) and block trading policies. Item 9 of Part 2 corresponds to Item 8 of Part 1, so advisers should make sure that answers to these two sections do not conflict.

ITEM 10

Item 10 asks advisers to disclose whether they require clients to have a minimum dollar amount to start or maintain an account with the adviser.

ITEM 11

Item 11A asks advisers to provide details on how it reviews its accounts and who reviews the accounts. Advisers should detail the frequency of account reviews and the factors that will trigger a review. Advisers also need to disclose the number of people who review accounts, the titles of those people, and how many accounts each reviewer is assigned.

Item 11B asks the adviser to disclose the nature and frequency of reports to clients. For example, client reports may be provided monthly, quarterly, or as requested by the client. If the adviser issues no regular reports unless requested, that should be clearly spelled out in Item 11.

ITEM 12

Items 12A and 12B of Part 2 are intended for advisers to disclose to clients (see question 1.20) the adviser's soft-dollar practices (see chapter 18).

Although Form ADV does not specifically ask for the information, the SEC also expects advisers in Item 12 to explain
   a. the adviser's proxy voting policies (see chapter 13)
   b. whether or not the adviser bunches trade transactions and splits fees among clients

These disclosures should be made on Schedule F and listed as a continuation of Item 12. Specifically, if an adviser has discretion to vote proxies for clients, then proxy voting policies must be disclosed on Schedule F under Item 12A. If an adviser does not vote proxies, then a statement must be made on Schedule F under Item 12A that the adviser does not vote proxies and that clients are expected to vote their own proxies.

Item 12A of Part 2 corresponds to Item 8C of Part 1, and Item 12B corresponds to Items 8D and 8E of Part 1. Advisers should answer these questions the same way.

ITEM 13

Advisers are required to disclose in Item 13A whether they receive any ancillary economic benefits, including soft dollars (see chapter 18). If the answer is yes, the adviser must describe the arrangements on Schedule F. Any additional cash or noncash compensation the adviser receives from someone who is not a client, which is related to the adviser giving advice to clients, must be disclosed, along with any referral arrangements. If the adviser receives research services or any other product or service in exchange for directing client transactions to a broker, the arrangement must be disclosed to clients. Advisers must disclose what products or services they receive, whether clients are paying commission rates that are above market, and whether the research received benefits all clients or only those paying for the service.

Advisers are required to disclose in Item 13 if and how they compensate anyone directly or indirectly for client referrals (see chapter 16).

Although not specifically asked for in the instructions, advisers are also required to disclose in Item 13 whether an employee who brings in business gets a percentage of the management fees generated by that account as a reward for bringing in that account.

Item 13A of Part 2 corresponds to Item 8E of Part 1, and Item 13B of Part 2 corresponds to Item 8F of Part 1. Advisers should answer such cross-referenced questions exactly the same way.

ITEM 14

Item 14 requires advisers to file a balance sheet on Schedule G if the adviser

   a. is not SEC registered and has custody of client funds or securities; or
   b. requires prepayment of fees or a retainer of more than $500 per client and 6 months or more in advance.

Form ADV Part 2 Schedules F and G

6.2   What is Schedule F and what is the correct way to complete it?
Schedule F is the continuation sheet for responses to Part 2 items.

Its purpose is to give clarification to Part 2 responses in a narrative form in plain English. Additionally, if an adviser has any potential conflicts of interest, Schedule F is the place to disclose them to clients. The rule of thumb is that more disclosure is better than less.

Schedule F is also the place for advisers to provide additional information that does not have a corresponding item number. For example, because there is no ADV item number that corresponds to an adviser's obligation to provide clients with a privacy notice (see chapter 19), it is generally recommended that it be put at the end of Schedule F. Furthermore, if an adviser receives shares in initial public offerings, the SEC expects to see IPO distribution procedures disclosed at the end of Schedule F even though there is no question in Part 2 asking for such information.

6.3 What is Schedule G and how should it be completed?

Schedule G is for the balance sheet required by Part 2 of Item 14.

7 RIA Compliance Programs and Codes of Ethics

- ◆ The Chief Compliance Officer
- ◆ Policies and Procedures
- ◆ The Compliance Program
- ◆ Record Keeping
- ◆ Code of Ethics
- ◆ Supervised Persons
- ◆ Access Persons

Registered investment advisers must consider their fiduciary and regulatory obligations and formalize policies and procedures to address these obligations. Firms must identify conflicts and other compliance factors creating risk exposure in light of the firm's particular operations, and then design policies and procedures to address those risks.

Under Rule 206(4)-7 of the Advisers Act, registered investment advisers must have written policies and procedures that are reasonably designed to prevent the adviser and its supervised persons (see question 7.7) from violating the Investment Advisers Act. Advisers must review these policies and procedures annually and appoint a chief compliance officer to ensure all steps are taken.

Additionally, Rule 204A-1 under the Investment Advisers Act requires registered investment advisers to adopt, maintain, and enforce codes of ethics. A code of ethics must remind advisers' workers, owners, and directors of their ethical and fiduciary obligations to clients and require them to report personal securities transactions and holdings. Personal securities transaction reporting and preclearance requirements are discussed in chapter 12.

The Chief Compliance Officer

7.1   Who can be a chief compliance officer and what are the responsibilities of the position?
Advisers must appoint a chief compliance officer who is competent and knowledgeable about the Investment Advisers Act and has a position of sufficient seniority and authority within the organization to compel others to follow the firm's policies and procedures. The chief compliance officer cannot be more than one individual. The SEC has stated that either an existing firm employee may be designated as chief compliance officer or the firm may designate an employee of an outside firm to fill the position.

The Advisers Act indicates that the chief compliance officer must administer the compliance program and should have a good working understanding of Advisers Act requirements and SEC policy statements and no action letters. The SEC has also indicated that the chief compliance officer should keep abreast of legal and regulatory changes.

Although above and beyond what is required under the Advisers Act, there are a number of specific duties or functions that the SEC has indicated chief compliance officer of advisers should perform or consider performing. They include the following:

a. Advise the firm's senior management on establishing and maintaining an effective firmwide culture of compliance.

b. Confer with and advise senior management on significant compliance matters and issues.

c. Be available to be consulted on compliance matters and issues by businesspeople throughout the firm.

d. Be the lynchpin on compliance matters.

e. Become involved in analyzing and resolving significant compliance issues.

f. Ensure the firm's compliance process is appropriate and implemented effectively.

g. Become personally involved in various steps of the process such as serving on committees that review or define risk or policies and procedures when necessary and appropriate.

h. Ensure that compliance policies and procedures are comprehensive, robust, current, and reflect business processes and conflicts of interest.

i. Ensure appropriate principles of management and control are observed in implementing policies and procedures, including separation of functions, assignment of responsibilities, measuring results against standards and reporting outcomes.

j. Ensure that personnel with compliance responsibilities are competently performing those functions.

k. Ensure that

    i. appropriate quality control (transactional) testing is conducted to detect deviations of actual transactions from policies or standards;

    ii. results of such tests are included on exception and other management reports; and

    ii. problems are promptly addressed, escalated when necessary, and resolved by responsible businesspeople.

l. Ensure timely and appropriate review of material and repetitive compliance issues to detect possible gaps and weaknesses in policies and procedures or risk-identification processes and use the information to keep the compliance program up to date.

m. Conduct periodic analyses and evaluation of compliance issues to obtain additional or corroborating evidence regarding the effectiveness of the firm's compliance program and the possible existence of disguised or undetected compliance issues.

n. Ensure that service providers have effective compliance programs so that services provided by these firms are consistent with the adviser's fiduciary obligations to clients.

o. Establish a compliance calendar that identifies all important dates by which regulatory, client reporting, tax, and compliance matters must be completed to ensure that these important deadlines are not missed.

p. Create a process for regularly mapping a firm's compliance policies and procedures and conflicts of interest to disclosures made to clients so that disclosures are current, complete, and informative.

q. Manage the adviser's compliance department or unit in ways that encourage proactive work, a practice of professional skepticism, and thinking outside the box by compliance staff.

r. Manage the adviser's code of ethics, which is a responsibility given to the chief compliance officer of advisers by Rule 204A-1 of the Advisers Act.

s. Undertake or supervise others in performing the required annual review of an adviser's compliance program. Every adviser is required to conduct a review at least annually of its compliance program. The review should consider any compliance matters that arose during the previous year, any changes in the business activities of the adviser or its affiliates, and any changes in the Advisers Act or applicable regulations that might suggest a need to revise the policies or procedures. Although the rule requires only annual reviews, advisers should consider the need for interim reviews in response to significant compliance events, changes in business arrangements, and regulatory developments.

t. Report results of the annual review to senior management and ensure that recommendations for improvements that flow from the review are implemented as appropriate.

u. Be a strong and persistent advocate for allocating an appropriate amount of a firm's resources to the development and maintenance of an effective compliance program and compliance staff.

v. Recognize the need to remain current on regulatory and compliance issues and participate in continuing education programs.

w. Ensure that the firm's staff members are appropriately trained in compliance-related matters.

x. Be the adviser's liaison and point of contact with SEC examination staff, both during exams and as part of the SEC's chief compliance officer outreach program.

Policies and Procedures

7.2   What written compliance policies and procedures does an adviser need to have in place?

Compliance policies and procedures need to accomplish three objectives:

a. Policies and procedures should be reasonably designed to prevent violations of the Advisers Act by the adviser or any of its supervised persons. Advisers must consider their fiduciary and regulatory obligations under the Advisers Act and formalize policies and procedures to address them.

b. The program should find violations or compliance issues that occur.

c. The program should promptly correct such violations or issues.

Compliance and supervisory policies and procedures should be sufficiently tailored to the firm's business and sufficiently specific in nature to be effective tools that firm management and personnel can and will refer to when conducting business on behalf of the firm. Advisers are not required to consolidate all compliance policies and procedures into a single document.

7.3 What topics should the policies and procedures cover?

Policies and procedures should address

a. portfolio management processes, including allocation of investment opportunities among clients and consistency of portfolios;

b. trading of both the registered investment adviser and supervised persons;

c. trading practices such as procedures the registered investment adviser uses to satisfy its best-execution obligations, use of "soft dollars" to obtain research and services, and allocation of aggregated trades among clients;

d. the accuracy of disclosures made to investors, clients, and regulators, including account statements and advertisements;

e. safeguarding of client assets from conversion or inappropriate use by firm owners and staff;

f. the accurate creation and maintenance of required records, which must be kept secure from unauthorized alteration or use and protected from untimely destruction; marketing, including the use of solicitors; processes to value client holdings and assess fees; safeguards for privacy protection; and business continuity plans.

7.4 Once an adviser sets up a compliance program for the firm, what reviews if any are required?

SEC-registered advisers must periodically review their policies and procedures to determine their adequacy and the effectiveness of their implementation. Specifically, advisers are required to review the adequacy and effectiveness of implementation of their policies within 18 months of their adoption and annually thereafter. The review should consider any compliance matters that arose during the previous year, any changes in business activities of the adviser or its affiliates, and any changes in the Advisers Act or applicable regulations that would suggest a revision to the policies or procedures is in order.

7.5 What records must the adviser maintain?

Advisers have to maintain copies of all compliance policies and procedures that are in effect or were in effect at any time during the last 5 years. Advisers also must keep any records documenting their annual review. These records may be maintained electronically.

The Code of Ethics

7.6   How does an adviser draft a code of ethics?

Under the SEC's rules, advisers have substantial flexibility in drafting codes of ethics to fit the structure, size, and nature of their business. An advisory firm's code of ethics, however, must contain

  a. standards of business conduct requiring supervised persons to comply with fiduciary obligations and securities laws;
  b. provisions requiring access persons to report, and firms to review, personal securities transactions and holdings;
  c. provisions requiring supervised persons to report violations and procedures for internally reporting code of ethics violations;
  d. provisions requiring advisers to provide supervised persons with the code of ethics and amendments and to obtain written acknowledgment of receipt;
  e. provisions requiring access persons to preclear personal investments in initial public offerings or private placements.

7.7   What are supervised persons?

Supervised persons (see question 1.19) are generally firm owners, directors, and workers and can include temporary staff or independent contractors if they are subject to the adviser's control or give advice on the adviser's behalf.

7.8   What are access persons?

Access persons are supervised persons with

  a. access to nonpublic information regarding clients' securities purchases or sales; or
  b. are involved in making securities recommendations to clients; or
  c. have access to nonpublic recommendations.

Access persons include portfolio managers as well as any employee who communicates investment advice to clients. Administrative, technical, and clerical personnel may also be access persons if they have any access to nonpublic information.

7.9   What topics should the code of ethics address?

The SEC requires adviser codes of ethics to set forth a standard of business conduct for supervised persons. The SEC doesn't dictate a particular standard, but the standard must reflect fiduciary obligations and require compliance with federal securities law. Advisers can set higher standards for staff, such as adopting the standards of a professional or trade group, as long as it meets the minimum standards required by the SEC.

The code of ethics must also require a complete report of each access person's securities holdings, initially within 10 days of that person's becoming an access person and then annually thereafter. Personal securities holding reporting requirements are discussed in chapter 12.

Codes of ethics must also require access persons to report personal securities transactions and holdings quarterly, and the adviser to review these reports. Personal securities trading rules are discussed in chapter 12.

Although the provisions are not required, the SEC recommends advisers consider including provisions in the code of ethics covering

   a. securities preclearance procedures beyond those for initial public offerings and private placement

   b. restrictions on short-swing trading and market timing

Additionally, advisers may want to consider addressing the following issues, if appropriate for their firm:

   a. prohibitions on employees' discussing client transactions in public areas

   b. prohibitions against client favoritism

   c. prohibitions against the acceptance of gifts or entertainment above a de minimis value without firm preapproval

   d. prohibitions against profiting, directly or indirectly, from knowledge about client trades

7.10 If an adviser belongs to a professional association that has a code of ethics, does that satisfy the SEC requirement on a code of ethics?

No, advisers must draft and implement an individual code of ethics for the firm.

7.11 Does an adviser have to give clients a copy of the firm's code of ethics?

Advisers are not required to give clients copies of the code of ethics, but they are required to have a description of it on Form ADV Item 9 in Part 2. The description should include the code provisions that have the greatest relevance for clients, such as those relating to securities transaction reporting and preclearance procedures.

7.12 Do employees have to be given a copy of the firm's code of ethics?

Advisers are required to give supervised persons copies of the code of ethics and obtain written acknowledgment of receipt. Advisers must also give supervised persons copies of any amendments made to the code and obtain and keep written acknowledgment of receipt. To be on the safe side, advisers may want to make it a policy to give all firm employees copies of the code of ethics and any amendments and get written acknowledgment of receipt.

7.13 Are advisers required to have ethics training sessions for employees?

There is no requirement to have periodic training sessions on ethics for employees, but the SEC recommends that such training be done.

7.14 What happens if someone doesn't comply with the code of ethics?

Advisers must have in place procedures for promptly reporting violations of the code of ethics to the chief compliance officer or someone else designated in the code of ethics. If someone other than the chief compliance officer is designated to receive reports of code of ethics violations, the chief compliance officer must still periodically receive reports of all violations.

Advisers are also required to create an environment that encourages and protects supervised persons who report violations and protects them from retaliation. For example, reporting of violations may be permitted to be done anonymously, or retaliation against a reporter may be made a further violation of the code of ethics.

7.15   What kind of records with respect to the firm's code of ethics must an adviser keep?

Advisers must keep

    a. records of code of ethics violations and actions taken as a result of the violations

    b. copies of written acknowledgments of code of ethics receipt by supervised persons

    c. a list of the names of access persons

    d. holding and transaction reports

    e. records of decisions approving securities acquisitions

These records must be kept for 5 years in an easily accessible place, with the first 2 years in an appropriate office of the adviser. Copies of codes of ethics must be kept for 5 years after the last date they were in effect. Supervised persons' acknowledgments of the receipt of the code of ethics must be kept for 5 years after the individual ceases to be a supervised person. The adviser's list of access persons must include every person who was an access person at any time within the past 5 years, even if they are no longer access persons.

8 | Investment Recommendations and Fiduciary Obligations

◆ **Fiduciary Responsibilities**
◆ **Fiduciary Defined**
◆ **Standards of Care**
◆ **Conflicts of Interest**
◆ **ERISA Plans**
◆ **Prudent Investments**

The Investment Advisers Act of 1940 imposes fiduciary obligations on registered investment advisers. ERISA also imposes fiduciary obligations on registered investment advisers dealing with ERISA plan assets (see chapter 17).

The Advisers Act prohibits investment advisers from engaging in fraudulent, deceptive, or manipulative conduct in their investment-planning activities. Every adviser has an affirmative duty of utmost good faith to act solely in the best interest of the client.

Under the Advisers Act, advisers are fiduciaries and have a fiduciary duty to provide only suitable investment advice to clients. Before making any investment for a client, an adviser should do due diligence, looking into the financial situation, investment experience, and investment objectives of the client to ensure that the investment is suitable for that particular client. Advisers must also clearly delineate to clients the level of risks assumed in making any investment.

When investing for retirement plans, ERISA requires that advisers make only "prudent" investments (see chapter 17). Furthermore, before making any investment for an ERISA plan, advisers should also ascertain whether such investment is allowed under the provisions of the plan document.

Fiduciary Responsibilities

8.1 How can advisers determine whether they are fiduciaries?

Every registered investment adviser is a fiduciary to its clients.

8.2 What does it mean to be a fiduciary?

As a fiduciary, an adviser has an obligation that becomes part of every decision and every transaction the adviser undertakes which affects or impacts its clients. An adviser's fiduciary obligation requires the adviser to always put the interests of clients first and its own interests second. Thus, whenever an adviser's interests or those of its staff conflict with the interests of clients, the client's interests must always come first; if not, the adviser has breached its fiduciary obligations. Furthermore, in discus-

> ### FIGURE 8.1   **Fiduciary Responsibilities**
>
> **As fiduciaries to their clients, advisers must**
> - **act in the best interest of clients** and must always put the interests of the client ahead of their own
> - **exercise a high standard of care** because clients are relying on them for advice
> - **disclose conflicts of interest to clients**
> - **disclose all fees and commissions** they receive on all investment and insurance products they recommend to clients
> - **honor the duty of confidentiality** and never disclose confidential information regarding clients without the clients' consent

sions with clients, advisers are just as liable for what is not said as for what is said.

8.3   By what standards of care must an adviser abide?

As part of investment advisers' fiduciary duty to clients, they should

   a. pay close attention to client goals

   b. develop an investment policy/strategy

   c. focus on management of risk and not just the avoidance of risk

   d. determine clients' risk tolerance

   e. diversify appropriately

Furthermore, the SEC has indicated that, as part of investment advisers' fiduciary duties to clients, they have a duty to

   a. have a reasonable, independent basis for any investment advice provided to clients

   b. ensure that investment advice is suitable to a client's objectives, needs, and circumstances

   c. be loyal to clients

   d. obtain best execution for clients' securities transactions when advisers direct brokerage transactions

8.4 What are advisers' fiduciary obligations to clients with respect to actual and potential conflicts of interest?

The Advisers Act fiduciary rules obligate advisers to disclose conflicts of interest to clients. If there are any real or potential conflicts of interest, advisers have a fundamental duty to make a full and fair disclosure of that real or potential conflict. Advisers must disclose what the conflict of interest is and how the adviser will handle each such conflict. According to the SEC, examples of conflicts of interest may include

a. using clients' brokerage to get anything that benefits the adviser, whether or not it may also benefit clients and whether or not the benefit to the adviser fits within the soft-dollar safe harbor (see chapter 18);

b. the personal trading activities of advisory firm insiders;

c. how the allocation of investment opportunities among clients is made.

ERISA Plans

8.5 Are there any special rules that apply to advisers that handle retirement plans for clients?

ERISA imposes a number of substantial fiduciary duties on investment advisers who are fiduciaries to the plan that deal with plan assets. Severe penalties can result from violating these rules. See chapter 17 for an explanation of the fiduciary rules governing investment of ERISA plan assets and the penalties for violating the prohibited transaction rules.

8.6 When is an investment suitable under the Advisers Act?

The Advisers Act does not have any provisions expressly defining what types of investments are or are not suitable. Whether or not an investment is suitable depends on the particular client. Advisers must consider the client's financial circumstances, investment goals, and risk tolerance. Whether or not an investment is suitable also depends on what types of investment the adviser is authorized to make, as outlined in the advisory contract (see chapter 9).

SEC staff has noted that advisers are required to reasonably determine that every investment recommendation they make to a client be suitable for that client. In other words, each piece of advice to every client has to be suitable, not just the adviser's investment advice in the aggregate. Whether or not advice is suitable should be evaluated in the context of the client's entire portfolio.

The SEC also takes the position that an adviser defrauds clients when it misrepresents the nature of investments to clients, makes investments contrary to clients' stated investment desires, fails to disclose the risks of the investments, or recommends investments that are unsuitable in light of the clients' assets, income, or degree of investment sophistication.

8.7 When is an investment considered prudent under ERISA?

When an adviser manages the entire portfolio of an ERISA plan, the adviser must determine whether each and every investment is reasonably designed to further the purposes of the plan, considering the risk of loss and opportunity for return associated with the investment or investment strategy. Before making any investment, advisers managing the entire portfolio must consider

a. the entire composition of the portfolio and how the investment diversifies the assets and determine if it minimizes the risk of large losses

b. the liquidity and current rates of return on the investment

c. the overall projected portfolio returns and plan objectives

Advisers must consider the same factors when they do not manage the entire portfolio of the plan. However, advisers may rely on information provided by the plan's fiduciary to make the determination as to whether or not the investment advice is prudent.

9 | Advisory Contracts and Fees

- ◆ Fee Structures
- ◆ Performance Fees
- ◆ Wealthy or Foreign Clients
- ◆ Asset-Based Fees
- ◆ Management Fees for Mutual Fund Investments
- ◆ Up-Front Fees
- ◆ Contract Termination
- ◆ Retirement Plan Assets
- ◆ Advisory Contracts
- ◆ Dispute Resolution
- ◆ Terminating, Assigning, or Amending a Contract

Contracts between advisers and clients, or advisory contracts, typically cover the topics of fees; scope of services; administrative issues; liabilities; controversy and dispute resolution; representations and acknowledgments; and termination, assignment, and amendment. There is nothing in the Advisers Act requiring a written contract, although it is generally considered good business practice to have written contracts. Many states also require written contracts, so advisers should check the laws of any states in which they do business.

Advisers must strictly adhere to the terms of the advisory contract once it is drafted. An adviser's failure to fulfill a contractual obligation may constitute a material misrepresentation in violation of the Advisers Act. Furthermore, all terms of contracts between advisers and clients must be consistent with the adviser's regulatory filings, and no terms or provisions may violate relevant laws and regulations. Specifically, all advisory contract provisions must match up with what is disclosed on Form ADV, and if Form ADV is amended to reflect new information or new business practices, advisory contracts should be amended as well.

Fees

9.1   What choices does an adviser have in structuring fees?

Although there are restrictions, advisers have wide latitude in structuring fees for clients, and the Advisers Act sets no limits as to how much clients may be charged. But all fee arrangements the adviser uses must be disclosed to clients on Form ADV Part 2 (see chapter 6).

9.2   May advisers calculate fees differently from the methodology agreed to in the advisory contract or on Form ADV?

No. Advisers must charge fees as agreed to in advisory contracts with clients and as disclosed on Form ADV.

9.3   May advisers charge performance fees?

The Investment Advisers Act states that adviser compensation from clients may not be based on a share of capital gains or capital appreciation of the client's funds—"performance fees." However, since the prohibition applies only to fees based on a share of capital gains or capital appreciation, advisers may charge fees based on other measures of performance.

9.4 Are there any exceptions to these rules for wealthy or foreign clients?

An adviser may enter into performance fee arrangements with a client of $1.5 million in net worth if the client is either an individual or a company that has $750,000 in assets under the adviser's management. Advisers may also charge performance fees to persons who are not U.S. residents.

9.5 May advisers charge asset-based fees?

Yes, the Advisers Act specifically permits advisers to base their fees on a percentage of the total assets in a client's account.

9.6 When advisers invest clients' assets in mutual funds that charge fees, may they charge management fees in addition to the mutual fund's fees?

If advisers invest client assets in mutual funds, the advisory contract should state that in addition to paying the adviser's fee, the client will pay mutual fund fees and charges. Additionally, if advisers are receiving fees from a mutual fund for investing client assets in that fund, advisers must disclose to clients that they are receiving those indirect fees in addition to the direct fees they receive from the clients.

9.7 Some advisers charge fees up front. If a client terminates the contract, may those advisers keep the fees paid? And may they charge a fee if the client terminates the contract early?

If a client pays fees in advance, those fees must be returned pro rata to the client if the contract is terminated before it expires. The SEC takes the position that charging clients fees for terminating an advisory contract violates the Advisers Act. However, the SEC also takes the position that advisers may charge termination fees for services the adviser has already provided.

9.8   Suppose an adviser is asked to manage a very large retirement plan for a client who is self-employed. The plan covers the client and his employees. Do any special rules apply regarding how the adviser may charge fees to the plan?
When dealing with plan assets, ERISA applies (see chapter 17). Performance fees are not always prohibited under ERISA. If a plan has at least $50 million in assets, an adviser may be able to charge performance fees if the compensation arrangement is reasonable and a fiduciary who is knowledgeable about the type of investment arrangement and the appropriate fees for it approves.

9.9   May advisers have their advisory fees automatically deducted from clients' accounts?
It is not prohibited, but if the advisory contract permits the adviser to deduct advisory fees directly from the client's account, custody issues may arise. (See question 10.2.)

Advisory Contracts

9.10   What information about fees should advisers include in the advisory contract?
The advisory contract should include a fee schedule and when fees are due and payable. If fees are based on a percentage of assets, the advisory contract should indicate how the market value of assets will be computed. Furthermore, the contract should outline such things as how brokerage commissions, stock transfer fees, and other charges will be paid.

9.11   How should advisers explain the scope of their services on the advisory contract?
In their advisory contracts, advisers should fully define the scope of the services that will be provided to clients. For example, if an adviser is managing client assets, the advisory contract should state whether the adviser is providing only investment recommendations or has the authority to execute those recommendations.

Similarly, if the client is designating a particular broker to execute trades, that designation should be made in the advisory contract, and if the client directs brokerage, the contract should note that the client may not be receiving best execution. If the client grants the adviser authority to pick brokers, that should be spelled out in the advisory contract as well, along with factors the adviser will use in meeting the duty of "best execution" (see question 11.2), whether the adviser may use an affiliated broker, and whether he may aggregate trades. The advisory contract should also outline whether or not the adviser will be voting proxies held in advisory accounts (see chapter 13).

9.12   How should administrative issues be explained on the advisory contract?

Advisers' advisory contracts should discuss administrative issues, including

a. who will act as custodian of client account assets;
b. frequency of investment reports;
c. client investment objectives, specifying any limits on investments;
d. what information provided by either the client or adviser is deemed confidential.

Furthermore, if the adviser is organized as a partnership, the Advisers Act requires the advisory contract to state that the client will be notified of any changes in members of the partnership.

9.13   How should advisers handle controversies and dispute-resolution provisions?

The advisory contract should specify which state laws are to be followed, if not otherwise preempted by federal laws, in the event controversies or disputes arise. Arbitration clauses are not prohibited, but there are questions as to their enforceability.

9.14   Are there any ways that advisers may legally limit their liability?

Advisory contracts may define the scope of both the adviser's and the client's liabilities. However, the SEC takes the position that "hedge clauses"—that is, contractual provisions, clauses, or legends that cause a client to waive rights of action—are prohibited by the antifraud provisions of the Advisers Act. The Advisers Act also declares void any advisory contract provisions waiving compliance with any provisions of the Advisers Act.

9.15 How may advisers draft provisions terminating, assigning, or amending the agreement or contract?

Advisory contracts may contain provisions specifying under what terms the contract may be terminated or amended. The SEC takes the position that the contract may not provide for a penalty if the advisory contract is terminated by the client. Therefore, if the adviser charges advisory fees received in advance, the fees must be returned pro rata to the client if the contract is terminated before it expires. The Advisers Act prohibits the adviser from assigning the contract without the client's consent.

10 Custody of Customer Accounts

- ◆ **Custody**
- ◆ **Qualified Custodian**
- ◆ **Custody Rules**
- ◆ **Account Statements**
- ◆ **An Independent Representative**

The Investment Advisers Act does not prohibit investment advisers from maintaining custody of client assets. However, some states do prohibit such arrangements, so investment advisers should check with their state securities authorities if they wish to hold client assets.

The Advisers Act imposes a number of requirements on advisers when they maintain custody of client assets, and advisers must disclose on Form ADV if they or a related person have custody of client funds or securities. Investment advisers with custody or possession of advisory client funds or securities must maintain books and records with respect to funds or securities held in custody. Advisers are also required to segregate client assets and are required to make disclosures to clients.

The Advisers Act has no bonding requirements when advisers have custody. Many states, however, impose bonding requirements. If the assets are ERISA plan assets, then ERISA rules apply (see chapter 17).

Custody

10.1   When are advisers deemed to be in custody of client funds or securities?

Advisers are deemed to have custody if they directly or indirectly hold client funds or securities, have any authority to obtain possession of them, or have the ability to appropriate them, even for a brief period. Advisers may also be deemed to have custody of client funds held by affiliates.

Advisers are considered to have custody of client accounts held by a custodian if they have the authority to withdraw client funds or securities from those accounts. Advisers are also deemed to have custody if they have a power of attorney to sign checks on clients' behalf, withdraw funds or securities from clients' accounts, or dispose of client funds or securities for any purpose other than authorized trading.

Actual possession of client funds or securities is not necessary for an adviser to be subject to the custody rule. For example, if a client sends an adviser a check payable to the adviser or a stock certificate for forwarding to a custodian, the adviser will be deemed to have custody unless the check or certificate is returned to the client within 3 days. Receiving checks for advisory fees, however, is not considered custody, nor is receiving from a client a check made payable to a third party for forwarding.

10.2 Does having advisory fees paid automatically from a client's account run afoul of the custody rules?

Advisers who are authorized to deduct advisory fees or other expenses directly from client accounts are deemed to have custody of client funds or securities in that account.

10.3 What rules do advisers need to be aware of when they have custody of client assets?

Advisers who have custody of client assets must
   a. maintain them with a "qualified custodian"
   b. provide clients with written notice identifying the custodian and describing the customer arrangement
   c. deliver to clients quarterly account statements that identify client assets held in custody and transactions that occurred

There are two exceptions to the rule that client assets must be held by a "qualified custodian." First, mutual fund shares that are purchased directly from the mutual fund's transfer agent do not have to be held by a qualified custodian. Second, privately offered securities that are not certified do not have to be held by a qualified custodian if the ownership is recorded only on the books of the issuer or its transfer agent in the name of the client and only if such securities are transferable only with prior consent of the issuer or shareholders. The exception for uncertificated, privately offered securities does not apply if the securities are held for the account of a pooled vehicle unless the pooled vehicle is audited annually in accordance with generally accepted accounting principles and the audited financial reports are distributed to all limited partners within 120 days of the end of the fiscal year.

10.4 What is a qualified custodian?

Qualified custodians are U.S.-based banks and savings associations, registered broker-dealers, registered futures commission merchants, and foreign financial institutions that hold financial assets for customers and who keep advisory clients' assets in segregated accounts. Affiliates of an adviser that are qualified custodians may hold client assets, as may the adviser if the adviser is a qualified custodian.

Account Statements

10.5   What information must the written notice to clients regarding custody contain?

Anytime an adviser opens an account with a qualified custodian on behalf of a client, the adviser must provide that client with written notice identifying the custodian, the address of the custodian, and describing the custody arrangement. Furthermore, the client must be notified promptly of any changes to the information provided in the original notice.

10.6   What information must the quarterly account statement contain and how may it be delivered?

Advisers are required to give clients quarterly account statements identifying client assets held in custody and transactions occurring during the reporting period. If the qualified custodian sends the client quarterly statements, the requirement is satisfied. The SEC takes the position that quarterly reports may be sent to clients electronically.

When the adviser is the one sending the quarterly statements, the adviser must undergo an annual surprise audit by an independent public accountant for the purposes of verifying client funds and securities. The accountant must conduct the audit without notifying the adviser and the accountant must file a certificate on Form ADV-E with the SEC within 30 days. If the accountant finds any material discrepancies, then the SEC must be informed within 1 business day of finding such discrepancy.

The surprise audit requirement can be avoided in cases where the adviser has a "reasonable basis" to believe that the qualified custodian sent the account statement. Advisers have a reasonable basis if the qualified custodian sends the adviser copies of the account statements sent to clients.

Clients may choose to have an independent representative (see question 10.7) receive their account statements.

10.7   What is an independent representative?
An independent representative is a person who
   a. acts as an agent for an advisory client and by law or contract is obligated to act in the best interest of the advisory client
   b. does not control, is not controlled by, and is not under common control with the adviser
   c. does not have and has not had within the past 2 years a material business relationship with the adviser

10.8   If an advisory firm advises a limited partnership, how should it comply with the quarterly statement requirement?
Advisers to pooled investment vehicles can, but are not required to, provide quarterly account statements themselves or through qualified custodians. Advisers to pooled investment vehicles, such as limited partnerships or limited liability companies, do not have to provide quarterly statements provided that the pooled investment vehicle is audited annually. For the exemption to apply, the audited financial statements must also be prepared in accordance with generally accepted accounting principles and be distributed to all limited partners, beneficial owners, or members within 120 days of the end of the fiscal year.

Other Custody Rules
10.9   Are there any other rules advisers need to be aware of when they have custody of client assets?
Any time an adviser or a person related to the adviser has custody of client accounts, that fact must be disclosed on the adviser's Form ADV. Furthermore, when advisers have custody of client accounts, they are required to
   a. keep records showing all purchases, sales, receipts, and deliv-

eries of securities, with certificate numbers, for all accounts over which they have custody;

b. keep separate ledger accounts for each client for whom the adviser has custody of assets showing all purchases, sales, receipts, and deliveries of securities, as well as the date and price of each purchase and sale and all debits and credits;

c. keep copies of confirmations of transactions;

d. keep a position record for each security in which the client has a position, showing the name of each client having an interest, the amount of the interest of each client, and the location of each security.

11 | Selecting Brokers and Executing Trades

- ◆ **Recommending Brokers**
- ◆ **Best Execution**
- ◆ **Conflicts of Interest**
- ◆ **Securities Transactions**
- ◆ **Aggregate Orders**
- ◆ **Nonpublic Information**
- ◆ **Broker Violations**
- ◆ **Disclosure**
- ◆ **Preexecution Consent**
- ◆ **Allocations**

Advisers have a number of obligations to clients when they execute client trades. In addition to the duty of best execution, they have to be cognizant of rules for transactions executed between the adviser and the client as well as between clients. The party that selects the broker to execute client trades should be specified in the advisory contract (see chapter 9).

When a registered investment adviser assumes the responsibility to select brokers to execute client trades, the adviser is subject to the duty of best execution (see question 11.2). Registered investment advisers must use client assets for the benefit of clients and must disclose certain information about their brokerage practices. If advisers use client brokerage to obtain research or other products and services, then the soft-dollar rules apply (see chapter 18) and the adviser must fully and accurately disclose this practice to clients.

Additional rules apply when advisers or their supervised persons trade for their own accounts (see chapter 12).

Broker Selection

11.1 What rules apply when advisers recommend brokers to clients?

Advisers have a fiduciary duty to seek to obtain the best net price reasonably available under the circumstances, and if they are not obtaining the best price and execution, they must disclose to clients that they are not obtaining the best price and execution.

11.2 What is the duty of best execution?

Executing securities transactions is a core service that investment advisers provide to clients, so best execution of client trades is a core fiduciary responsibility. Best execution, however, does not mean best price. Although obtaining the lowest transactional cost should be a consideration, advisers need to review and consider the full range and quality of the broker's service in placing brokerage, including execution capability, the value of the research provided, commission rate, financial responsibility, and responsiveness.

To that end, advisers should document conclusions as to how trades are carried out, noting

   a. commission rates

   b. execution capability of brokers

   c. whether any soft dollars were received

   d. affiliated brokers

   e. client-directed brokerage

Advisers are also required in Part 2 of Form ADV to disclose the factors considered in determining best execution (see chapter 6).

11.3 What conflicts of interest may arise in the selection of a broker to execute a client transaction and how should advisers disclose them?

If advisers use client brokerage to obtain research or other products and services (soft dollars), they must fully and accurately disclose this practice (see chapter 18).

When advisers direct transactions to brokers with whom they're affiliated, it can lead to conflicts. The Advisers Act does not specifically prohibit advisers from executing client trades through affiliated brokers. The SEC, however, recognizes that there are potential conflicts. An adviser should execute client trades through an affiliated broker only if it satisfies the adviser's duty of best execution. That the adviser executes trades through an affiliated broker must also be adequately disclosed to clients in Part 2 of Form ADV.

If the client is an ERISA plan, and the assets are plan assets, executing a trade through an affiliated broker could be a prohibited transaction (see chapter 17). The Department of Labor, however, has exempted affiliated broker transactions if specific requirements are met. To be eligible for the exemption, the affiliated brokerage may not be excessive under the circumstances, either in the amount or frequency. Furthermore, the transactions must be executed pursuant to a written authorization executed by an independent plan fiduciary, and the written authorization must be terminable at will by the plan with no penalty. The affiliated broker also must make annual disclosure to the fiduciary.

Securities Transactions

11.4   Suppose an adviser's client wants to sell a security. Another of the adviser's clients wants to buy the same security at the same time that the first client is selling his interest. May an adviser complete the transaction between the clients through an unaffiliated broker?

The transaction is allowed, but the Advisers Act requires that prior to effectuating the transaction, the conflict be disclosed in writing to both clients and consent obtained from them. In addition, an adviser may not receive any additional compensation, beyond the customary advisory fee for the transaction.

11.5   Sometimes advisers recommend the same security to a number of clients. May advisers aggregate orders to get the best transaction prices?

Advisers may aggregate or bunch trades. However, there are potential fiduciary issues and conflicts of interest when doing so. Advisers should take care to not violate fiduciary duties to clients in allocating securities or expenses among clients. For example, advisers should not allocate trades based on what is most profitable to the adviser. Furthermore, advisers should be cautious and avoid the appearance of favoring certain clients over others.

The SEC staff takes the position that trades may be aggregated or bunched as long as

a. prior to entering the aggregated order, the adviser prepares a written statement specifying the participating client accounts and how the order will be allocated;

b. if the order is partially filled, it will be allocated pro rata;

c. if the allocation differs from the written statement, the reasons for the difference will be explained in writing and approved in writing by the firm's compliance officer no later than 1 hour after the markets open on the next trading day.

11.6   Suppose an adviser is on the board of directors of a public company whose stock is owned by several of his clients. Suppose, also, that the adviser learned some nonpublic infor-

mation about the company that could hurt the clients' investment. May the adviser sell their stock?

If the adviser sells stock based on the nonpublic information,
the transaction would constitute insider trading. Advisers are
required to have procedures in place to prevent insider trading.
Advisers are also required to establish, maintain, and enforce
written policies and procedures to prevent the misuse of nonpublic information by the investment adviser or any person
associated with the investment adviser. When an adviser has
access to inside information on a public company, the SEC has
stated that it will examine the adequacy of these procedures
to guard against misuse of nonpublic information about companies.

11.7 What are some examples of brokerage practices that the SEC has found to violate the Advisers Act?

Examples of brokerage activity that the SEC has determined violate the Advisers Act include the following:

a. An adviser allocates client brokerage to a broker in exchange
for client referrals without full disclosure of the practice, or without revealing that allocating client brokerage to this broker in
exchange for client referrals costs clients higher brokerage commissions and does not give them the best price and execution.

b. An adviser allocates client brokerage to a broker in exchange
for research or other products (for more on soft dollars, see chapter
18) without disclosing the practice.

Disclosure of Sales to or From Firm Inventory

11.8 When an adviser either buys securities for the firm's own inventory from a client or sells securities from the firm's inventory to a client, are there any potential conflicts of interest the adviser needs to be aware of?

The Advisers Act does not specifically prohibit advisers from buying or selling securities to or from clients. However, the act does
require that advisers disclose to clients, in writing, that this is a
conflict and obtain a consent from the client before effectuating

the transaction. If the client is an ERISA plan, the transaction could be a prohibited transaction (see chapter 17).

Furthermore, the SEC takes the position that not only are advisers prohibited from engaging in buying or selling securities to or from clients without disclosure and consent, but any affiliate of the adviser is similarly restricted from doing so.

11.9 What information must the disclosure described in question 11.8 contain?

Depending on their relevance to a particular transaction and the extent to which the client is relying on the adviser for investment advice, executions, and trades, the disclosure should specify

- **a.** the capacity in which the investment adviser proposes to act
- **b.** the cost of the security to the adviser if sold to the client
- **c.** the price at which securities could be resold if purchased from a client
- **d.** the best price at which the transaction could be effected by or for the client elsewhere if the price is more advantageous to the client than the actual purchase or sale

11.10 What should advisers do when asking for the preexecution consent described in question 11.8 if they can't provide execution price, best price, or final commission charges?

SEC staff recognizes that sometimes advisers may not be able to provide a client with a final execution price, best price, or final commission charges when soliciting the preexecution consent described in question 11.8. In such cases, the SEC has indicated that advisers should provide comparable information that is sufficient to identify and explain the potential conflicts of interest arising from the capacity in which the adviser is acting. When soliciting a client's postexecution, presettlement consent, the adviser should provide the client with information regarding pricing and final commission charges. The adviser should also provide a client with sufficient information to inform the client of the adviser's conflicts of interest in engaging in the transaction.

11.11   At what point do advisers have to make these disclosures and receive these consents?
The SEC staff takes the position that the disclosure described in question 11.8 must be made and consents received prior to settlement of the transaction.

11.12   Do advisers have to make the disclosures and obtain consents detailed in question 11.8 each time they engage in these types of transactions?
Yes, the SEC takes the position that a blanket disclosure not tied to any specific securities transaction is insufficient.

Allocations of Initial Public Offerings

11.13   If advisers sometimes participate in initial public offerings, are there any rules regarding how they should allocate those shares to client or employee accounts?
If advisers participate in initial public offerings (IPOs) and the IPO opportunities are disproportionately allocated to favored client accounts, advisers are required to disclose those circumstances to clients. However, the SEC recommends that IPO opportunities be allocated equally among client accounts (see question 11.14).

11.14   How should advisers allocate trades among clients' accounts?
The SEC recommends that advisers adopt strict trading policies and procedures to prevent allocating trades inequitably among clients. The SEC takes the position that an adviser might defraud clients if it disproportionately allocates initial public offerings to favored accounts without disclosing the practice.

12 Personal Securities Trading and Reporting

- ◆ Prohibited Practices
- ◆ Disclosure and Consent
- ◆ Preclearance of Employee Investments
- ◆ Reporting of Employee Personal Securities Trades and Holdings
- ◆ Holding and Transaction Reports
- ◆ Reportable Securities
- ◆ Trading for Family Members

A number of rules apply to owners, directors, and employees of an adviser engaged in personal trading. For one thing, certain kinds of trading practices are specifically prohibited. Furthermore, advisers are required to maintain records of transactions undertaken by specific firm personnel, and the adviser code of ethics must contain specific rules regarding both the reporting of securities transactions and obtaining preclearance for those transactions (see chapter 7).

Prohibited Practices

12.1 Are there any trading practices that are prohibited by the Advisers Act?

Advisers are specifically prohibited from trading securities for personal accounts or for the accounts of family members or affiliates shortly before trading the same securities for clients. Directing clients to trade in securities in which the adviser has an undisclosed interest is also prohibited. Although there are no specific prohibitions on advisers' buying or selling thinly traded securities, it would be prudent to adopt waiting periods for access persons to trade thinly traded securities if the firm has traded the same securities for a client.

Sales of Adviser Securities to Clients

12.2 Are there any other restrictions on adviser trading in the Advisers Act?

If an adviser sells or buys a security to or from the adviser's personal account to a client, the Advisers Act requires the adviser to disclose that transaction to the client and to obtain the consent of the client before effectuating the transactions.

12.3 What information does the disclosure and consent detailed in question 12.2 have to contain?

In addition to identifying and explaining to the client the potential conflicts of interest, the disclosure, at a minimum, must contain

    a. the capacity in which the investment adviser proposes to act

    b. the cost of the security to the adviser if sold to the client

c. the price at which the securities could be resold if purchased from a client

d. the best price at which the transaction could be effected by or for the client elsewhere if the price is more advantageous to the client than the actual purchase or sale price

12.4 May advisers who sell or buy securities to or from their personal accounts have clients sign one consent for all future transactions?

No, a new disclosure and consent must be given and written confirmation obtained for each specific transaction.

Preclearance of Employee Investments

12.5 Are advisers required to set up preclearance procedures for employee trades?

Yes, advisers are required to set up procedures for certain employees to receive prior written approval (or preclearance) for personal investments in initial public offerings and private placements.

12.6 Which members of the firm must comply with these preclearance procedures?

Owners, directors, and employees who are access persons must obtain preclearance (see question 7.8 for a definition of access person). To be prudent, however, an adviser may want to have all firm workers obtain preclearance.

Reporting of Employee Personal Securities Trades and Holdings

12.7 Do advisers have to report employee trades or keep records of them?

The Advisers Act requires an adviser to keep records of every securities transaction in which it or its advisory representative (see question 12.8) has or acquires any direct or indirect beneficial ownership. These records must indicate the title and amount of the security involved; the date and nature of the transaction; the price; and the name of the broker, dealer, or bank through which the transaction was effectuated. The transaction record must be recorded within 10 days of the end of the calendar quarter in which the transaction was effectuated. The Advisers Act provides that securities that are direct obligations of the United States are not subject to these rules.

Certain firm owners, directors, and employees are also required to report personal securities transactions and holdings to the firm's chief compliance officer (see question 7.1). Advisers are required to review and retain these transaction reports.

12.8   What is an advisory representative?

The following individuals are considered advisory representatives:

    a. any partner, officer, or director of the adviser;

    b. any employee who is involved in making investment recommendations;

    c. any employee who obtains information about securities recommendations;

    d. any control person or affiliated person of such control person;

    e. any affiliate of such affiliated person.

12.9   Which employees are required to file the holding and transaction reports detailed in question 12.7?

Firm owners, directors, and employees who are access persons (as described in question 7.8). However, depending on the size and setup of a firm, an adviser may want to have all firm workers file holding and transaction reports.

12.10   What kind of transactions and holdings must be reported?

SEC rules require that access persons submit holding and transaction reports for any security that is a reportable security in which the access person has or acquires any direct or indirect beneficial ownership, such as in a trust.

12.11   What are reportable securities subject to the holding and transaction reporting requirement?

Reportable securities are all securities with the exception of
  a. direct obligations of the U.S. government;
  b. bankers' acceptances, bank certificates of deposit, commercial paper, repurchase agreements and high-quality, short-term debt instruments;
  c. shares of money market funds;
  d. shares of open-end mutual funds, unless the adviser or an affiliate acts as the investment adviser or principal underwriter for the fund;
  e. units of a unit investment trust if the unit investment trust is invested exclusively in unaffiliated open-end mutual funds.

12.12 How often must the holding and transaction reports detailed in question 12.7 be filed?

Employees, directors, and owners must file their initial holding reports within 10 days of becoming an access person (see question 7.8) and annually thereafter. Personal securities transaction reports must be filed no later than 30 days after the close of the calendar quarter and contain all transactions during the quarter. An adviser's code of ethics (see chapter 7) may excuse access persons from submitting transaction reports that would duplicate information contained in trade confirmations or account statements that the adviser holds in its records, provided that the confirmations or statements were received no later than 30 days after the close of the calendar quarter in which the transaction takes place.

12.13 What information must holding reports contain?

Holding reports must be accurate to within 45 days of filing and contain
  a. the title and type of security, exchange ticker symbol, or CUSIP number, number of shares, and principal amount;
  b. the name of any broker, dealer, or bank with which the access person maintains an account;
  c. the date the report was submitted.

12.14   What information must transaction reports contain?
Transaction reports must contain

a. the date of the transaction, the title and exchange ticker symbol or CUSIP number, interest rate and maturity date, number of shares, and the principal amount of each reportable security involved;

b. the nature of the transaction (that is, purchase, sale, or any other type of acquisition or disposition);

c. the price of the security at which the transaction was effected;

d. the name of the broker, dealer, or bank with or through which the transaction was effected;

e. the date the report was submitted.

12.15   Who is in charge of receiving preclearance requests and transactions reports?
Unless another person is designated in the adviser's code of ethics, all transaction and holding reports detailed in question 12.7 must be received by the chief compliance officer (see chapter 7). The chief compliance officer or other designated person must review these reports. That review should not only assess whether the access person followed any required internal procedures, but also

a. compare personal trading to any restricted lists

b. assess whether access persons are trading for their accounts in the same securities they are trading for clients

c. analyze the access persons' trading for patterns that may indicate abuse

d. investigate substantial disparities between the percentage of trades that are profitable when access persons trade for their own accounts and the percentage that are profitable when they place trades for clients

12.16   Are there any requirements regarding how these reports should be filed?
Reports may be filed electronically, and software exists to ensure filing and review.

12.17 Are solo practitioners required to report their securities transactions to themselves?

Firms with only one access person are exempt from reporting and obtaining preclearance, but they must keep records of holdings and transactions. Firms with more than one access person, even if related, such as husband or wife, should fully comply.

12.18 If an adviser and some of the firm's employees trade for family members or have family members who trade, what rules apply?

For purposes of holding and transaction reports an access person is presumed to be a beneficial owner of securities that are held by his or her immediate family members who are sharing the access person's household. Therefore, any trades that the access person initiates or which are initiated by a family member must be reported, and any holdings by such family members must be reported as well.

12.19 Are there any other exceptions to the personal securities reporting rules?

No reporting is required

   a. with respect to transactions effected pursuant to an automatic investment plan, such as a 401(k) plan;
   b. with respect to securities held in accounts over which the access person had no direct or indirect influence or control.

13 Voting Client Proxies

◆ **Policies and Procedures**

◆ **Addressing Conflicts of Interest**

◆ **Voting Retirement Plan Proxies**

◆ **Fiduciary Rules**

◆ **Record-Keeping Requirements**

Whether or not the adviser will vote proxies for clients with respect to securities held in clients' accounts should be spelled out in the advisory contract (see chapter 9). The Investment Advisers Act has no provisions regarding how advisers should vote proxies for client securities. The SEC, however, does take the position that advisers have a fiduciary duty to vote or not vote proxies in the best interests of clients. Furthermore, the duty of care requires advisers with voting authority to monitor corporate actions and vote client proxies, so advisers should have procedures designed to ensure that this duty is fulfilled.

Policies and Procedures

13.1   What regulatory requirements must advisers be aware of if they vote client proxies?
The SEC requires that advisers that exercise voting authority over client proxies

   a. adopt policies and procedures reasonably designed to ensure that the adviser votes proxies in the best interests of clients;
   b. disclose to clients information about those policies and procedures
   c. disclose to clients how they may obtain information on how the adviser voted their proxies

13.2   If advisers vote client proxies, must they have a formal proxy voting policy?
Registered investment advisers that exercise voting authority with respect to client securities are required to adopt and implement written policies and procedures

   a. reasonably designed to ensure that votes are cast in the best interest of clients;
   b. describing how, when voting proxies, the adviser addresses material conflicts between its interests and those of its clients.

The SEC does not have any specific policies and procedures that advisers are required to adopt, and advisers may have different policies and procedures for different clients.

13.3 What should an adviser do if a conflict of interest exists?

The SEC recommends that advisers addressing material conflicts of interest

a. disclose to clients the conflict prior to voting and obtaining the client's consent
b. vote proxies in accordance with a predetermined policy that provides the adviser with little discretion
c. vote in accordance with a predetermined policy in accordance with the recommendations of an independent third party
d. suggest to the client that another party be hired to vote the proxies

13.4 Do clients have to be given a copy of the adviser's proxy voting policy?

The Advisers Act requires that advisers describe their proxy voting policies and procedures to clients and provide them with copies on request as well as disclose to clients how they can obtain information about how the adviser voted their proxies.

13.5 If an adviser makes it a policy to never vote clients' proxies, even for clients who have asset management accounts, must the adviser tell clients that they have to vote their own proxies?

The Advisers Act requires that advisers describe their proxy voting policies and procedures to clients. This means that advisers should make it clear to clients if they do not vote proxies, and the advisory contract should contain provisions spelling out that proxies will not be voted.

13.6 Do any special rules apply when voting proxies for retirement plans?

Fiduciary duties are also implicated when advisers vote proxies for securities held in retirement plan accounts. When voting proxies for securities held in ERISA plan accounts, advisers have to vote proxies in the best interests of plan participants (see chapter 17).

When advising for ERISA plans, it is important to ensure that the advisory contract spells out who is responsible for voting proxies and that such provisions do not conflict with provisions of the plan. The Department of Labor takes the position that when both the ERISA plan document and the advisory contract are silent as to who is responsible for voting proxies, the person responsible for managing the shares, that is, the adviser, is responsible for voting. The Department of Labor also takes the position that proxies should be voted only if it is expected that the effect on the value of the plan's investment exceeds the cost of voting.

13.7   What fiduciary rules are applicable when voting proxies?
Under the Advisers Act, an adviser is a fiduciary that owes each client the duty of care and loyalty. Proxies have to be voted in the client's best interest and must not subrogate client interests to the adviser's own interests. The SEC takes the position that an adviser with proxy voting authority should monitor corporate events and vote proxies. An adviser, however, does not breach its fiduciary duty if it does not vote proxies. For example, sometimes not voting proxies can be in a client's best interest, such as when the cost of voting exceeds the expected benefit to the client.

13.8   Are there any special record-keeping requirements when advisers vote client proxies?
Advisers with the authority to vote proxies for clients are required to maintain the following records:

    a. their proxy voting policies and procedures

    b. all client security proxy statements received (although the adviser is not required to retain proxy statements available on EDGAR)

    c. all records of votes cast on behalf of clients (although the adviser does not need to retain proxy statements and records of votes cast by the adviser if they're maintained by a third party)

    d. records of client requests for proxy voting information

    e. all documents the adviser prepared that were material to making the decision on how to vote, or which establish how the decision regarding how to vote was made

Proxy voting records are subject to the same retention requirements that apply to other books and records that advisers must maintain (see chapter 14).

13.9   What information must advisers supply to clients with respect to how they voted their proxies, and how should advisers describe their policies and procedures to clients?

The Advisers Act requires advisers to disclose to clients how they can obtain information as to how the adviser voted their securities. Advisers are not required to disclose their votes publicly.

Proxy voting policies and procedures must be described in Part 2 of the adviser's Form ADV. This description of the adviser's policies and procedures should be a concise summary of the proxy voting process and should indicate that a copy of the policies and procedures is available upon request.

14 | Record-Keeping Requirements

- ◆ **Accounting and Financial Records**
- ◆ **Written Communications**
- ◆ **Third-Party Record Keepers**
- ◆ **E-mail Correspondence**
- ◆ **Advertisements**

The Advisers Act requires that investment advisers keep and maintain records of their business and business transactions. Advisers must also have business continuity plans in place. Business continuity plans are procedures for the maintenance and preservation of, and access to, records, so as to reasonably safeguard records from loss, alteration, or destruction.

The Advisers Act rules cover what records must be kept, as well as the location where the records are to be maintained and the length of time the records must be kept. The SEC also has standards as to the type of media in which the records may be preserved. Finally, the Advisers Act also gives the SEC the authority to inspect those records (see chapter 22).

14.1   What records are advisers required to keep?

Advisers are required to maintain extensive business records, including:

a. accounting and financial records—that is, records forming the basis of entries in any ledger;

b. general and auxiliary ledgers reflecting asset, liability, reserve, capital, income, and expense accounts;

c. all written communications received or sent relating to recommendations or advice given or proposed to be given; the receipt, disbursement, or delivery of funds or securities; and the placing or execution of any securities order;

d. all electronic communications and media;

e. all checkbooks, bank statements, canceled checks, and cash reconciliations;

f. bills or statements paid or unpaid, trial balances, financial statements, internal audit working papers, and memoranda of each order for purchase or sale of any security;

g. all corporate records;

h. all accounts, books, internal working papers, records, or documents necessary to form the basis for or demonstrate the calculation of the performance rate of return of any or all managed accounts;

i. Form ADV Part 2 or written brochure and all amendments or revisions as well as a record of the dates that Form ADV Part 2 or a written brochure with amendments and revisions was given or offered to clients;

    j. a list of all accounts in which the adviser has any discretionary authority with respect to the funds, securities, or transactions of any client;

    k. all powers of attorney and other evidences of the granting of any discretionary authority by any client to the adviser;

    l. copies of documents delivered to clients by solicitors and written client acknowledgments of the receipt of the adviser's disclosure document and the solicitor's written disclosure document;

    m. records showing securities purchased and sold, and the date, amount, and price for each such purchase and sale for each client who receives investment supervisory or management services;

    n. copies of compliance policies and procedures.

Additional record-keeping requirements are discussed in chapters 7, 10, 12, 13, 15, and 16.

14.2 How long do the records have to be maintained?

The Advisers Act generally requires that records be kept for at least 5 years.

14.3 Where may advisers maintain them?

All required books and records must be maintained in the adviser's office for 2 years after the last entry date and for 3 to 5 additional years in an easily accessible place. Generally, books and records should be retrievable within 24 hours.

14.4 In what form may advisers maintain the records?

Records may be maintained and preserved in hard copy or on microfilm, microfiche, or other electronic storage media, but they must be arranged and indexed so that they can be located and retrieved easily (generally within 24 hours). Furthermore, if records are stored photographically or electronically on a computer or other electronic format, advisers must have a second copy of such records stored separately from the original and have procedures for the maintenance and preservation of, and access to, the records so as to reasonably safeguard them from loss, alteration, or destruction. If the records are stored on photographic film, they must be available for regulatory examination with facilities for immediate, easily readable projection of the film and for producing easily readable facsimile enlargements. If records are stored in an electronic format, the SEC has also indicated that advisers, as part of their business continuity plans, should have procedures in place to address network failure and appropriate backup of records, although the SEC has not indicated specific procedures to be followed.

If the SEC or other examiner requests a copy of a record stored on any photographic film or other electronic storage media, the adviser must be able to provide a legible, true, and completely accurate hard copy of the record in the medium and format in which it is stored.

14.5   May advisers hire a third party as record keeper?

Yes, the SEC allows advisers to delegate some of its record-keeping responsibilities. However, advisers are not relieved of liability if the records are not properly maintained by the third party. If the adviser is relying on an outside vendor for services, for example, hosting a website, it would be prudent to determine the adequacy of the vendor's backup disaster-recovery plans. Advisers should try to verify the adequacy of the plan and have the records of any such determination on file.

14.6   Advisers correspond frequently with clients via e-mail. How long must they keep e-mails, and what are the requirements for maintaining these records?

E-mail falls under the heading of correspondence and is subject to the same record-keeping rules. All e-mail, including any corresponding attachments, should be retained for at least 5 years. If requested by the SEC, advisers should be able to produce e-mail in a timely manner (generally within 24 hours) in an electronic, not paper, format. Spam may be purged from the firm's files, but the firm may not have an overall policy to delete all e-mail.

14.7 Do any special record-keeping rules apply with respect to an adviser's advertisements?

Advisers must keep copies of notices, circulars, advertisements, newspaper articles, investment letters, bulletins, and any other communication that they circulate or deliver to at least ten people. If a communication recommends the purchase or sale of any security, and does not give a reason for the recommendation, then a separate memorandum stating the reasons for the recommendation must also be kept.

If an adviser makes performance claims in an advertisement or in any communication circulated to ten or more people, books, records, internal working papers, and any other document or record that may be needed to demonstrate how the performance claim was made need to be kept for at least 5 years as well.

15 Advertising and Client Communications

- ◆ Advertising Defined
- ◆ False or Misleading Statements
- ◆ Testimonials
- ◆ Use of RIA Designation
- ◆ Performance Results
- ◆ Model Portfolios
- ◆ State Laws
- ◆ Internet and E-mail
- ◆ Fiduciary Obligations
- ◆ Advertising Brochures

The Investment Advisers Act and the SEC impose stringent rules regarding advertising on registered investment advisers. The SEC has historically been very active in reining in advertisements it deems fraudulent or misleading, and violations of the advertising rules are frequently found by the SEC when it examines advisers (see chapter 22). Advisers also have fiduciary obligations to their clients when they communicate with clients.

The term "advertising" has been defined very broadly under the Advisers Act, and the SEC's guidance has further broadened the definition. The advertising rules cover not only standard paid advertisements in newspapers, on television, radio, and other media forms, but a number of activities not normally considered advertising. Anytime an adviser communicates with more than one current or prospective client, it is considered advertising. Any material designed to maintain current clients or solicit new clients is also considered advertising by the SEC.

Advertising

15.1 How does the Investment Advisers Act define advertising?

Essentially, any form of communication that is sent or can be accessed by more than one person should be considered advertising under the Advisers Act. The SEC's definition of advertising is broad, including not only paid advertisements in newspapers or on television but also almost any form of communication given to current or prospective clients. "Advertising" includes any communication addressed to more than one person and any notice or announcement in any publication or on any form of media; for example, a letter or e-mail addressed to one person is correspondence, whereas group mailings or e-mails are advertising.

Information disseminated by audio or video such as radio and television or through electronic media is advertising, as are firm newsletters, standardized cover letters of client performance reports, mass mailings, group or blast e-mails, electronic communications such as websites and blogs, which all must conform to Investment Advisers Act rules.

However, the SEC takes the position that written adviser communications responding to an unsolicited request by a client, prospective client, or consultant for specific information regarding the adviser's past specific recommendations are not advertising.

15.2   What are some of the basic rules regarding advertising?

Advertisements may not contain any untrue statement or material fact or any other statement that could be interpreted as being false or misleading. Advisers may not make statements in their advertisements that any report, analysis, or other service is free unless it is actually free and there is no further obligation on the part of the client or potential client. Finally, advertisements may not contain any graph, chart, formula, or other device reputed to show which securities to buy and which to sell, or represent that such graph, chart, formula, or other device assists in the decision-making process without also disclosing the limits of the graph, chart, formula, or other device.

The SEC also believes that misrepresentation of assets under management, credentials, length of time in business, or the use of a predecessor's performance results in current performance results is false or misleading.

15.3   May advisers use testimonials from current clients in their advertising?

Any statement by a person that endorses an adviser is a testimonial, and the SEC does not permit registered investment advisers to use testimonials by past or former clients directly or indirectly in any advertisements. Any statements from current or former clients indicating satisfaction with the adviser's service are testimonials and are thus prohibited. For example, a statement by a current client that the adviser provides excellent services and that he is satisfied with the service he receives is a testimonial and is not allowed to be used in the adviser's advertising.

Advisers also may not use testimonials attesting to the adviser's moral character even if the person making the statement is not a current or former client. For example, a statement from the adviser's minister, who is not a client, stating that the adviser is of high moral character may not be used in the adviser's advertising.

Certain communications, however, are not considered testimonials. For example, the SEC has allowed advisers to include a list of clients in advertisements, as well as third-party ratings of advisers. The SEC has also allowed an adviser to include an article concerning the adviser's performance written by an unbiased third party, as long as the article does not include statements regarding any client's experiences or endorsements. Advisers are also permitted to provide client testimonials in response to an unsolicited request by a client, potential client, or consultant.

15.4   May advisers advertise that they are registered with the SEC as a registered investment adviser?

The SEC discourages the use of the initials "RIA" following a registered investment adviser's name on printed materials. Furthermore, the SEC does not allow advisers to make representations or implications that they have been sponsored, recommended, or approved, or that their abilities or qualifications have been authorized by the SEC.

Performance Results

15.5   Suppose an adviser has achieved very good results for clients on their portfolios and wants to use these real-life examples in advertising. May the adviser talk about such past performance with other clients?

Public communication of actual performance of actual accounts is permitted in advertising, provided that the exclusion of certain accounts does not cause the presentation to be misleading. Unless composite illustrations are used reflecting the actual performance of all accounts, advisers must disclose that the performance results of only selected accounts are being presented, and they must disclose the basis for which the accounts were selected as well as any other material facts that would affect the results portrayed. Actual performance results must be presented net-of-fees. Furthermore, when using the actual performance results of actual accounts in advertising, the following disclosures, to the extent applicable, must be made:

    a. the effect of material market or economic conditions on the results;

    b. the extent to which the results reflect the reinvestment of dividends and other earnings;

    c. the probability of losses, but only if claims as to potential for profits are made;

    d. material facts relevant to the comparison if the model results are compared to an index;

    e. any material conditions, objectives, or investment strategies used to obtain the results portrayed;

    f. a prominent disclaimer "that the results portrayed relate only to a select group of the adviser's clients," the basis on which the selection was made, and the effect of this practice on the results portrayed.

15.6 In an advertisement, may advisers portray performance results based on a model portfolio?

Performance information based on a model portfolio is also allowed if

    a. the information deducts advisory fees, brokerage and other commissions, and any other applicable charges; and

    b. the following disclosures, to the extent applicable, are made:

        i. the effect of material market or economic conditions on the results;

        ii. the extent to which the results reflect the reinvestment of dividends and other earnings;

        iii. the probability of losses, but only if claims as to potential for profits are made;

        iv. material facts relevant to the comparison if the model results are compared to an index;

        v. any material conditions, objectives, or investment strategies used to obtain the results portrayed;

vi. the limitations inherent in the model results, that the results do not represent actual trading, and may not reflect the impact that material economic and market factors had on the adviser's decision making;

vii. that the conditions, objectives, or investment strategies of the model portfolio changed materially during the time period portrayed in the advertisement, and the effect of any such change on the results portrayed;

viii. that any of the securities contained in, or the investment strategies followed with respect to, the model portfolio do not relate, or only partially relate, to the type of advisory services currently offered by the adviser;

ix. that the adviser's clients had investment results materially different from the results portrayed in the model.

Furthermore, advisers must maintain records that substantiate performance claims.

15.7   What are some examples of performance claims that the SEC has said may be fraudulent?

According to the SEC, questionable performance claims include

   a. creating distorted performance results by constructing composites that include only selected profitable accounts, or are for selected profitable periods;

   b. comparing the adviser's performance to inappropriate indices such as stating or implying that a dissimilar index is comparable to the adviser's investment strategies;

   c. representing or implying that model or back-tested performance is actual performance;

   d. failing to deduct the adviser's fees from performance calculations without disclosure;

   e. representing falsely the adviser's total assets under management, credentials, or length of time in business;

   f. incorporating a predecessor adviser's performance into the adviser's advertised performance returns in a misleading manner, or when it is otherwise inappropriate.

15.8 If an adviser's past recommendations have paid off well for clients, may the adviser use examples of past recommendations in advertising?

If past specific recommendations are used in communications, the advertisement must also set out or offer to furnish a list of all adviser recommendations for a particular period, including all unsuccessful recommendations. The SEC has stated that providing prospective clients with past copies of an adviser's newsletter could violate this rule.

An advertisement that includes only the adviser's current recommendations is not subject to this rule, as is an advertisement that includes an unbiased third-party article that refers to past specific recommendations, provided that neither contains any untrue statement of a material fact or is otherwise false or misleading.

The Advisers Act permits an advertisement to include, or contain an offer to furnish, a list of all recommendations made by the adviser for the past year, provided that the following information is also included:

 a. the name of every security recommended in the period
 b. the date and nature of each recommendation
 c. the market price of the security at the time it was recommended
 d. the price on which the adviser recommended the security be acted on
 e. the current market price of every recommended security
 f. a disclaimer that "it should not be assumed that recommendations made in the future will be profitable or will equal the performance of the securities on this list"

15.9 What other state laws or industry rules regulate advertising for advisers?

Unlike NASD requirements, there is no requirement that registered investment advisers who are registered with the SEC file advertisements with the SEC.

Most states have enacted rules that regulate adviser advertising. Advisers should contact the securities regulatory bodies in every state in which they do business to find out what requirements they must meet when advertising. Additionally, industry groups like NASD have rules advisers should be aware of as well.

Internet and E-mail

15.10   An adviser may want to put information about the firm on a website and possibly prospect for new clients via e-mail. What rules govern advertising on the Internet?
If something is not allowed in print, video, or audio, it may not be done on the Internet. Thus, postings on electronic bulletin boards, chat rooms, or blogs as well as e-mails or websites must conform to the rules of the Advisers Act.

Websites may be construed as soliciting business in all fifty states, the District of Columbia, and foreign jurisdictions unless an adviser is not transacting business via the Internet but only offering information about products and services. Websites should post notices stating that an adviser transacts business or renders personalized investment advice to clients only in specific states. If an adviser does transact business via the Internet, that adviser needs to follow the registration and/or licensing procedures for multiple states and foreign jurisdictions.

15.11   Suppose an adviser wants to start a blog. Do advisers need to follow the Advisers Act advertising rules?
Blogs are a form of advertising and must conform with the Advisers Act's rules. Additionally, advisers need to take care not to violate other Advisers Act rules or securities laws. Touting stocks on a blog to manipulate the market is prohibited, as is touting a stock currently being recommended to clients or which the adviser holds in a personal account. Furthermore, if the adviser gives any commentary on the stock market, the adviser must be fully identified with all the appropriate disclaimers.

If a firm has a number of advisers, the chief compliance officer may want to consider having procedures in place to avoid having advisers violating the law.

15.12 What fiduciary obligation do advisers have when they advertise?

Advisers have an affirmative obligation of utmost good faith and full and fair disclosure of all material facts to clients. Advisers are required to disclose any facts that might cause the adviser to render advice that is not disinterested.

15.13 If an adviser does a mass mailing to current and potential clients, is there any information that must be included in this correspondence?

A mass mailing is considered advertising and the adviser must ensure that any mass communication to current or prospective clients conforms to the advertising rules requirements.

15.14 Are there rules advisers need to be aware of if they draft high-end, glossy advertising brochures?

As with mass mailings and communications, the rules regarding advertising apply. Furthermore, if the adviser is intending that the brochures fulfill the firm's disclosure obligations of Part 2 of Form ADV, the brochure must contain all the information required on the actual form (see chapter 6).

15.15 Many advisers now do the bulk of their firm's correspondence via e-mail and the Internet and many have set up websites. Are there rules governing these media that advisers need to be aware of?

The SEC takes the position that the Internet, e-mail, and other means of electronic media are acceptable means of communicating information to clients and prospective clients. Advisers, however, need proof of delivery. Paper versions of any documents or communications sent electronically must be delivered to clients or prospective clients on request.

When sending e-mail correspondence to current and potential clients or when engaging in any other forms of electronic communications, whether via e-mail, websites, blogs, instant messaging, chat rooms, or message boards, registered investment advisers must comply with the Advisers Act advertising rules. Anything that an adviser is prohibited from doing under the advertising rules is also prohibited in adviser electronic communications.

Advisory firm electronic communications must also comply with ethical rules and standards and are subject to record-keeping requirements (see chapter 14). Generally, e-mail correspondence with all corresponding attachments must be kept for 5 years.

16 | Referrals

- ◆ Solicitation Activity
- ◆ Cash Referral Fees
- ◆ Solicitation Fees
- ◆ Written Agreements
- ◆ Disclosure
- ◆ Supervision of Solicitors
- ◆ Record-Keeping Requirements

Investment advisers who are registered with the SEC are not prohibited from paying referral fees. However, if an adviser directly or indirectly does pay cash referral fees for client referrals or solicitations, the SEC imposes several requirements. Specifically, if a solicitor engages in solicitation activity on behalf of an adviser, and the adviser pays cash referral fees to that solicitor, the adviser must disclose the referral arrangements and must maintain certain books and records. Furthermore, certain persons are prohibited from engaging in solicitation activity for a fee on behalf of an adviser, and only certain types of solicitation activities are sanctioned. If referrals are made for noncash payments, the SEC does not specifically require that its rules be followed, but it is considered prudent to follow the rules anyway.

16.1   What is a solicitor and what is solicitation activity?

A solicitor is any person who directly or indirectly solicits any client for or refers any client to an adviser. Persons are solicitors if they supply the names of clients to a registered investment adviser, even if they do not specifically recommend to clients that they retain that adviser.

Any activity that seeks to steer a prospective client to a particular adviser or provides names of potential clients to an adviser is solicitation activity. However, activities in which a person or a professional association merely helps another to identify advisers or provides a list of advisers is not solicitation activity if the person or association identifying the advisers has no real interest in whether a particular adviser is selected. For example, the SEC has stated that the referral program of the International Association for Financial Planning is not solicitation activity. The program allowed potential clients to obtain the names of financial advisers in their geographic area through the IAFP's website or through a toll-free number. The IAFP merely provided individuals with a random list of advisers and did not steer the individuals to a particular adviser. The SEC staff has also stated that merely providing a prescreened list of advisers to individuals is not activity subject to the referral rules.

16.2 What are the requirements associated with an adviser's paying cash referral fees to a solicitor?

The SEC imposes four requirements on advisers who want to pay cash referral fees:

a. The adviser must be registered in accordance with the Advisers Act.

b. Advisers are prohibited from paying cash referral fees to solicitors who are subject to a statutory disqualification, which generally means that the solicitor may not be one who has been censored in some way by the SEC or has been convicted in either a U.S. court or foreign jurisdiction. Specifically, the solicitor may not be someone

i. against whom the SEC has issued an order under Section 203(f) of the Advisers Act, which bars certain persons from associating with advisers;

ii. who has within the previous 10 years been convicted of any felony or misdemeanor involving conduct described in Section 203(e)(2)(A)–(D) of the Advisers Act;

iii. who has been found by the SEC to have engaged or has been convicted of engaging in any of the conduct specified in paragraphs (1), (4), or (5) of Section 203(e) of the Advisers Act; or

iv. who is subject to an order, judgment, or decree described in Section 203(e)(3) of the Advisers Act. The SEC may grant requests allowing persons subject to a statutory bar to serve as a solicitor.

c. Cash referral fees must be paid pursuant to a written agreement to which the adviser is a party.

d. Even if requirements (a.) through (c.) are met, cash referral fee payments are still prohibited unless one of the following three conditions is met:

i. **Impersonal advisory services.** Advisers are permitted to pay cash referral fees to solicitors who solicit clients only for impersonal advisory services. Impersonal advisory services are

A. written materials or oral statements that do not purport to meet the objectives or needs of specific clients;

B. statistical information containing no expression of opinions as to the investment merits of particular securities; or

C. any combination of (A.) and (B.).

If advisers offer a full range of financial services, the solicitation activity must be exclusively for the adviser's impersonal advisory services.

ii. **Affiliated solicitor.** Advisers may pay cash referral fees to a solicitor who is

A. a partner, officer, director, or employee of the adviser; or

B. a partner, officer, director, or employee of a company that controls, is controlled by, or is under common control with, the adviser. Solicitors, in this case, are required to disclose their affiliation.

iii. **Third-party solicitor.** Advisers may pay cash referral fees to third-party solicitors. Third-party solicitors are solicitors who are not partners, officers, directors, or employees of the adviser or persons affiliated with the adviser. Furthermore, advisers may make cash referral fees to third-party solicitors only if three additional requirements are met:

A. The adviser must enter into a written contract with the solicitor which

- describes the solicitation activities to be engaged in on behalf of the adviser;

- contains a provision requiring the solicitor to perform its duties under the agreement in a manner consistent with the adviser's instructions and the provisions of the Advisers Act and the rules under the Advisers Act; and

- requires that the solicitor, at the time the client is solicited, deliver a copy of the adviser's current brochure or Form ADV Part 2 to the client along with a separate written disclosure document. The separate written disclosure document is usually referred to as the solicitor's brochure, and the requirements for this document are outlined in question 16.5.

B. Prior to entering into any oral or written advisory contract with the client, the adviser must obtain from the client a signed and dated acknowledgment or receipt of the adviser's brochure and the solicitor's written disclosure document.

C. The adviser must make a bona fide effort to ascertain whether the solicitor is in compliance with the requirements of (iii. A.) above.

FIGURE 16.1 **Solicitation Fees**

Advisers may pay cash referral fees if
1. the advisers are registered under the Advisers Act;
2. the solicitor is not disqualified;
3. the referral fees are paid pursuant to a written agreement; and
4. either
   a. the clients are solicited only for impersonal advisory services; or
   b. the solicitor is affiliated with the adviser; or
   c. the solicitor is a third-party solicitor, if
      i. there is a written contract; and
      ii. the client gets the adviser's brochure and the solicitor's disclosure statement; and
      iii. the adviser makes a bona fide effort to ascertain that the solicitor is in compliance with the written contract.

16.3   What kinds of referral fees are covered by the rules?

Any fees paid for referrals are referral fees even if called by another name. For example, the SEC has determined that a consulting fee was a referral fee, as were fees that were categorized as fees paid for services.

16.4   Do advisers need written agreements with their solicitors?

Yes. The Advisers Act requires that there be a written agreement between the adviser and a third-party solicitor if cash payments are made for referrals.

16.5 Must advisers disclose to clients any arrangements they have for obtaining referrals?

Advisers who pay cash solicitation fees must disclose those referral arrangements to clients. Disclosure is required at the time of the solicitation and is made by the solicitor. The disclosure statement must include

  a. the name of the solicitor;
  b. the name of the adviser;
  c. the nature of the relationship between the solicitor and the adviser;
  d. a statement that the solicitor will receive compensation for the referral from the adviser and a description of the compensation arrangement;
  e. if the client will pay a specific charge or a higher advisory fee because of the solicitation arrangement, that must be disclosed as well.

16.6 Advisers sometimes recommend a broker who gives them free research in exchange for a referral. Is that a compliance problem?

If you recommend a broker who gives you free research in exchange for the referral, then the soft-dollar rules apply (see chapter 18).

16.7 Are advisers under any obligation to supervise their solicitors?

The SEC takes the position that advisers have a duty to supervise solicitors with respect to solicitation activities performed on the adviser's behalf.

Advisers are also required to make a bona fide effort to determine whether a third-party solicitor has complied with the terms of the written agreement between the solicitor and the adviser. This requires that advisers, at a minimum, make inquiries to clients referred by the solicitor to ascertain whether the solicitor has made improper representations or has otherwise violated the agreement.

16.8 Are there any additional record-keeping requirements if advisers pay cash referral fees?

Advisers must maintain copies of written agreements between the adviser and the solicitor, the solicitor's written disclosure to clients, and all client acknowledgments of receipt of written disclosure documents.

17 | ERISA Plans

- **Rules Governing ERISA Plans**
- **Plan Assets**
- **Prohibited Transactions**
- **Prohibited Transaction Exemptions**
- **Liability**
- **Investment Advice and Investment Managers**
- **Acting as Fiduciary**
- **Indemnity**
- **Audits**
- **The Prudence Rule**
- **Diversifying Investments**
- **Plan Documents**
- **Trust Requirement**
- **Indicia of Ownership**
- **Exclusive Benefit Rule**
- **Fidelity Bonds**

Under ERISA, a person who for compensation provides investment advice regarding ERISA plan assets is a fiduciary to the plan. Registered investment advisers who deal with ERISA plan assets must abide by ERISA's rules, including the fiduciary duty and prohibited transaction rules. However, if a named fiduciary selects an investment adviser to be an investment manager to manage plan assets, there is limited relief from the ERISA fiduciary rules.

Rules Governing ERISA Plans

17.1   What is an ERISA plan?

All retirement, health and welfare plans, and other benefit arrangements are ERISA plans if they cover a substantial portion of the client's workforce. Generally, arrangements that cover one or two top people are not ERISA plans. Plans that cover only self-employed individuals and their spouses are not ERISA plans. Individual retirement accounts and Keogh plans are typically not ERISA plans, although both are still subject to the prohibited transaction rules. Plans located outside the United States that cover only nonresident aliens are not ERISA plans. Plans sponsored by governmental agencies are not subject to ERISA, although they are often subject to state laws that mirror ERISA. Plans offered by churches are also exempt from ERISA, although they can elect to be subject.

17.2   What are plan assets and how are they relevant to regulatory compliance?

Registered investment advisers are ERISA plan fiduciaries and investments are subject to ERISA requirements, including the prohibited transaction rules, only to the extent that advisers are dealing with ERISA plan assets. In other words, if the investment is not made with ERISA plan assets (see question 17.1), the ERISA rules do not apply and the adviser is not acting as an ERISA plan fiduciary. Essentially, all securities, cash, and other assets owned directly by an ERISA plan are plan assets. Thus, all publicly offered equities and debt instruments owned by the

---

FIGURE 17.1 **Plans Not Protected Under ERISA**

Generally, the following types of employee retirement or health and welfare plans are not ERISA plans:

- Top-hat plans
- Self-employed plans
- Individual retirement accounts or Keogh plans
- Foreign plans covering nonresident aliens
- Government plans
- Church plans

Note: Even though these plans are not ERISA plans, they may still be subject to the prohibited transaction rules and/or the ERISA fiduciary rules.

---

plan are plan assets. For example, if an adviser invests publicly owned securities owned by an ERISA plan trust, then that adviser is an ERISA plan fiduciary and the investment must meet all of ERISA's requirements.

Sometimes assets owned indirectly by an ERISA plan through equity investments are plan assets as well, and care needs to be taken that buying an equity investment does not lead unintentionally to the underlying investment being deemed a plan asset. Investment in certain entities always leads to the underlying investments being deemed plan assets. These entities include group trusts such as bank collective investment funds and most insurance company separate accounts. Furthermore, any entity owned 100 percent either by a single ERISA plan or a group of related ERISA plans is deemed to be a plan asset.

Other ERISA plan equity investments can lead to the underlying assets being declared plan assets unless the equity is

a. a registered investment company;

b. an insurance company guaranteed benefit contract;

c. a publicly offered security which is freely transferable and widely held by more than 100 unrelated holders and either registered with the SEC or subsequent to an initial public offering;

d. a de minimis holding, or any investment in an entity that does not have more than 25 percent benefit plan investor participation;

e. an investment in an operating company that develops or markets goods and services other than the investment of capital, plus hybrid entities known as "venture capital operating companies" and "real estate operating companies."

17.3 Are there any transactions that are off-limits to advisers responsible for plan assets?

ERISA and the Internal Revenue Code prohibit both ERISA plan fiduciaries and nonfiduciaries from engaging in a broad range of activities. Note that even though they're technically not ERISA plans, Keogh plans and individual retirement accounts are subject to these rules. These prohibited activities are called prohibited transactions. There are three basic types of prohibited transactions, which are

a. any direct or indirect transactions, such as a sale, lease, exchange, loan, furnishing goods or services, or transferring assets between an ERISA plan and a party in interest, or disqualified person. A party in interest, or disqualified person, includes

i. all plan fiduciaries;

ii. any fiduciary or nonfiduciary providing services to the plan;

iii. any employer or union whose employees are covered by the plan;

iv. any other party affiliated with (i.), (ii.), or (iii.) in any way.

b. the acquisition or holding by an ERISA plan of certain types of employer securities;

c. fiduciary conflicts, including self-dealing, direct conflicts such as representing the plan and an adverse party in the same transaction, or accepting compensation or kickbacks from a third party dealing with the plan. Self-dealing conflicts arise when a fiduciary uses plan assets for his own interest or account.

Fiduciaries are not per se prohibited from being retained by the plan to provide services for a fee, but fiduciaries may not use their authority to get themselves or any affiliate hired, even if it is just for additional plan services.

With certain exceptions, ERISA also prohibits a plan from acquiring and holding employer securities or real property leased to the employer. However, to the extent allowed by plan documents, a defined-benefit plan may acquire qualifying employer securities and qualifying employer real property if in the aggregate they do not exceed 10 percent of total plan assets. The 10 percent limitation does not apply to defined-contribution plans such as 401(k) plans, although the plan must specifically authorize such investments, and if the plan is a self-directed plan under ERISA 404(c), certain other conditions apply.

Prohibited Transaction Exemptions

17.4 Are there any exemptions to these prohibited transaction rules?

ERISA exempts the following from the prohibited transaction rules:

a. A party in interest can contract with an ERISA plan to provide services that are appropriate and helpful to the plan in carrying out its functions to the extent that compensation is reasonable. The arrangement must be terminable by the plan with reasonably short notice without penalty.

b. A purchase or sale of securities between a plan and a party in interest if the sale or exchange is a blind transaction on a security exchange and neither party, nor their broker agents, knows the identity of the other.

The Department of Labor has also issued many broad class exemptions to the prohibited transaction rules, which are available to any party in interest that meets the terms and conditions of a particular class exemption. Examples of Department of Labor prohibited transaction class exemptions include

a. PTE-75-1, which exempts some principal transactions, underwriting, and extensions of credit by nonfiduciary broker-dealers as well as some market-making transactions by parties in interest who may be fiduciaries;

b. PTE 80-83, which exempts purchases of securities in an initial public offering in which the issuer uses proceeds of the sale to reduce or retire indebtedness to a party in interest;

c. PTE 81-8, which permits a plan to enter into short-term investment transactions with parties in interest, including

i. bankers' acceptances

ii. commercial paper

iii. repurchase agreements that are not reverse repurchase agreements;

d. PTE-83-1, which allows investments in mortgage pool investment trusts;

e. PTE 84-14, which exempts from the prohibited transaction rules plan transactions done at the direction of a qualified professional asset manager (QPAM). A QPAM is an ERISA-defined investment manager with total client assets under its discretionary management of $50 million and shareholders' or partners' equity of $750,000. Plan assets of all ERISA plans may represent no more than 20 percent of the QPAM's discretionary client assets;

f. PTE 86-128, which allows the receipt of fees, including brokerage commissions by a fiduciary or its affiliate for effecting or executing securities transactions as agent for the plan. However, the trading may not be excessive in amount or frequency. If the fiduciary is acting as a discretionary trustee, plan administrator, or plan sponsor, this exemption applies only if all profits earned on trades are repaid to the plan;

g. PTE 2002-12, which permits certain kinds of passive cross-trading among client accounts.

These are merely general descriptions of several prohibited transaction class exemptions. Advisers should consult legal counsel before engaging in any of these activities.

17.5   What can happen if advisers invest the plan's assets in investments that are prohibited or violate ERISA rules in any way?

Registered investment advisers can be held personally liable to compensate the plan for any losses resulting from a transaction that the advisers knew or should have known is prohibited, and they may have to pay additional excise taxes. Prohibited transaction violations have two tiers of penalty. First, a fine of 15 percent of the amount involved in the transaction is assessed. Second, if the transaction is not corrected after notice, an additional 100 percent penalty is applied. Correction is generally defined as undoing the transaction.

The Department of Labor can even prevent a registered investment adviser from acting as an ERISA plan fiduciary in the future. Willful breaches of ERISA are also potentially subject to criminal penalties of up to 10 years of imprisonment and fines of up to $100,000 for an individual and $500,000 for nonindividuals per violation.

17.6   If a client with an individual defined-benefit plan wants to invest assets in an investment that appears to be a prohibited transaction, may the adviser apply for an exemption?

Yes, an adviser may apply to the Department of Labor to get an individual prohibited transaction exemption to allow a transaction that would otherwise violate the prohibited transaction rules.

Investment Advice and Investment Managers

17.7   How is investment advice defined under ERISA?

The definition of investment advice under ERISA is narrower than under the Advisers Act. For recommendations to be considered investment advice under ERISA, the recommendations must

a. be rendered regularly;

b. be rendered for a direct or indirect fee;

c. be provided pursuant to an agreement, arrangement, or understanding;

d. be individualized for the plan's particular needs;

e. serve as a primary basis for another plan fiduciary's investment decisions.

Registered investment advisers may provide 401(k) plan or other

individual account plan participants with investment education and
not have those services be deemed investment advice if

    a. the information is basically descriptive information;

    b. it is general financial and investment information regarding
investment concepts, terminology, risk assessment, etc.;

    c. it provides generic asset allocation models along with generic
information regarding the means by which participants may assess
which model to use;

    d. it discusses interactive investment models that participants
can access to assess their personal retirement needs, goals, and risk
tolerance and allows participants to apply assessments to available
plan investment options.

17.8 How does ERISA define an investment manager?

A plan fiduciary who properly appoints an investment manager
or any trustee who follows an investment manager's directions
is generally not liable for investment decisions of the investment
manager. The fiduciary appointing the investment manager must
be a named fiduciary under the plan who remains liable for the
selection and oversight of the investment manager.

Only banks, insurance companies, or advisers registered under
the Advisers Act or state law are eligible to be investment managers. A registered investment adviser who has actual authority to
acquire, manage, or dispose of plan assets may be an ERISA plan's
investment manager. To acquire investment manager status, registered investment advisers must acknowledge in writing that they
are fiduciaries to the ERISA plan.

Registered investment advisers with discretionary management
of ERISA plan assets maintain investment manager status under
ERISA by filing Form ADV via the IARD.

A registered investment adviser serving as an investment manager is obligated to provide to the plan administrator financial
information for the filing of the plan's annual 5500 reports and to
cooperate with independent annual plan audits. That the registered
investment adviser is serving as the investment manager must also
be disclosed to plan participants.

Acting as Fiduciary

17.9 How do advisers know if they're considered fiduciaries to an ERISA plan?

Registered investment advisers are ERISA plan fiduciaries if they

    a. exercise any authority or control over the management or disposition of plan assets;

    b. provide investment advice (see question 17.7) for a fee with respect to plan assets or have the authority or responsibility to do so; or

    c. administer the plan.

The Department of Labor takes the position that advisers who give individual investment advice for a fee to participants in defined-contribution, individual account plans, such as 401(k)s, can be fiduciaries to the plan. Advisers can be fiduciaries even if employed directly by the participant with no other connection to the plan.

Specifically, advisers who render investment advice to individual account ERISA plan participants for a fee are fiduciaries if

    a. they have discretionary authority to manage a participant's plan investments; or

    b. they do not have discretionary authority over accounts, but give regular individualized investment advice to a participant with the expectation that the participant will act on it.

Merely advising a participant to roll over an account balance to an individual retirement account, however, does not constitute investment advice under ERISA.

If deemed plan fiduciaries, advisers can be held liable as fiduciaries for imprudent investment recommendations, even if the plan is an ERISA 404(c) plan in which the participant is technically responsible for all investment decisions. ERISA would preempt any contractual or state-law limits on the advisers' exposure.

Additionally, advisers working with individual participants would also be subject to the prohibited transaction rules (see question 17.3), including self-dealing. For example, if an adviser who is a fiduciary advises a client to roll over assets from the plan to an IRA from which the adviser will earn management or other investment fees, that adviser may have engaged in a prohibited transaction subjecting the adviser to penalties (see question 17.5). However, if an adviser who is not otherwise a fiduciary recommends that a participant withdraw funds from a plan and invest the funds in an IRA from which the adviser will earn management or other investment fees, that adviser has not engaged in a prohibited transaction.

17.10   Should advisers be concerned about what other fiduciaries to the plan are doing?

An ERISA fiduciary may be held jointly and severally liable for the breach of another fiduciary if

a. the fiduciary knowingly participates in or knowingly undertakes to conceal another fiduciary's act or omission, provided that the first fiduciary knows that the other fiduciary's act or omission is a fiduciary breach;

b. the first fiduciary, in committing the breach, allows the second fiduciary also to commit a breach; or

c. the fiduciary knows of the second fiduciary's breach, unless the first fiduciary makes a reasonable effort, given the circumstances, to remedy it.

17.11   Can advisers get indemnified for sanctions imposed on them for breaches of fiduciary duty?

ERISA prohibits fiduciaries from entering into agreements that relieve them of liabilities for their wrongdoings, and no indemnification may be paid from plan assets. If a fiduciary is held liable for another fiduciary's breach, there is no implied right to seek indemnification from the other fiduciary.

ERISA does not specifically preclude fiduciaries from obtaining fiduciary insurance to cover financial losses from fiduciary breaches. ERISA also does not specifically preclude fiduciaries from contracting with one another or the plan sponsor for indemnification. However, some courts have even held that ERISA preempts an express agreement between fiduciaries for contribution or indemnification.

17.12 May advisers that invest ERISA plan assets be audited by the Department of Labor?

Yes, the Department of Labor has extremely broad powers to audit or to request the review of any books and records relating to the filing of any return or report required by ERISA.

17.13 What other rules apply when advisers act as fiduciaries to an ERISA plan?

ERISA imposes a number of obligations, including the following rules:

a. The prudence rule. Registered investment advisers who are ERISA plan fiduciaries must act with the care, skill, prudence, and diligence under the circumstances then prevailing that a reasonably prudent person acting in a like capacity and familiar with such matters would use in the conduct of an enterprise of like character and like aims. In general, individual investment must meet the prudence rule on a stand-alone basis rather than as part of an overall portfolio.

b. The duty to diversify investments rule. ERISA requires fiduciaries to diversify plan investments to minimize the risk of large losses, unless, under the circumstances, it is clearly prudent not to do so. To the extent that a registered investment manager is responsible for only a portion of a plan's total assets, its obligation to diversify should be clearly spelled out in an agreement, but the assets still need to be diversified within those limits.

c. The compliance with plan documents rule. Fiduciaries are required to act in accordance with the documents governing a plan to the extent that those plan documents are not inconsistent with ERISA. This means that if the plan's trust document prohibits certain types of investments, a registered investment adviser who invests plan assets in prohibited investments has violated ERISA's fiduciary duty rules, even if the investment agreement allows such investments.

d. The trust requirement rule. ERISA plan assets must always be held in trust, except *i.* when holding securities in nominee or street name with a custodial bank, insurance company, registered broker-dealer, or clearing agency, or their nominees, provided that a trustee is the ultimate beneficial owner of the securities;

ii. upon the creation of certain single owner or commingled investment vehicles, such as a corporation, partnership, or limited liability company, which hold the plan assets, if the interests in the vehicles is held in trust;

iii. when assets are held by insurance companies.

e. The indicia of ownership rule. ERISA requires the indicia of ownership of plan assets be held within the jurisdiction of U.S. federal district courts. Indicia of ownership is determined under securities and state laws. Certain foreign securities and currencies may be held outside the United States provided that they are held

i. under the management or control of a qualified fiduciary—a U.S. bank, insurance company, or registered investment adviser with at least $50 million in assets under management and $750,000 equity; or

ii. in the physical possession or control of certain qualifying financial institutions—a U.S. bank, insurance company, or broker-dealer that is a U.S. domestic entity whose principal place of business is in the United States. Foreign agents of banks or insurance companies may hold ownership if certain other requirements are met as to the plan's ability to assert and enforce its ownership rights.

f. The exclusive benefit rule. Fiduciaries must discharge their duties solely in the interest of the plan and its participants and beneficiaries, for the exclusive purpose of providing plan benefits and defraying reasonable plan expenses. Fiduciaries have a duty not to mislead plan participants when discussing plan-related matters, including misleading participants by omission. Material information should always be disclosed to participants.

17.14 Must advisers be bonded to invest ERISA plan assets?

Fiduciaries handling ERISA plan assets must be covered by a fidelity bond. The amount of the bond must not be less than 10 percent of the funds under management with a minimum of $1,000 and a maximum of $500,000 per plan. Generally, registered investment advisers would need to obtain their own individual coverage for their employees and agents, naming each ERISA plan as an insured party.

18 | Soft Dollars

- ◆ Soft-Dollar Arrangements
- ◆ Soft-Dollar Safe Harbor Rules
- ◆ Safe Harbor Brokerage and Research Services
- ◆ Safe Harbor Broker Agreements
- ◆ Transactions Outside the Scope of the Safe Harbor
- ◆ Riskless Principal Transactions Within the Scope of the Safe Harbor
- ◆ Disclosure
- ◆ SEC Enforcement Actions
- ◆ Retirement Plan Assets

The term "soft dollars" describes a brokerage practice in which investment advisers use client brokerage commissions to pay for services. Soft dollars are, in effect, credits brokers give advisers to purchase goods and services such as research, IT equipment, performance-measurement services, economic analysis, and publications.

When using soft dollars to purchase goods and services, questions regarding an adviser's fiduciary duties to clients are called into question. When advisers cause clients to pay more for brokerage so that the adviser can get research or other services, questions arise as to whether the adviser has met the duty of best execution and duty of loyalty. The Securities and Exchange Act of 1934 provides advisers with a safe harbor when advisers pay more than the lowest available brokerage commission in exchange for research.

Essentially, if an adviser receives brokerage or research services from the broker effecting the transaction and the adviser determines in good faith that the brokerage or research services are reasonable in relation to the commissions paid, then that transaction falls within the scope of the safe harbor. If the soft dollars received fall within the scope of the safe harbor, then the adviser has technically not violated his fiduciary duties to clients.

18.1   What forms do soft-dollar arrangements take?

Soft-dollar arrangements fall into three main categories:

a. Brokers provide advisers with services that the broker or an affiliate has produced such as in-house or bundled research.

b. Advisers receive services produced by a third party whom the broker pays.

c. Directed brokerage arrangements are made in which the client instructs an adviser to direct transactions to a particular broker and the client then receives goods and services directly from the broker.

18.2   Is it legal for advisers to use soft dollars to purchase services and goods?

The Securities Exchange Act of 1934 provides a safe harbor for advisers who participate in soft-dollar arrangements. The safe harbor allows advisers to pay more than the lowest available commission to a broker from whom they are accepting research without breaching their fiduciary duties to clients under state or federal laws. The safe harbor allows advisers to consider the receipt of research in determining the reasonableness of the commissions. In making the determination, the safe harbor allows advisers to consider all client accounts collectively. In other words, advisers do not have to consider on a client-by-client basis whether the exchange is reasonable.

18.3   How can an adviser determine if a transaction falls within the soft-dollar safe harbor rules?

Transactions come within the soft-dollar safe harbor if

    a. soft-dollar goods and services are provided by the broker effecting the transactions

    b. soft-dollar goods and services are provided to a party having investment discretion

    c. the recipient of the goods and services has made a good faith determination that the commissions paid are reasonable in relation to the value of the brokerage and research services provided

    d. the goods and services received must be brokerage and research services

18.4   How do advisers determine whether they are parties having investment discretion for purposes of the soft-dollar safe harbor rules?

Investment advisers who manage client accounts on a discretionary basis come within the safe harbor rules.

18.5   How do the soft-dollar safe harbor rules define brokerage and research services?

Brokerage and research services include

    a. advice about securities;

    b. analyses and reports concerning issuers, industries, securities, economic factors and trends, portfolio strategy, and the performance of accounts;

c. services to complete securities transactions and incidental services, for example, settlement, custody, or clearance.

18.6 What services qualify as research services for the safe harbor?

The SEC has stated that the appropriate test to determine whether a service constitutes legitimate research for the purposes of the safe harbor is whether or not it provides "lawful and appropriate assistance to the money manager in performance of his investment decision-making responsibilities." Newspaper and magazine subscriptions and other publications are legitimate research for the safe harbor, as are market, financial, economic, and similar data. Purchases of computer equipment, software, or phone and data transmission lines with soft dollars are generally outside the scope of the safe harbor. The SEC, however, has stated that computer hardware and quotation equipment may be purchased with soft dollars to the extent that the equipment is, in fact, used by the adviser to make investment decisions for clients.

Mixed-use items purchased with soft dollars—that is, items that are used for both research and nonresearch purposes—must be reasonably allocated between eligible and ineligible uses, and the allocation must be documented so as to enable the adviser to make a good-faith determination of the reasonableness of commissions in relation to the value of the brokerage and research services. For example, fees for research conferences and seminars may be purchased with soft dollars. Nonresearch categories of trip expenses such as air fares, hotels, and meals, however, do not fall within the scope of the safe harbor if purchased with soft dollars.

If something is mixed use, that is, for both research and nonresearch, only the percentage of the product or service that assists the adviser's investment decision-making process is covered by the safe harbor. For example, if a seminar covers both the making of investment decisions and improving advisers' marketing skills, only an amount equal to the percentage of time the seminar is devoted to investment decision making is eligible for the safe harbor. The adviser may satisfy this requirement by making a good-faith attempt to allocate the correct amount and must back up the decision with adequate books and records documenting the allocation decision.

18.7   How are brokerage services defined for the safe harbor?

Brokerage is defined as services effecting securities transactions and performing functions incidental thereto, such as clearance, settlement, and custody. The SEC takes the position that advisers using soft dollars to correct errors made in placing a trade for a client's account do not qualify for the safe harbor.

18.8   When are services considered to be "provided by" the broker for purposes of the soft-dollar safe harbor rules?

Services are "provided by" the broker when the broker provides the adviser with services that the broker or an affiliate of the broker produced. If the research is actually produced by a third party, it must still be the broker, and not the third party, that actually provides the research. The broker, however, may have the goods shipped directly from the third party to the adviser.

18.9   Specifically, what kinds of agreements may advisers enter into with brokers?

The SEC takes the position that an adviser's duty of best execution may be breached if it is motivated to generate trades with a particular broker because the adviser is obligated to pay for research from the broker with future client commissions. Advisers may also breach their fiduciary duties of best execution when they are obligated to pay off commission shortfalls. Thus, it is prudent to structure agreements so that they are based on anticipated brokerage and not on brokerage for which the adviser is obligated to pay.

18.10   What kinds of securities transactions fall within the soft-dollar safe harbor?

The SEC takes the position that broker transactions executed on an agency basis for commissions comes within the scope of the safe harbor. Certain types of "riskless principal transactions" also come within the scope of the safe harbor (see question 18.12).

18.11 What kinds of transactions do not fall within the soft-dollar safe harbor?

The SEC takes the position that the safe harbor does not apply to commodity futures transactions. The SEC also takes the position that broker-dealer transactions executed on a principal basis—for a markup or markdown—are outside the scope of the safe harbor. A principal trade is a trade in which the broker-dealer buys or sells for an account in which the broker-dealer has a beneficial ownership interest, such as a proprietary account. Even if the fee paid to the dealer is denominated as something other than a markup or markdown, the transaction still does not come within the scope of the safe harbor.

However, certain types of "riskless principal transactions" do come within the scope of the safe harbor. A qualifying riskless principal transaction is one in which a broker-dealer, after getting a customer's order, executes an offsetting transaction as principal with another customer or broker-dealer to fill the customer's order and both transactions are executed at the same price (see question 18.12).

So-called interpositioning transactions also fall outside the scope of the safe harbor. Interpositioning is a practice whereby instruments that traditionally trade on a principal basis such as debt securities and over-the-counter equities are traded in agency transactions. Such transactions are considered a breach of the adviser's fiduciary duty if the adviser could have gone directly to a dealer and received better execution without using a broker. Such transactions are not prohibited per se, but advisers must keep records proving that the client received best execution.

18.12 When do "riskless principal transactions" come within the scope of the safe harbor?

In 2001, in response to a request from Nasdaq, the SEC expanded the soft-dollar safe harbor to cover "flat riskless principal trades" by market makers in Nasdaq trades. "Flat riskless principal trades" are trades in which both the buyer and seller pay the same price. Specifically, the SEC clarified that a commission for purposes of coming within the soft-dollar safe harbor includes a markup, markdown commission equivalent, or other fee paid by a managed account to a dealer for executing a trade where there is adequate transparency of both price and trading costs to enable the money manager to make a reasonableness determination. The transparency requirement is met if

a. the commission and trade price are "fully and separately disclosed on the confirmation";
b. the trade is "reported under conditions that provide independent and objective verification of the transaction price subject to self-regulatory organization oversight."

The SEC takes the position that this broadening of the safe harbor rule applies only to riskless principal transactions in Nasdaq securities. It does not extend to riskless principal trades in over-the-counter bulletin board stocks, pink sheet stocks, convertible securities, or other securities that may be subject to similar reporting requirements but not the same confirmation disclosure requirements for market makers. The SEC, however, takes the position that "as other markets develop equivalent regulations to ensure equivalent transparency, transaction charges in those markets that meet the requirements of this interpretation will be considered to fall within the interpretation."

18.13 How should advisers disclose soft-dollar arrangements to clients?

Form ADV Part 2 disclosure requires that advisers disclose any products or services provided to them that may have influenced the selection of brokers. Advisers must disclose

a. what products and services they received
b. whether clients pay commission rates that are above market rates

c. whether the research benefits all adviser clients or only those paying for the service

d. what procedures the adviser used during the past fiscal year to direct clients' transaction to a particular broker

The SEC has proposed a new Form, ADV-B, for advisers to fill out if they receive soft dollars. If adopted, Form ADV-B would have to be filed annually with the SEC, with a copy delivered to clients. At the close of 2005, it was unclear when or if Form ADV-B would be adopted.

18.14   What happens if advisers' soft-dollar arrangements do not meet the requirements of the safe harbor?

Soft-dollar arrangements that do not meet the requirements of the safe harbor are not prohibited. Such arrangements, however, may be interpreted as breaching fiduciary duties to clients.

18.15   What kinds of enforcement actions against advisers has the SEC taken with respect to soft dollars?

SEC enforcement actions focus on disclosure of soft-dollar practices. In one action, the SEC found that an adviser violated the Advisers Act when it did not adequately disclose that it used soft-dollar credits to pay expenses such as rent and employee salaries. In another action, the SEC again found Advisers Act violations because of inadequate disclosure when the adviser used soft dollars to pay telephone bills, client-solicitation fees, accounting expenses, and marketing expenses as well as to purchase office equipment. The SEC has also brought an administrative proceeding against an adviser for failing to disclose to clients on Form ADV its use of soft dollars to pay for nonresearch expenses. The adviser had used soft dollars to pay for credit card bills, car services, messenger services, rent, telephone bills, furniture rentals, office supplies, and accounting expenses as well as research services.

18.16   Do any special rules apply to retirement plan assets?

Soft-dollar payments from a broker to a registered investment adviser that is an ERISA plan fiduciary would appear to be a prohibited transaction. However, the Securities and Exchange Act of 1934 safe harbor preempts ERISA's prohibited transaction rules if the transaction is an agency transaction in which the only soft dollars provided are for research services. The Department of Labor, however, takes the position that even if a transaction is covered by the soft-dollar safe harbor, the plan's named fiduciary is not relieved from the ongoing duty to monitor the adviser's performance to assure that best execution is received. Named fiduciaries, therefore, should require soft-dollar reporting from their plan advisers.

When ERISA plan assets (see question 17.2) are involved, advisers are more restricted in accepting soft dollars that fall outside the soft-dollar safe harbor. The SEC takes the position that if a soft-dollar arrangement falls outside the safe harbor, an adviser must demonstrate that the research covers an expense or other obligation of the ERISA plan exclusively. The soft dollars may not be for other clients or for the plan sponsor. If an ERISA plan soft-dollar transaction falls outside the scope of the safe harbor, it would be prudent to document how the ERISA plan benefited.

Commissions paid must be reasonable in relation to the value of the brokerage and research services provided by the broker. For other types of goods and services, the Department of Labor has indicated that a plan may be directed to a specific broker to procure goods and services for the benefit of the plan paying the commissions.

19 | Protecting Clients' Privacy

- ◆ Defining the Client
- ◆ Clients Considered Consumers
- ◆ Clients Considered Customers
- ◆ Nonpublic Personal Information
- ◆ Personally Identifiable Financial Information
- ◆ Publicly Available Information
- ◆ Privacy Protection
- ◆ Policies and Procedures
- ◆ Privacy Notices
- ◆ Opt-Out Rules

The Gramm-Leach-Bliley Financial Services Modernization Act of 1999 and SEC Regulation S-P require registered investment advisers to adopt and disclose privacy policies and practices with respect to sharing client information with both affiliates and nonaffiliated third parties.

Specifically, without proper notice, advisers are prohibited from disclosing client "nonpublic personal information." Advisers must notify current and prospective clients under what conditions the adviser would disclose nonpublic personal information to affiliates and nonaffiliated third parties, and provide clients an opportunity to opt out of such disclosure of personal information. Different rules apply depending on whether the client is a customer or a consumer.

Defining the Client

19.1   Which clients are covered by these rules?

Only individual clients are covered by the rules. The privacy rules under Regulation S-P apply only to individual clients who obtain financial products or services primarily for personal, family, or household purposes. The privacy rules do not apply to information from those who obtain financial services and products primarily for business, commercial, or agricultural purposes.

19.2   Which clients or prospective clients are considered consumers?

A consumer is any individual, or the legal representative of the individual, who obtains or has obtained a financial product or service from the adviser to be used primarily for personal, family, or household purposes. Individuals are consumers even if they do not ultimately obtain the financial product. Merely transmitting personal information to an adviser for the purpose of obtaining a financial product or service is enough to deem an individual a consumer, even if the individual never opens an account. However, individuals are not consumers if they merely provide an address and general area of investment interest in connection with requesting an adviser's brochure.

19.3   Which clients are considered customers?

A customer is a consumer with whom the registered investment adviser has an ongoing relationship. For example, any individual with an advisory contract is a customer. Although all customers are consumers, not every consumer is a customer.

Personal Financial Information and Publicly Available Information

19.4   What is nonpublic personal information?

Nonpublic personal information is
  a. personally identifiable financial information;
  b. any list, description, or other grouping of consumers that is derived using personally identifiable financial information.

Publicly available information is generally excluded from the definition of nonpublic personal information.

19.5   How does the SEC define personally identifiable financial information?

According to the SEC, personally identifiable financial information includes the following:
  a. any information provided by the consumer to obtain a financial product or service
  b. any information that results from a transaction with the consumer involving a financial product or service
  c. any information otherwise obtained in connection with providing a product or service to the consumer

Personally identifiable financial information does not include nonidentifying aggregate or blind data.

19.6   What are some examples of personally identifiable financial information?

The SEC staff considers material a consumer supplies to an adviser when entering into an investment advisory contract to be personally identifiable financial information. The same applies to any information regarding account balances, securities positions, financial products purchased or sold. Even something as simple as whether or not the consumer is a client of the firm is considered personally identifiable financial information.

19.7   How does the SEC define publicly available information?

The SEC staff defines publicly available information as information an adviser reasonably believes is lawfully made available to the general public through

   a. federal, state, or local government records;
   b. widely distributed media;
   c. disclosures to the public required by federal, state, or local law.

Privacy Protection

19.8   Must advisers have policies and procedures in place to protect clients' records and information?

Yes, advisers must have policies and procedures in place to address the protection of customer records and information. These policies and procedures must be reasonably designed to

   a. ensure the security and confidentiality of customer records and information
   b. protect against any anticipated threats or hazards to the security or integrity of customer records and information
   c. protect against unauthorized access to or use of customer records or information that could result in substantial harm or inconvenience to any customer

19.9   What rules apply to customers?

Advisers must provide customers with an initial privacy notice and thereafter annual privacy notices during the term of the customer relationship. Specifically, advisers must provide customers annually with a clear and conspicuous notice that accurately reflects the firm's privacy policies. If an adviser wants to disclose nonpublic information in a way that is not accurately described in the previous notice, the adviser must provide a new revised notice to customers prior to disclosing such information.

19.10   What rules apply to consumers?

Advisers are not required to provide an initial privacy notice to consumers if they do not disclose any nonpublic personal information about the consumer to any nonaffiliated third party. If an adviser does disclose consumer nonpublic personal information to a nonaffiliated third party, then the adviser must first provide the consumer with

a. a short-form initial notice (see question 19.11) and an opt-out notice

b. a reasonable opportunity to opt out

c. access to the firm's privacy policies

19.11   What information must be provided in the short-form initial notice to consumers?

The short-form notice must clearly and conspicuously (see question 19.15) state that information regarding the adviser's privacy policies and procedures is available on request as well as the means by which the consumer can obtain such policies and procedures. Note, however, that once a consumer becomes a customer, the full initial privacy disclosure must be delivered.

19.12   What kind of notice and disclosures are advisers required to provide clients?

Advisers are required to provide initial privacy notices to customers and consumers regarding the adviser's privacy policy and procedures. Advisers are also required to provide customers with annual privacy notices for the term of the customer relationship.

The notice requirements have four elements:

a. content—notices have specific information requirements

b. timing of delivery

c. method of delivery

d. clarity—notices must be made clear and conspicuous

Advisers who do not intend to divulge consumer information can provide such clients with simplified notices. Revised privacy notices must be provided if advisers' disclosure policies change.

19.13 What kind of information must the privacy notices contain?

Advisers must disclose anything that they may do with a consumer's or customer's nonpublic personal information. The following information must be included in the initial, annual, and revised privacy notices:

a. the categories of nonpublic personal information that the adviser collects;

b. the categories of nonpublic personal information that the adviser discloses;

c. the categories of affiliates and nonaffiliates to whom the adviser discloses nonpublic personal information, other than those to whom information is disclosed pursuant to an exception;

d. the registered investment adviser's policies with respect to sharing information about former customers;

e. the categories of information that are disclosed under agreements with third-party service providers and joint marketers and the categories of third parties providing services;

f. an explanation of a consumer's right to opt out of the disclosure of nonpublic personal information to nonaffiliated third parties and the methods by which the consumer may exercise that right;

g. any disclosures the adviser may have to make under the Fair Credit Reporting Act;

h. the adviser's policies and practices with respect to protecting the confidentiality of nonpublic personal information; and

i. if disclosures are made to third parties pursuant to the exceptions in question 19.14, a statement that disclosures are made to other nonaffiliated third parties as permitted by law.

19.14 Are there any exceptions?

There are exceptions to both the notice and opt-out requirement for the disclosure of nonpublic personal information if

a. it is necessary to effect, administer, or enforce certain transactions that the consumer requests or authorizes; or

b. disclosures are made for the purpose of administering, processing, servicing, and selling a customer's account or if made with the customer's approval for the customer's personal use, such as asset verification to a lender.

19.15 When are notices considered clear and conspicuous?

A notice is clear and conspicuous when it is reasonably understandable (see question 19.16) and designed to call attention to the nature and significance of the information of the notice. In Regulation S-P, the SEC provides a number of examples as to what is reasonably understandable and designed to call attention to a notice (see question 19.17).

19.16 When is a notice reasonably understandable?

Notices are reasonably understandable if
   a. information is provided in clear, concise sentences, paragraphs, and sections;
   b. short explanatory sentences or bulleted lists are used whenever possible;
   c. definite, concrete, everyday words and active voice are used whenever possible;
   d. the use of multiple negatives is avoided;
   e. legal and highly technical business terminology is avoided whenever possible;
   f. explanations that are imprecise and readily subject to different interpretations are avoided.

19.17 When are notices seen as "designed to call attention to"?

Notices are designed to call attention to the nature and significance of the information if
   a. the notice uses a plain-language heading to call attention to the notice;
   b. the notice uses a typeface and type size that are easy to read;
   c. the notice provides wide margins and ample line spacing;
   d. the notice uses boldface or italics for key words;

e. the notice uses distinctive type size, style, and graphic devices, such as shading or sidebars, when the notice is combined with other information.

19.18   May advisers provide the notice on their websites?

Notices can be provided on a web page. To be considered clear and conspicuous, the notice must be designed to use text or visual cues to encourage scrolling down the page if it is necessary to view the entire notice and ensure that other elements on the website do not distract from the notice. Advisers should place the notice on a screen that consumers frequently access or place a link on a screen that consumers frequently access that connects directly to the notice and is appropriately labeled to convey the importance, nature, and relevance of the notice.

19.19   If an adviser does not intend to divulge any nonpublic information about consumers to any affiliate or nonaffiliate, does the adviser still have to provide the privacy notices?

Advisers who do not want to reserve the right to disclose consumer nonpublic personal information to affiliates or nonaffiliates may provide a simplified privacy notice. The notice must be clear and conspicuous (see question 19.15) and state that the adviser does not disclose and does not wish to reserve the right to disclose, nonpublic personal information, except as permitted in certain exceptions. Furthermore, the notice must also include

a. the categories of nonpublic personal information that the adviser collects;

b. the adviser's policies and practices with respect to protecting the confidentiality of nonpublic personal information; and

c. if disclosures are made pursuant to the exceptions to the rules, a statement that disclosures are made to other nonaffiliated third parties as permitted by law (see question 19.14).

19.20   When must advisers provide the initial privacy notice to customers and consumers?

Advisers are generally required to provide the initial privacy notice to a customer no later than when the customer relationship is established. Advisers are required to provide an initial privacy notice to a consumer prior to sharing nonpublic personal information about that consumer with a nonaffiliated third party.

Opt-Out Rules

19.21   May clients opt out of sharing their nonpublic personal information with nonaffiliated third parties?

Individuals, both consumers and customers, must be given a reasonable opportunity to prevent the adviser from disclosing the individual's nonpublic personal information to nonaffiliated third parties. Specifically, advisers must provide consumers and customers a reasonable opportunity to opt out of any potential disclosure of their nonpublic personal information to third parties before disclosing such material to third parties. If the client decides to opt out after the adviser has already begun disclosing such information, the adviser must honor the opt-out as soon as reasonably practicable. Once a client exercises the right to opt out, an adviser may not disclose nonpublic personal information about that client unless the client retracts the opt-out.

19.22   What form must the opt-out notice take?

Prior to disclosing any nonpublic personal information about any consumer or customer, advisers must provide an opt-out notice, which must be clear and conspicuous (see question 19.15) and state

   a. that the adviser reserves the right to disclose nonpublic personal information to third parties

   b. that the consumer or customer has the right to opt out of the disclosure

   c. a reasonable means by which the consumer or customer may exercise that opt-out right

Furthermore, the SEC requires that opt-out notices identify

   a. all of the categories of nonpublic personal information that the adviser discloses or reserves the right to disclose, and all the categories of nonaffiliated third parties to which the adviser discloses information and states that the consumer may opt out of the disclosure of that information;

   b. the financial products or services that the consumer obtains from the adviser to which the opt-out direction applies.

19.23   What are some examples of a reasonable means for the consumer or customer to exercise the opt-out right?

Generally, advisers should give clients at least 30 days after providing them with the opt-out notice to exercise or not exercise their right to opt out. Advisers provide a reasonable means to allow clients to opt out of disclosure if

   a. the adviser designates check-off boxes in prominent positions on forms provided with the opt-out notice;

   b. the adviser includes a reply form with the opt-out notice;

   c. the adviser provides an electronic means to opt out, including a form that can be filled out and sent electronically on a website; or

   d. the adviser provides a toll-free telephone number that clients can call to opt out.

For example, if an adviser mails an opt-out notice to a client and allows the client to opt out by mailing in a form or calling a toll-free telephone number within 30 days after the adviser mailed the notice, the SEC considers that a "reasonable opportunity" to opt out. Requiring clients to write their own letters to opt out, however, is not reasonable.

19.24   How must advisers deliver privacy and opt-out notices?

Notices must be delivered in a manner in which the consumer or customer "can be reasonably expected to actually receive actual notice" in writing or, if the consumer agrees, electronically. The notice may be incorporated into another document such as Form ADV Part 2. There is no ADV item number that correlates to this requirement, so it is generally recommended that it be put at the end of Schedule F. However, since the privacy notice has to be delivered annually to clients, whereas the ADV only has to be offered, it would be advisable to have a separate notice for delivery as well.

19.25 Under what circumstances may advisers reasonably expect that consumers or customers received actual notice?
An adviser may reasonably expect that the client received actual notice if the adviser

   a. hand-delivers a printed copy of the notice to the consumer or customer;

   b. mails a printed copy of the notice to the last known address of the consumer or customer;

   c. posts the notice on the firm's website and requires the consumer to acknowledge receipt of the notice as a necessary step to obtaining a particular financial product or service. However, this can only be done for customers or consumers with whom the adviser conducts transactions electronically. If the notice is the annual notice, the customer need not acknowledge receipt of the notice if the firm continuously posts a current notice of its privacy policies and practices in a clear and conspicuous manner on the website and the customer has agreed to accept notices at the firm's website. It is not a reasonable expectation to send notices electronically to a consumer or customer who does not customarily obtain financial products or services from the firm electronically.

19.26 Are there any exceptions to either the opt-out or notice requirements?
The SEC provides exceptions to the opt-out or both the notice and opt-out requirements so that advisers can disclose information to nonaffiliated third parties in circumstances such as maintaining or servicing a customer's account or complying with federal, state, or local laws.

19.27 How may advisers service accounts or do joint marketing if a client opts out?
The SEC provides an exception to the opt-out requirements if the

adviser shares information with outside vendors or service providers who service client accounts and for joint marketing. Note that advisers still must notify clients that this information is being shared. Advisers may share information with a nonaffiliated third party without providing the customer with a right to opt out if the third party performs services for or functions on behalf of the adviser, including marketing the adviser's products or services under a joint agreement between the adviser and other advisers or financial institutions. The adviser must still fully disclose to the consumer that it will provide this information to the nonaffiliated third party prior to sharing the information. Furthermore, the adviser is required to enter into a contract with that third party, requiring the third party to maintain the confidentiality of the information.

19.28 How should the contract with the third party be drafted?

The contract should be drafted to ensure that the third party

a. will maintain the confidentiality of the information at least to the same extent as is required for the adviser to disclose it; and

b. will use the information solely for the purposes for which the information is disclosed or otherwise permitted.

19.29 May advisers process and service transactions under the privacy and opt-out rules?

The rules include exceptions to both the notice and opt-out requirements for processing and servicing transactions. Advisers are not required to provide initial or annual privacy notices or provide clients with an opportunity to opt out of disclosure of nonpublic personal information as necessary to effect, administer, or enforce a transaction that the consumer requests or authorizes, or a transaction in connection with

a. processing or servicing a financial product or service that a consumer requests or authorizes;

b. maintaining or servicing the consumer's account with the adviser, or with another entity as part of a private label credit card program or other extension of credit on behalf of such entity; or

c. a proposed actual securitization, secondary market sale, including the sales of servicing rights, or similar transaction related to a transaction of the consumer.

19.30 Are there any other exceptions to the notice and opt-out requirements?

The SEC has adopted a number of exceptions to the notice and opt-out requirements that would otherwise apply before an adviser would be permitted to disclose client nonpublic personal information. The privacy and opt-out requirements do not apply when advisers provide nonpublic personal information

a. with the consent or at the direction of the consumer, provided that the consumer has not revoked the consent or direction;

b. to protect the confidentiality or security of the adviser's records pertaining to the consumer, service, product, or transaction; to protect against or prevent fraud, unauthorized transaction, claims or other liabilities; for required institutional risk control or for resolving consumer disputes or inquiries; to persons holding legal or beneficial interest relating to the consumer; to persons acting in a fiduciary or representative capacity on behalf of the consumer;

c. to provide information to insurance rate-advisory organizations, guaranty funds or agencies, agencies that are rating the adviser, persons that are assessing the adviser's compliance with industry standards, and the adviser's attorneys, accountants, and auditors;

d. to the extent specifically required under other provisions of the law, to law enforcement agencies, a state insurance authority, self-regulatory organization, or for an investigation on a matter related to public safety;

e. to a consumer reporting agency, or a consumer report reported by a consumer reporting agency;

f. in connection with a proposed or actual sale, merger, transfer, or exchange of all or a portion of a business or operating unit if the disclosure of all nonpublic personal information concerns solely consumers of such business or unit;

g. to comply with federal, state, or local laws, rules and other applicable legal requirements; to comply with a properly authorized civil, criminal, or regulatory investigation, subpoena, or summons by federal, state, or local authorities; to respond to judicial process or government regulatory authorities having jurisdiction over the adviser for examination, compliance, or other purposes as authorized by law.

20 | Money Laundering

- ◆ **Anti–Money Laundering Program**
- ◆ **Screening Prospective Clients**
- ◆ **A High-Risk Client**
- ◆ **Monitoring for Suspicious Activities**
- ◆ **Responsibilities of the Compliance Officer**
- ◆ **Training**
- ◆ **Audits**
- ◆ **Due Diligence**

Anti–money laundering rules for registered investment advisers had yet to be finalized as of late 2005. Nonetheless, registered investment advisers should develop and implement an anti–money laundering program reasonably designed to prevent the firm from being used to launder money or finance terrorist activities. It is against the law for advisers to participate knowingly in the transfer of funds that are connected to a crime, so advisers should have programs designed to keep that from happening.

20.1 What is money laundering?

Money laundering is a scheme designed to conceal or disguise the source of money obtained illegally. Funds are moved through financial systems to distance them from their criminal sources and make it appear that the funds came from legitimate sources.

Money laundering also encompasses the movement of funds to support terrorism or terrorist organizations. In this case, the funds may derive from legitimate sources, and the money is laundered to disguise the identity of the source of the funds or to move the money to places or organizations prohibited under U.S. or international laws.

20.2 At a minimum, what is an anti–money laundering program required to do?

Registered investment advisers must report any transactions in cash or currency that exceed $10,000, regardless of whether or not they believe the funds to be connected to a crime. Advisers' supervisory procedures should include anti–money laundering policies regarding the receipt of cash to ensure that the rule is not broken, and a compliance officer should oversee the program. The procedures should require firm employees who suspect or detect suspicious activity to promptly report that activity to their immediate supervisors and the adviser's compliance officer.

Advisers should but are not required to develop anti–money laundering programs for their firms. Specifically, advisers should

    a. establish and implement policies, procedures, and internal controls reasonably designed to prevent the adviser from being used to launder money or finance terrorist activities;

b. provide for periodic independent testing of compliance with these controls to be conducted by company personnel or by a qualified outside party;

c. designate a person or persons responsible for implementing and monitoring the operations and internal controls of the program;

d. provide ongoing training for appropriate persons in detecting and avoiding money laundering activities.

20.3 Do advisers have to screen prospective clients for possible money laundering involvement?

It would be prudent for advisers to have procedures in place to identify prospective clients, screen for prohibited clients, and identify clients who are at a high risk for potentially laundering money. Advisers should conduct some due diligence to ensure that clients are indeed who they represent themselves to be and to verify that the client does not appear on any list of known or suspected terrorists published by any governmental agency.

As part of the due diligence, when clients are opening accounts, advisers should ascertain

a. the reason for opening the account;

b. anticipated account activity;

c. the source that generated the money deposited into the account;

d. the estimated net worth of the individual or entity who owns the account;

e. the source of the funds as well as by what means and from where the funds were transferred into the account. Gathering references and other information on the prospective client is prudent as well.

20.4 What is a high-risk client?

High-risk clients include persons

a. who are residents of or have funds sourced from countries identified by the U.S. Department of Treasury as noncooperative jurisdictions

b. who engage in any activity deemed by the U.S. Department of Treasury to be a "primary money laundering concern"

c. whose source of wealth emanates from activities known to be susceptible to money laundering

d. who have positions of public trust in developing countries.

Additionally, advisers should be cautious when a client or a beneficiary of an account has a questionable background, which could include prior criminal charges or convictions, or is having difficulty explaining the nature of his business.

20.5 Do advisers have an affirmative obligation to monitor for suspicious activities?

Registered investment advisers should monitor clients and accounts for suspicious activities that could suggest that the client is attempting to launder money. Suspicious activities include any transactions that appear to

a. involve proceeds from an illegal activity

b. be attempting to evade currency transaction reporting requirements

c. vary significantly from the client's normal investment activities

d. have no business or apparent lawful purpose and the adviser knows of no reasonable explanation for the transaction

20.6 What kind of activities should raise advisers' suspicions?

Activities such as

a. frequent wires in and out of an account where such activity is unusual for that particular account

b. a request to wire money to an Office of Foreign Assets Control (OFAC)-blocked country

c. several money orders received within a short span of time after an account is opened

d. multiple accounts under a single name or multiple names with frequent interaccount transfers

e. a high level of account activities with low levels of securities transactions

f. large wire transfers immediately followed by withdrawal by check or debit card

g. transactions in which the client appears to be acting as an agent for an undisclosed principal

h. cash transactions of a large dollar amount

i. transactions that appear to lack business sense or that are inconsistent with the client's stated investment strategy

j. transactions about which the client exhibits an unusual concern for secrecy

k. large or frequent wire transfers to unrelated third parties

20.7 What requirements must an employee meet to be a firm's compliance officer, and what are the responsibilities of the compliance officer?

The compliance officer should have sufficient responsibility, authority, and support to implement and operate the anti–money laundering program. The compliance officer should be charged with monitoring the adviser's anti–money laundering compliance program, conducting training sessions, and reviewing reports of suspicious activity.

20.8 What kind of training must advisers conduct to help detect money laundering?

Advisory firms are required to provide anti–money laundering training to senior management and to any employees who have contacts with clients or responsibilities for client accounts. It would be prudent for the firm to hold training for all employees on how to detect and prevent money laundering and to conduct periodic audits of the anti–money laundering program. Periodic training sessions should teach employees about the anti–money laundering statutes and regulations, how to recognize suspicious activities, and employees' responsibilities if they detect such activities.

20.9 Are there any required audits?

Anti–money laundering programs should be periodically audited—
at least annually—by an independent auditor. The audit must
review the adequacy of the compliance program, the system and
records maintained, and regulatory forms filed.

20.10 What are advisers required to do if they encounter suspicious activity?

If a client's activities appear suspicious, advisers should explore
and conduct due diligence. Although banks and broker-dealers
must file a suspicious activity report (SAR) related to a transaction involving funds or assets of $5,000 or more with the U.S.
Department of Treasury's Financial Crimes Enforcement Network,
advisers are not subject to this requirement. However, advisers may
voluntarily file SARs if they detect suspicious activity.

21 | Supervising Employees

◆ **Liability**
◆ **Supervisory Responsibilities and Procedures**
◆ **Internal Controls**
◆ **Reporting Violations**

An adviser's employees must be supervised to ensure that all the firm's activities comply with disclosures made to clients and with the provisions of applicable securities laws. The SEC considers that supervision to be a primary responsibility of a registered investment adviser. The SEC has the power to sanction an adviser and an associated person for failure to supervise.

Specifically, if federal securities laws have been violated, the SEC may seek to sanction an advisory firm if it establishes that the violation could have been prevented if the firm had not failed to reasonably supervise. An individual can also be sanctioned for failure to supervise if that individual was responsible for supervising the person who did not effectively carry out the necessary steps to comply with the law.

21.1 How can advisers keep from being held liable for failure to supervise?

There is a safe harbor in the Advisers Act. Advisers cannot be deemed to have failed reasonably to supervise a person if they

a. establish procedures that could be expected to prevent and detect, insofar as practicable, any violation by such person;

b. reasonably discharge the duties and obligations incumbent on advisers by reason of such procedures and systems and have no reasonable cause to believe that such procedures and systems were not being complied with.

During inspections, the SEC will evaluate advisers' internal controls and supervisory procedures. Note that while the safe harbor says that advisers may be able to avoid liability "if" they establish procedures, advisers no longer have the option not to. They are now required to have compliance programs in place (see chapter 7).

21.2 Who is considered a supervisor?

The Advisers Act does not define the term "supervisor." An advisory firm, however, is generally always considered to be a supervisor and therefore is subject to the failure to supervise sanctions. Individuals are also generally considered to be supervisors if they are in the firm's management chain. The SEC has also attempted to expand supervisory responsibility to persons outside the advisers' direct management chains, such as legal and compliance personnel.

21.3 How must advisers discharge their supervisory responsibility?

Advisers must establish and implement adequate procedures to prevent and detect violations of the law. When there are indications that procedures are not being followed, there must be meaningful follow-up.

21.4 How may advisers design and implement adequate procedures?

Under Rule 206(4)-7 of the Advisers Act, registered investment advisers must establish and maintain comprehensive compliance policies (see chapter 7).

21.5 What constitutes meaningful follow-up?

The SEC staff takes the position that supervisors are required to respond immediately whenever a wrongdoing or possible indications of wrongdoing come to their attention. Supervisors must take steps such as reporting to their supervisors and the firm's legal/compliance department or informing the head of the firm. At that point, steps such as conducting an investigation should be taken. If supervisors cannot get people up the chain to act on a wrongdoing or on indications of potential wrongdoing, they need to consider resigning from the firm and disclosing the conduct to regulatory authorities.

Once it's been determined that there has been wrongdoing, meaningful follow-up includes taking steps such as

    a. notifying regulatory agencies

    b. disciplining the people involved

    c. making clients whole and/or implementing new procedures to make sure the wrongdoing does not happen again

21.6   What are some examples of poor internal controls?

The SEC has indicated that the following examples illustrate weaknesses in internal controls:

a. Without any independent review, an adviser's portfolio managers may value recommended securities or override values provided by a custodian, for purposes of reporting to clients and calculating advisory fees. The SEC has indicated that it would be preferable to provide for a separation of duties and proper management oversight of pricing overrides.

b. An adviser establishes comprehensive written control procedures but does not monitor for compliance. For example, the insider trading policy states that access persons may not trade shares issued by companies on a restricted list, yet the adviser does not review personal securities transactions.

c. An investment adviser does not have an oversight process—other than that performed by the portfolio manager responsible for managing an account—to determine whether risks taken in managing client portfolios are consistent with each client's stated investment objectives and/or to measure and evaluate each client's risk tolerance.

21.7   If a member of an adviser's staff violates the rules, is the adviser required to report the person to the SEC?

The SEC staff takes the position that in determining enforcement actions it will take into account whether or not an adviser reported a violation to the SEC. In other words, if the SEC finds a violation during the course of an examination, it may give a firm credit for reporting the violation. Conversely, if the SEC finds a violation during an examination and the firm did not self-report, the SEC will take that into account. (See chapter 22 for a discussion of enforcement actions by the SEC.)

22 | SEC Examinations and Enforcement Actions

- ◆ Routine Examinations
- ◆ Suspected Wrongdoing
- ◆ Sweep Examinations
- ◆ Common Problems Uncovered
- ◆ Documents, Books, and Records
- ◆ Client Confidentiality Rules
- ◆ Preparing for an Examination
- ◆ Confidential Treatment
- ◆ Enforcement Action
- ◆ Disciplinary Actions
- ◆ A No-Action Letter

In recent years, the SEC has been stepping up audits of registered investment advisers. The Advisers Act authorizes the SEC to conduct reasonable, periodic, special, or other examinations of advisers at any time or from time to time. The SEC does not have to suspect wrongdoing to conduct an examination. Furthermore, although the SEC typically does inform an adviser in advance that it will come and inspect, such notice is not required and the SEC can show up unannounced.

Advisers should always be truthful to SEC examiners. Lying to the SEC is a criminal offense that can subject an adviser to up to 5 years' imprisonment and fines.

The Advisers Act gives the SEC wide latitude in enforcement. The SEC has the power to bring administrative sanction, initiate civil injunctions, and together with the U.S. Attorney General, criminally prosecute. The SEC can bring enforcement actions in the U.S. federal courts or before an independent administrative law judge.

The SEC, however, cannot seek criminal penalties and sanction on its own, but it can refer a matter to the Department of Justice with a recommendation that an adviser be indicted and prosecuted. If the Department of Justice concurs, the matter is referred to a grand jury. If an indictment follows, the adviser will then be prosecuted.

22.1   Who conducts the examinations?

The SEC's Office of Compliance Inspections and Examinations administers the SEC's nationwide examination and inspection program for registered investment advisers. The SEC conducts examinations through its field offices located throughout the United States. See the appendix to this chapter for a list of regional offices and contact information.

22.2   Are there different kinds of examinations?

The Office of Compliance Inspections and Examinations conducts inspections to
   a. foster compliance with the securities laws

b. detect violations of the law

c. keep the SEC informed of developments in the regulated community

Among the goals of the SEC's examination program is the quick and informal correction of compliance problems. When the office finds deficiencies, it issues a deficiency letter identifying the problems that need to be rectified and monitors the situation until compliance is achieved. Violations that appear too serious for informal correction are referred to the Division of Enforcement.

22.3   What are periodic, routine examinations?

Periodic, routine exams can last several weeks. The SEC's examination staff conducts periodic, routine examinations of registered investment advisers to determine

a. if advisers are conducting their activities in accordance with the law and making disclosures to clients

b. whether they have adequate systems and procedures in place to ensure that their operations are in compliance with the law

SEC staff has indicated that the SEC exam cycle ranges from 2 to 10 years. An individual investment adviser's exam cycle is determined by the perceived risk the SEC believes the adviser presents.

22.4   Are examinations conducted because of suspected wrongdoing?

Yes, in addition to routine, periodic examinations, the SEC may investigate an adviser because of complaints by investors or referrals from state securities regulators or self-regulatory bodies such as the NYSE. Press reports may even trigger an exam, as may SEC staff initiatives. If the SEC is examining an adviser for cause, the SEC must inform the adviser that the exam is for cause, but it does not have to state the reason the adviser is being examined.

Investigative examinations tend to address issues such as alleged accounting deficiencies, insider trading, illegal trading and/or sales practices, offerings of unregistered securities, soft-dollar practices, or disclosure problems. Generally, investigations begin as informal investigations in which the adviser cooperates voluntarily. If the informal investigation turns up suspicious activities or the adviser does not cooperate, the SEC could move to the formal investigation stage.

22.5 What is a sweep examination?

The SEC conducts sweep examinations as fact-finding missions to gather information and learn about industry practices. For example, the SEC conducted sweep examinations focusing on soft dollars.

22.6 During the course of a routine exam, what are some of the common problems that the SEC finds?

The SEC has indicated that among the common deficiencies it finds when it conducts exams of advisers are the following:

   a. violations of the advertising rules;

   b. deficiencies in books and records;

   c. personal trading violations;

   d. problems with referral arrangements;

   e. problems with the use of brokerage;

   f. failure to remedy deficiencies noted in previous examinations;

   g. inaccurate disclosures on Form ADV;

   h. failure to offer Form ADV annually to clients;

   i. failure to maintain advisory contracts;

   j. failure to fully disclose advisory fees, including how fees are charged and whether fees are negotiable;

   k. failure to maintain complaint or litigation files;

   l. inaccurate or misleading websites;

   m. failure to disclose that initial public offerings are disproportionately allocated to favored accounts;

   n. fraudulent performance claims including false representation of assets under management, credentials, length of time in business, or use of a predecessor's performance in current performance returns;

o. failure to comply with the custody rules;

p. failure to fulfill a contractual obligation in the advisory contract including calculating advisory fees differently from the methodology specified in the contract or failing to comply with clients' wishes concerning directed brokerage arrangements and causing clients to invest in securities that are inconsistent with the level of risk they have agreed to assume.

22.7　What kinds of documents, books, and records may advisers expect the SEC or state agency to ask to examine?

The examination staff will review an adviser's filings with the SEC and other materials provided to clients to ensure that disclosures are accurate, timely, and do not omit material information. The SEC has been known to request items such as business contingency plan documents, e-mail correspondence from specific people in the firm, copies of the compliance manual and code of ethics, as well as records of trades over a specified period of time.

The SEC staff is required to provide a notice to advisers prior to the audit, informing the adviser of

a. the SEC's authority to request the information

b. whether providing the information is mandatory or voluntary

c. why the SEC is requesting the information

d. the consequences of not producing the requested information

e. whether the SEC is requesting the information under its inspection powers or its law enforcement powers

It should be noted that the SEC takes the position that it has authority to examine all records of an investment adviser, not just those the adviser is required to keep under the Advisers Act. For example, it could ask an adviser for records on the educational and experience background of the chief compliance officer as well as details on the chief compliance officer's compensation package. Many lawyers and other experts, however, take the position that the SEC is not entitled to see books and records beyond those advisers are required to keep under the Advisers Act. In any event, it is generally considered not prudent to refuse an examiner's request.

22.8   What kinds of client confidentiality rules apply during an examination?

There are exceptions to the requirements to provide privacy notices and opt-out options prior to revealing client information to comply with state or federal laws or to comply with inspections under those laws. See question 19.30.

22.9   How should advisers prepare for the examination?

Before the exam, advisers should review records of previous exams and internal audits to make sure that any previously noted deficiencies have been corrected. Advisers should also communicate with staff, telling them of the upcoming exam and that they should cooperate fully.

The SEC will most likely send a letter in advance with a list of documents the adviser must furnish to the examiners. The SEC will also ask that adequate accommodations be provided for staff wherever the inspection is taking place. Under the Freedom of Information Act, third parties may request copies of documents that are in the SEC's possession, and the SEC is required to grant that request unless the documents are exempt from disclosure. An adviser may ask that SEC staff return documents produced during an inspection, although the SEC staff is not obligated to return such documents. At a minimum, an adviser should request confidential treatment of any material that involves sensitive nonpublic, client information.

22.10   What is confidential treatment and how do advisers request it?

Under the Freedom of Information Act, advisers submitting documents and information to the SEC may seek confidential treatment for certain categories of documents and information. For example, commercial or financial information that is not customarily disclosed to the public may be given confidential treatment. If confidential treatment is given and a third party requests the information, the SEC will notify that party that confidential treatment of the material was requested and ask for additional information from the party making the request. The SEC will then determine whether confidential treatment is warranted and whether to turn the information over to the third party.

If an adviser wants to request that the SEC treat certain documents and information as confidential and exempt from Freedom of Information requests, the adviser must do so in writing and submit the request at the time the information or documents are submitted to the SEC. Advisers may make the request directly to SEC staff on premises to do the inspection.

Such documents and information should be separated from nonconfidential items and labeled as confidential. Additionally, a copy of the request for confidentiality must be sent to the SEC's Freedom of Information Officer. Copies of the actual documents, however, need not be submitted to the SEC's Freedom of Information Officer.

22.11   Once the SEC staff are on-site, what can advisers expect?
Once on premises, SEC staff will likely ask to speak with key personnel of the firm. After that, they will begin to examine books and records as well as other requested information and ask for additional books and records as the exam progresses.

22.12   Once the staff completes their examination, what can advisers expect?
After the completion of the exam, SEC staff are likely to discuss their preliminary findings with the adviser. However, even if the SEC staff find no problems in the office examination, they may still find deficiencies in an adviser's practice later, when they review the books and records at the SEC's offices. Sometimes advisers are asked additional questions or to provide additional books and records.

If the SEC finds any minor problems with the adviser's business operations during the office exam, those issues will be addressed in a deficiency letter, which will discuss the violations that the SEC staff found and the steps the adviser will need to take to correct the violations. There are usually no monetary penalties for such deficiencies, although you can expect the SEC staff to follow up and verify that they have been corrected.

If the SEC finds anything it deems to be a serious violation, the violation will be referred to the SEC's Division of Enforcement for action. Proceedings will be brought before an administrative law judge, and sanctions can include censure, limitation of practice, suspension, and revocation of registration. The administrative law judge can also fine the adviser up to $100,000 if the adviser is an individual, or up to $500,000 if the adviser is a corporation or partnership and the charge is fraud, deceit, manipulation, or deliberate or reckless disregard of the law or underlying regulations. Cease and desist orders, injunctions, and additional monetary penalties can also be imposed.

If the SEC finds no deficiencies, sometimes an adviser will get an official letter saying so, but hearing absolutely nothing is the more common result of the staff's finding nothing to correct.

22.13   When may the SEC bring an enforcement action?

The Advisers Act empowers the SEC to discipline an adviser, or any person associated with the adviser, if the SEC finds that the adviser or a person associated with an adviser, did any of the following:

   a. made false statements on an application for registration or in an SEC report
   b. had been convicted of certain felonies or misdemeanors within 10 years preceding the filing of any application for registration or thereafter
   c. had been convicted of any crime punishable by imprisonment for at least 1 year within 10 years preceding the filing of any application for registration or thereafter
   d. had been enjoined by a court from engaging in activity in the financial services industry

e. had violated the federal securities laws or related statutes
f. had aided and abetted a violation of the federal securities laws or related statutes or had failed to reasonably supervise someone who commits a violation of such laws
g. had been barred or suspended by the SEC from associating with an investment adviser
h. had been found by a foreign financial regulatory authority to have engaged in certain conduct

22.14 What kind of disciplinary actions may the SEC take?
The SEC can take the following disciplinary actions against advisers or persons associated with an adviser:
a. censure
b. impose limitations on the adviser's activities
c. suspend the adviser for up to a year
d. revoke or suspend the adviser's registration or bar or suspend a person from employment in the securities industry
e. impose permanent or temporary cease and desist orders
Additionally, the SEC may enter into administrative proceedings to
a. impose civil monetary penalties
b. enter into disgorgement orders requiring disgorgement of all ill-gotten profits
Since 2004, the SEC has ratcheted up enforcement actions. Whereas in the past the SEC was more likely to issue deficiency letters or warnings, in recent years it has begun cracking down. Even small one-man advisory firms are now held to stringent compliance standards and face monetary penalties if found not to comply with the Advisers Act or other securities laws and regulations.

22.15 What is a no-action letter?
An adviser who is not certain whether a particular product, service, or action would constitute a violation of the federal securities laws may request a no-action letter from the SEC. No-action letters, which are published by the SEC and are generally available on the SEC website, describe the request, analyze the facts and circum-

stances involved, and discuss applicable laws and rules. If the SEC grants the request for no action, the no-action letter will state that the SEC would not recommend taking enforcement action against the adviser based on the facts and representations described in the letter.

22.16   If an adviser's employee violates a rule, can the SEC discipline the adviser?
The SEC can sanction an adviser for failure to supervise (see chapter 21).

Appendix A

Contact Information for the SEC and Securities Regulators

SEC Headquarters
100 F Street, NE
Washington, DC 20549
Office of Investor Education and Assistance
202-551-6551
e-mail: help@sec.gov

Office of Investment Adviser Regulation
202-551-6999
e-mail: IARDLive@sec.gov

Northeast Regional Office
Mark Schonfeld, Regional Director
3 World Financial Center, Room 4300
New York, NY 10281
212-336-1100
e-mail: newyork@sec.gov

Boston District Office
Walter G. Ricciardi, District Administrator
73 Tremont Street, Suite 600
Boston, MA 02108-3912
617-573-8900
e-mail: boston@sec.gov

Philadelphia District Office
Arthur S. Gabinet, District Administrator
The Mellon Independence Center
701 Market Street
Philadelphia, PA 19106-1532
215-597-3100
e-mail: philadelphia@sec.gov

Southeast Regional Office
David Nelson, Regional Director
801 Brickell Ave., Suite 1800
Miami, FL 33131
305-982-6300
e-mail: miami@sec.gov

Atlanta District Office
Richard P. Wessel, District Administrator
3475 Lenox Road, NE, Suite 1000
Atlanta, GA 30326-1232
404-842-7600
e-mail: atlanta@sec.gov

Midwest Regional Office
Merri Jo Gillette, Regional Director
175 W. Jackson Blvd., Suite 900

Chicago, IL 60604
312-353-7390
e-mail: chicago@sec.gov

Central Regional Office
Randall J. Fons, Regional Director
1801 California Street, Suite 1500
Denver, CO 80202-2656
303-844-1000
e-mail: denver@sec.gov

Fort Worth District Office
Harold F. Degenhardt
District Administrator
801 Cherry Street, 19th Floor
Fort Worth, TX 76102
817-978-3821
e-mail: dfw@sec.gov

Salt Lake District Office
Kenneth D. Israel, Jr.
District Administrator
15 W. South Temple Street, Suite 1800
Salt Lake City, UT 84101
801-524-5796
e-mail: saltlake@sec.gov

Pacific Regional Office
Randall R. Lee, Regional Director
5670 Wilshire Blvd., 11th Floor
Los Angeles, CA 90036-3648
323-965-3998
e-mail: losangeles@sec.gov

San Francisco District Office
Helane L. Morrison, District Administrator

44 Montgomery Street, Suite 1100
San Francisco, CA 94104
415-705-2500
e-mail: sanfrancisco@sec.gov

STATE SECURITIES REGULATOR CONTACTS

Alabama
Securities Commission
770 Washington Avenue, Suite 570
Montgomery, AL 36130-4700
Joseph P. Borg, Esq., Director
334-242-2984
800-222-1253
334-242-0240 (Fax)

Alaska
Dept. of Community and Economic
   Development
Div. of Banking, Securities & Corporations
150 Third Street, Room 217
PO Box 110807
Juneau, AK 99811-0807
Mark R. Davis, Director
907-465-2521
907-465-1230 (Fax)

Arizona
Corporation Commission Securities
   Division
1300 West Washington Street
3rd Floor
Phoenix, AZ 85007
Matthew J. Neubert, Director
602-542-4242
602-594-7470 (Fax)

Arkansas

Securities Department
Heritage West Building
201 East Markham, Room 300
Little Rock, AR 72201-1692
Michael Johnson
Securities Commissioner
501-324-9260
501-324-9268 (Fax)

California

Department of Corporations
1515 K Street, Suite 200
Sacramento, CA 95814
Timothy L. Le Bas, Assistant Commissioner
   & General Counsel
Office of Law & Legislation
916-445-7205
916-445-7975 (Fax)

Colorado

Division of Securities
1580 Lincoln Street, Suite 420
Denver, CO 80203
Fred J. Joseph, Securities Commissioner
303-894-2320
303-861-2126 (Fax)

Connecticut

Department of Banking
260 Constitution Plaza
Hartford, CT 06103-1800
Ralph A. Lambiase, Director of Securities
860-240-8230
860-240-8295 (Fax)

Delaware

Department of Justice
Division of Securities
Carvel State Office Building
820 North French Street, 5th Floor
Wilmington, DE 19801
James B. Ropp, Securities Commissioner
302-577-8424
302-577-6987 (Fax)

District of Columbia

Department of Insurance & Securities
   Regulation
Securities Bureau
810 First Street, NE, Suite 622
Washington, DC 20002
Theodore A. Miles
Director Securities Bureau
202-727-8000
202-535-1199 (Fax)

Florida

Office of Financial Regulation
200 East Gaines Street
The Fletcher Building
Tallahassee, FL 32399-0372
Don Saxon, Director
850-410-9805
850-410-9748 (Fax)

Georgia

Office of the Secretary of State
Division of Business Services and
   Regulation
Two Martin Luther King, Jr. Drive SE
802 West Tower

Atlanta, GA 30334
Tonya Curry, Director
Division of Securities
404-656-3920
404-651-6451 (Fax)

Hawaii
Department of Commerce & Consumer
  Affairs
Division of Business Regulation
335 Merchant Street, Room 203
Honolulu, HI 96813
Corinna Wong
Commissioner of Securities
808-586-2744
808-586-2733 (Fax)

Idaho
Department of Finance
700 West State Street, 2nd Floor
Boise, ID 83702
Marilyn T. Chastain
Securities Bureau Chief
208-332-8004
208-332-8099 (Fax)

Illinois
Office of the Secretary of State
Securities Department
69 West Washington Street, Suite 1220
Chicago, IL 60602
Tanya Solov, Director of Securities
312-793-3384
800-628-7937

Indiana
Office of the Secretary of State
  Securities Division
302 West Washington, Room E-111
Indianapolis, IN 46204
Wayne Davis
Securities Commissioner
317-232-6681
317-233-3675 (Fax)

Iowa
Insurance Division
Securities Bureau
340 E. Maple Street
Des Moines, IA 50319-0066
Craig A. Goettsch
Superintendent of Securities
515-281-4441
515-281-3059 (Fax)

Kansas
Office of the Securities Commissioner
618 South Kansas Avenue
Topeka, KS 66603-3804
Chris Biggs, Commissioner
785-296-3307
785-296-6872 (Fax)

Kentucky
Department of Financial Institutions
1025 Capital Center Drive, Suite 200
Frankfort, KY 40601
Colleen Keefe, Director of Securities
502-573-3390
800-223-2579
502-573-8787 (Fax)

Louisiana

Securities Commission

Office of Financial Institutions

8660 United Plaza Blvd., 2nd Floor

Baton Rouge, LA 70809-7024

Rhonda Reeves

Deputy Securities Commissioner

225-925-4512

225-925-4548 (Fax)

Maine

Securities Division

State House Station 121

Augusta, ME 04333

Christine A. Bruenn

Securities Administrator

207-624-8551

207-624-8590 (Fax)

Maryland

Office of the Attorney General

Division of Securities

200 Saint Paul Place

Baltimore, MD 21202-2020

Melanie Senter Lubin

Securities Commissioner

410-576-6360

410-576-6532 (Fax)

Massachusetts

Securities Division

One Ashburton Place, Room 1701

Boston, MA 02108

Bryan Lantagne, Director

617-727-3548

617-248-0177 (Fax)

Michigan

Conduct Review & Securities Division

Office of Financial & Insurance Services

Dept. of Labor & Economic Growth

611 West Ottawa Street, 3rd Floor

Lansing, MI 48933

Linda A. Watters, Commissioner

Office of Financial & Insurance Services

877-999-6442

517-241-3953 (Fax)

Minnesota

Department of Commerce

85 East 7th Place, Suite 500

Saint Paul, MN 55101

Scott P. Borchert, Director

Enforcement Division

651-296-4026

651-296-4328 (Fax)

Mississippi

Office of the Secretary of State

Business Regulation & Enforcement
  Division

700 North Street

Jackson, MS 39202

James O. Nelson, II

Assistant Secretary of State

Business Regulation & Securities Division

601-359-6371

601-359-2663 (Fax)

Missouri

Office of the Secretary of State

600 West Main Street

Jefferson City, MO 65101

David Cosgrove, Securities Commissioner
573-751-4704
573-526-3124 (Fax)

Montana
Office of the State Auditor
Securities Department
840 Helena Avenue
Helena, MT 59601
John Morrison, Securities Commissioner
406-444-2040
406-444-5558 (Fax)

Nebraska
Nebraska Department of Banking &
   Finance
Commerce Court
1230 "O" Street, Suite 400
PO Box 95006
Lincoln, NE 68509-5006
Jack E. Herstein, Assistant Director
402-471-3445

Nevada
Secretary of State
Securities Division
555 East Washington Avenue
5th Floor, Suite 5200
Las Vegas, NV 89101
Charles Moore, Securities Administrator
702-486-2440
702-486-2452 (Fax)

New Hampshire
Bureau of Securities Regulation
State House Annex

Suite 317A, 3rd Floor
Concord, NH 03301
Mark Connolly
Deputy Secretary of State
Director of Securities Regulation
603-271-1463
603-271-7933 (Fax)

New Jersey
Department of Law & Public Safety
Bureau of Securities
153 Halsey Street, 6th Floor
Newark, NJ 07102
Franklin L. Widmann, Chief
973-504-3600
973-504-3601 (Fax)

New Mexico
Regulation & Licensing Department
Securities Division
2550 Cerrillos Road
Santa Fe, NM 87505
Bruce R. Kohl, Director of Securities
505-476-4580
505-984-0617 (Fax)

New York
Office of the Attorney General
Investor Protection & Securities Bureau
120 Broadway, 23rd Floor
New York, NY 10271
Gary Connor, First Deputy Bureau Chief
212-416-8200
212-416-8816 (Fax)

North Carolina
Department of the Secretary of State
Securities Division
300 North Salisbury Street, Suite 100
Raleigh, NC 27603-5909
David S. Massey
Deputy Securities Administrator
919-733-3924
919-821-0818 (Fax)

North Dakota
Securities Commission
600 East Blvd.
State Capitol, 5th Floor
Bismarck, ND 58505-0510
Karen Tyler, Commissioner
701-328-2910
701-255-3113 (Fax)

Ohio
Division of Securities
77 South High Street, 22nd Floor
Columbus, OH 43215
Dale A. Jewell, Commissioner
614-644-7381
614-466-3316 (Fax)

Oklahoma
Department of Securities
1st National Center, Suite 860
120 N. Robinson
Oklahoma City, OK 73102
Irving Faught, Administrator
405-280-7700
405-280-7742 (Fax)

Oregon
Department of Consumer & Business
  Services
Div. of Finance & Corp. Securities
350 Winter Street, NE, Room 410
Salem, OR 97301-3881
Floyd Lanter, Division Administrator
503-378-4387
503-947-7862 (Fax)

Pennsylvania
Securities Commission
Eastgate Office Building
1010 North 7th Street, 2nd Floor
Harrisburg, PA 17102-1410
Robert M. Lam, Commissioner
717-787-8061
717-783-5122 (Fax)

Puerto Rico
Commission of Financial Institutions
1492 Ponce de Leon Avenue, Suite 600
San Juan, PR 00907
Felipe B. Cruz, Esq.
Assistant Commissioner
787-723-3131 ext. 2222

Rhode Island
Department of Business Regulation
233 Richmond Street , Suite 232
Providence, RI 02903-4232
Maria D'Alessandro, Associate Director
  & Superintendent of Securities
401-222-3048
401-222-5629 (Fax)

South Carolina
Office of the Attorney General
Securities Division
Rembert C. Dennis Office Building
1000 Assembly Street
Columbia, SC 29201
T. Stephen Lynch
Deputy Securities Commissioner
803-734-4731
803-734-0032 (Fax)

South Dakota
Division of Securities
445 E Capitol Avenue
Pierre, SD 57501-2000
Gail Sheppick, Director
605-773-4823
605-773-5953 (Fax)

Tennessee
Department of Commerce & Insurance
Securities Division
Davy Crockett Tower, Suite 680
500 James Robertson Parkway
Nashville, TN 37243-0575
Daphne D. Smith
Assistant Commissioner for Securities
615-741-2947
615-532-8375 (Fax)

Texas
State Securities Board
208 East 10th Street, 5th Floor
Austin, TX 78701
Denise Voigt Crawford
Securities Commissioner

512-305-8300
512-305-8310 (Fax)

Utah
Department of Commerce
Division of Securities
160 East 300 South, 2nd Floor
Salt Lake City, UT 84111
Jason Perry, Deputy Director
801-530-6600
801-530-6980 (Fax)

Vermont
Department of Banking, Insurance,
    Securities & Health Care Administration
89 Main Street, Drawer 20
Montpelier, VT 05620-3101
Tanya Durkee
Deputy Commissioner of Securities
802-828-3420
802-828-2896 (Fax)

Virginia
State Corporation Commission
Division of Securities & Retail Franchising
1300 East Main Street, 9th Floor
Richmond, VA 23219
Ronald W. Thomas, Director
804-371-9051
804-371-9911 (Fax)

Washington
Department of Financial Institutions
Securities Division
150 Israel Road, SW
Tumwater, WA 98501

Michael E. Stevenson
Director of Securities
360-902-8760
360-902-0524 (Fax)

West Virginia
Office of the State Auditor
Securities Division
Building 1, Room W-100
Charleston, WV 25305-0230
Chester F. Thompson
Deputy Commissioner of Securities
304-558-2257
877-982-9148
304-558-4211 (Fax)

Wisconsin
Department of Financial Institutions
Division of Securities
345 W. Washington Avenue, 4th Floor
Madison, WI 53703
Patricia D. Struck
Administrator
608-266-1064
608-264-7979 (Fax)

Wyoming
Secretary of State
Securities Division
State Capitol, Room 109
200 W. 24th Street
Cheyenne, WY 82002-0020
Thomas Cowan, Division Director
307-777-7370
307-777-5339 (Fax)

CANADIAN AND MEXICAN SECURITIES REGULATORS

CANADA
Alberta
Securities Commission
Suite 400, 300-5th Avenue SW
Calgary, AB T2P 3C4
Canada
Stephen Sibold, Q.C., Chair
403-297-6454
403-297-6156 (Fax)

British Columbia
Securities Commission
PO Box 10142, Pacific Centre
701 West Georgia Street
Vancouver, BC V7Y 1L2
Canada
Adrienne Salvail-Lopez, Commissioner
604-899-6500
604-899-6506 (Fax)

Manitoba
Securities Commission
1130-405 Broadway
Winnipeg, MB R3C 3L6
Canada
Donald G. Murray, Chairman
204-945-2548
204-945-0330 (Fax)

New Brunswick
Department of Justice
Securities Administration Branch
133 Prince William Street, Suite 606
St. John, NB E2L 2B5

Canada
Rick Hancox, Executive Director
506-658-3060
506-658-3059 (Fax)

Newfoundland and Labrador
Government of Newfoundland and
   Labrador
PO Box 8700
Confederation Building, West Block
St. John's, NL A1B 4J6
Canada
Winston Morris
Assistant Deputy Minister
Consumer & Commercial Affairs
Chair, Securities Commission
709-729-2571
709-729-4151 (Fax)

Northwest Territories
Securities Registry
Department of Justice
1st Floor, Stuart M. Hodgson Building
5009 49th Street
Yellowknife, NT X1A 2L9
Canada
Tony Wong, Registrar of Securities
867-873-7490
867-873-0243 (Fax)

Nova Scotia
Securities Commission
1690 Hollis Street
2nd Floor, Joseph Howe Building
Halifax, NS B3J 3J9
Canada
H. Leslie O'Brien, Vice-Chair

902-424-7768
902-424-4625 (Fax)

Nunavut
Department of Justice
Legal Registries Division
PO Box 1000, Station 570
1st Floor, Brown Building
Iqaluit, NU X0A 0H0
Canada
Gary Crowe, Registrar of Securities
867-975-6190
867-975-6194 (Fax)

Ontario
Securities Commission
20 Queen Street West, Suite 1900
Box 55
Toronto, ON M5H 3S8
Canada
David Brown, Chair
416-593-8200
416-593-8241 (Fax)

Prince Edward Island
Office of the Attorney General
95 Rochford Street
4th Floor, Shaw Building
Charlottetown, PE C1A 7N8
Canada
Edison Shea, Registrar of Securities
902-368-4552
902-368-5283 (Fax)

Québec
Autorité des Marchés Financiers
800 Square Victoria, 22nd Floor

Stock Exchange Tower
Montreal, PQ H4Z 1G3
Canada
Daniel Laurion, Superintendent
Securities Market
Regulation Directorate
514-940-2150
514-873-0711 (Fax)

Saskatchewan
Securities Commission
800-1920 Broad Street
Regina, SK S4P 3V7
Canada
Barbara Shourounis, Director
306-787-5645
306-787-5899 (Fax)

Yukon
Department of Justice
PO Box 2703
Corporate Affairs J-9
Whitehorse, YK Y1A 2C6
Canada
Richard M. Roberts, Registrar of Securities
867-667-5225
867-393-6251 (Fax)

MEXICO

Mexico
Comisión Nacional Bancaria y de Valores
Dirección General de Asuntos Int'l
Av. Insurgentes Sur 1971, Torre Sur
Piso 9
Plaza Inn, Col. Guadalupe Inn, CP 01020
Mexico
Miguel Angel Garza, Director General
   (International Affairs)
011-525-724-6578
011-525-724-6220 (Fax)

APPENDIX B
Form ADV

ADVISERS MUST FILE Form ADV to register with the Securities and Exchange Commission or with one or more state securities authorities or to amend prior Form ADV registrations. To register with the SEC, all advisers are required to file Form ADV Part 1 electronically through IARD, an Internet-based data system. Once an adviser establishes an IARD account, the adviser can access and complete Part 1 of Form ADV and submit it electronically to the SEC through IARD. Filing fees apply. Part 2 of Form ADV is completed in paper form.

The SEC generally has 45 days after receipt of the Form ADV to declare an applicant's registration effective. The SEC will mail what's called an effective order to an adviser once the adviser's registration is declared effective. An adviser can also check on IARD under the heading "Registration Status" to see if the registration has been declared effective by the SEC.

Form ADV has two parts. Part 1 requests information on an adviser's business, the persons who own or control the adviser, and whether the adviser or certain of its personnel have been sanctioned for violating securities laws or other laws. Part 1 is available in electronic format and is both filed and amended through IARD. Form ADV Part 2 is a written disclosure statement that provides information about business practices, fees, and conflicts of interest the adviser may have with its clients. Part 2 must be completed on paper rather than electronically. As of March 2006, IARD was still not accepting electronic filing of Part 2. Advisers are required: (1) to deliver a copy of Part 2 (or a brochure containing comparable information) to prospective clients; and (2) to offer a copy of Part 2 (or a brochure containing comparable information) to all current customers annually. A copy of Part 2 must be maintained in the adviser's file at all times and made available to the SEC staff upon request.

A full discussion of Form ADV Parts 1 and 2, including step-by-step instructions on how to complete the form, can be found in chapters 4, 5, and 6.

FORM ADV (Paper Version)
UNIFORM APPLICATION FOR INVESTMENT ADVISER REGISTRATION

PART 1A
WARNING: Complete this form truthfully. False statements or omissions may result in denial of your application, revocation of your registration, or criminal prosecution. You must keep this form updated by
filing periodic amendments. See Form ADV General Instruction 3.

Check the box that indicates what you would like to do (check all that apply):

☐ Submit an initial application to register as an investment adviser with the SEC.

☐ Submit an initial application to register as an investment adviser with one or more states.

☐ Submit an *annual updating amendment* to your registration for your fiscal year ended _____.

☐ Submit an other-than-annual amendment to your registration.

Item 1 Identifying Information
Responses to this Item tell us who you are, where you are doing business, and how we can contact you.

A. Your full legal name (if you are a sole proprietor, your last, first, and middle names):

_____

B. Name under which you primarily conduct your advisory business, if different from Item 1.A.

_____

List on Section 1.B. of Schedule D any additional names under which you conduct your advisory business.

C. If this filing is reporting a change in your legal name (Item 1.A.) or primary business name (Item 1.B.),
enter the new name and specify whether the name change is of ☐ your legal name or ☐ your primary
business name:

_____

D. If you are registered with the SEC as an investment adviser, your SEC file number: 801-_____

E. If you have a number ("*CRD* Number") assigned by the NASD's CRD system or by the IARD system, your
CRD number:

_____

*If your firm does not have a CRD number, skip this Item 1.E. Do not provide the CRD number of one of your offi-
cers, employees, or affiliates.*

F. *Principal Office and Place of Business*
    (1) Address (do not use a P.O. Box):

    _____
                              (number and street)

    _____   _____   _____
         (city)   (state/country)   (zip+4/postal code)

    If this address is a private residence, check this box: ☐

    List on Section 1.F. of Schedule D any office, other than your principal office and place of business, at which you conduct investment advisory business. If you are applying for registration, or are registered, with one or more state securities authorities, you must list all of your offices in the state or states to which you are applying for registration or with whom you are registered. If you are applying for registration, or are registered only, with the SEC, list the largest five offices in terms of numbers of employees.

    (2) Days of week that you normally conduct business at your *principal office and place of business:*
        ☐ Monday – Friday   ☐ Other: _____
        Normal business hours at this location: _____

    (3) Telephone number at this location: _____
                                            (area code)   (telephone number)

    (4) Facsimile number at this location: _____
                                            (area code)   (telephone number)

G. Mailing address, if different from your *principal office and place of business* address:

    _____
                              (number and street)

    _____   _____   _____
         (city)   (state/country)   (zip+4/postal code)

    If this address is a private residence, check this box: ☐

H. If you are a sole proprietor, state your full residence address, if different from your *principal office and place of business* address in Item 1.F.:

    _____
                              (number and street)

    _____   _____   _____
         (city)   (state/country)   (zip+4/postal code)

FORM ADV   Your Name: _____   *CRD* No.: _____

Part 1A   Date: _____   SEC 801-Number: _____

Page 3 of 16

I. Do you have World Wide Web site addresses?   Yes ☐   No ☐

If "yes," list these addresses on Section 1.I. of Schedule D. If a web address serves as a portal through which to access other information you have published on the World Wide Web, you may list the portal without listing addresses for all of the other information. Some advisers may need to list more than one portal address. Do not provide individual electronic mail addresses in response to this Item.

J. Contact *Employee:*

_____
(name)

_____
(title)

_____   _____
(area code)   (telephone number)   (area code)   (facsimile number)

_____
(number and street)

_____   _____   _____
(city)   (state/country)   (zip+4/postal code)

_____
(electronic mail (e-mail) address, if contact *employee* has one)

The contact employee should be an employee whom you have authorized to receive information and respond to questions about this Form ADV.

K. Do you maintain some or all of the books and records you are required to keep under Section 204 of the Advisers Act, or similar state law, somewhere other than your *principal office and place of business*?
Yes ☐   No ☐

If "yes," complete Section 1.K. of Schedule D.

L. Are you registered with a *foreign financial regulatory authority*?   Yes ☐   No ☐

Answer "no" if you are not registered with a foreign financial regulatory authority, even if you have an affiliate that is registered with a foreign financial regulatory authority. If "yes," complete Section 1.L. of Schedule D.

Item 2 SEC Registration

Responses to this Item help us (and you) determine whether you are eligible to register with the SEC. Complete this Item 2 only if you are applying for SEC registration or submitting an *annual updating amendment* to your SEC registration.

A. To register (or remain registered) with the SEC, you must check at least one of the Items 2.A(1) through 2.A(11), below. If you are submitting an *annual updating amendment* to your SEC registration and you are no longer eligible to register with the SEC, check Item 2.A(12). You:

☐ (1) have *assets under management* of $25 million (in U.S. dollars) or more;

See Part 1A Instruction 2.a. to determine whether you should check this box.

☐ (2) have your *principal office and place of business* in the U.S. Virgin Islands or Wyoming;

☐ (3) have your *principal office and place of business* outside the United States;

☐ (4) are an investment adviser (or sub-adviser) to an investment company registered under the Investment Company Act of 1940;

See Part 1A Instruction 2.b. to determine whether you should check this box.

☐ (5) have been designated as a nationally recognized statistical rating organization;

See Part 1A Instruction 2.c. to determine whether you should check this box.

☐ (6) are a pension consultant that qualifies for the exemption in rule 203A-2(b);

See Part 1A Instruction 2.d. to determine whether you should check this box.

☐ (7) are relying on rule 203A-2(c) because you are an investment adviser that *controls*, is *controlled* by, or is under common *control* with, an investment adviser that is registered with the SEC, and your *principal office and place of business* is the same as the registered adviser;

See Part 1A Instruction 2.e. to determine whether you should check this box. If you check this box, complete Section 2.A(7) of Schedule D.

☐ (8) are a newly formed adviser relying on rule 203A-2(d) because you expect to be eligible for SEC registration within 120 days;

See Part 1A Instruction 2.f. to determine whether you should check this box. If you check this box, complete Section 2.A(8) of Schedule D.

FORM ADV   Your Name: _____   *CRD* No.: _____

Part 1A   Date: _____   SEC 801-Number: _____

Page 5 of 16

☐ (9) are a multi-state adviser relying on rule 203A-2(e);

See Part 1A Instruction 2.g. to determine whether you should check this box. If you check this box, complete Section 2.A(9) of Schedule D.

☐ (10) are an Internet investment adviser relying on rule 203A-2(f);

See Part 1A Instructions 2.h. to determine whether you should check this box.

☐ (11) have received an SEC *order* exempting you from the prohibition against registration with the SEC;

If you checked this box, complete Section 2.A(11) of Schedule D.

☐ (12) are no longer eligible to remain registered with the SEC.

See Part 1A Instructions 2.i. to determine whether you should check this box.

B. Under state laws, SEC-registered advisers may be required to provide to *state securities authorities* a copy of the Form ADV and any amendments they file with the SEC. These are called *notice filings.* If this is an initial application, check the box(es) next to the state(s) that you would like to receive notice of this and all subsequent filings you submit to the SEC. If this is an amendment to direct your *notice filings* to additional state(s), check and circle the box(es) next to the state(s) that you would like to receive notice of this and all subsequent filings you submit to the SEC. If this is an amendment to your registration to stop your *notice filings* from going to state(s) that currently receive them, circle the unchecked box(es) next to those state(s).

☐ AL	☐ CT	☐ HI	☐ KY	☐ MN	☐ NH	☐ OH	☐ SC	☐ VA
☐ AK	☐ DE	☐ ID	☐ LA	☐ MS	☐ NJ	☐ OK	☐ SD	☐ WA
☐ AZ	☐ DC	☐ IL	☐ ME	☐ MO	☐ NM	☐ OR	☐ TN	☐ WV
☐ AR	☐ FL	☐ IN	☐ MD	☐ MT	☐ NY	☐ PA	☐ TX	☐ WI
☐ CA	☐ GA	☐ IA	☐ MA	☐ NE	☐ NC	☐ PR	☐ UT	
☐ CO	☐ GU	☐ KS	☐ MI	☐ NV	☐ ND	☐ RI	☐ VT	

If you are amending your registration to stop your notice filings from going to a state that currently receives them and you do not want to pay that state's notice filing fee for the coming year, your amendment must filed before the end of the year (December 31).

Item 3 Form of Organization

A. How are you organized?

☐ Corporation   ☐ Sole Proprietorship   ☐ Limited Liability Partnership (LLP)

☐ Partnership   ☐ Limited Liability Company (LLC)

☐ Other (specify):_____

If you are changing your response to this Item, see Part 1A Instruction 4.

B. In what month does your fiscal year end each year? _____

C. Under the laws of what state or country are you organized? _____

If you are a partnership, provide the name of the state or country under whose laws your partnership was formed. If you are a sole proprietor, provide the name of the state or country where you reside.

If you are changing your response to this Item, see Part 1A Instruction 4.

Item 4 Successions

A. Are you, at the time of this filing, succeeding to the business of a registered investment adviser?

☐ Yes ☐ No

If "yes," complete Item 4.B. and Section 4 of Schedule D.

B. Date of Succession: _____
    (mm/dd/yyyy)

If you have already reported this succession on a previous Form ADV filing, do not report the succession again. Instead, check "No." See Part 1A Instruction 4.

Item 5 Information About Your Advisory Business

Responses to this Item help us understand your business, assist us in preparing for on-site examinations, and provide us with data we use when making regulatory policy. Part 1A Instruction 5.a. provides additional guidance to newly-formed advisers for completing this Item 5.

Employees

A. Approximately how many *employees* do you have? Include full and part-time *employees* but do not include any clerical workers.

☐ 0   ☐ 1–5   ☐ 6–10   ☐ 11–50   ☐ 51–250   ☐ 251–500   ☐ 501–1,000
☐ More than 1,000

If more than 1,000, how many? _____ (round to the nearest 1,000)

B. (1) Approximately how many of these *employees* perform investment advisory functions (including research)?

☐ 0   ☐ 1–5   ☐ 6–10   ☐ 11–50   ☐ 51–250   ☐ 251–500   ☐ 501–1,000
☐ More than 1,000

If more than 1,000, how many? _____ (round to the nearest 1,000)

(2) Approximately how many of these *employees* are registered representatives of a broker-dealer?

☐ 0   ☐ 1–5   ☐ 6–10   ☐ 11–50   ☐ 51–250   ☐ 251–500   ☐ 501–1,000
☐ More than 1,000

If more than 1,000, how many? _____ (round to the nearest 1,000)

If you are organized as a sole proprietorship, include yourself as an employee in your responses to Items 5.A(1) and 5.B(2). If an employee performs more than one function, you should count that employee in each of your responses to Item 5.B(1) and 5.B(2).

FORM ADV   Your Name: _____   *CRD* No.: _____

Part 1A   Date: _____   SEC 801-Number: _____

Page 7 of 16

---

(3) Approximately how many firms or other *persons* solicit advisory *clients* on your behalf?

    ☐ 0   ☐ 1–5   ☐ 6–10   ☐ 11–50   ☐ 51–250   ☐ 251–500   ☐ 501–1,000

    ☐ More than 1,000

       If more than 1,000, how many? _____ (round to the nearest 1,000)

In your response to Item 5.B(3), do not count any of your employees and count a firm only once – do not count each of the firm's employees that solicit on your behalf.

Clients

C. To approximately how many *clients* did you provide investment advisory services during your most recently completed fiscal year?

    ☐ 0   ☐ 1–10   ☐ 11–25   ☐ 26–100   ☐ 101–250   ☐ 251–500

    ☐ More than 500

       If more than 500, how many? _____ (round to the nearest 500)

D. What types of *clients* do you have? Indicate the approximate percentage that each type of *client* comprises of your total number of *clients*.

	None	Up to 10%	11–25%	26–50%	51–75%	More Than 75%
(1) Individuals (other than high net worth individuals)	☐	☐	☐	☐	☐	☐
(2) High net worth individuals	☐	☐	☐	☐	☐	☐
(3) Banking or thrift institutions	☐	☐	☐	☐	☐	☐
(4) Investment companies (including mutual funds)	☐	☐	☐	☐	☐	☐
(5) Pension and profit sharing plans (other than plan participants)	☐	☐	☐	☐	☐	☐
(6) Other pooled investment vehicles (e.g., hedge funds)	☐	☐	☐	☐	☐	☐
(7) Charitable organizations	☐	☐	☐	☐	☐	☐
(8) Corporations or other businesses not listed above	☐	☐	☐	☐	☐	☐
(9) State or municipal *government entities*	☐	☐	☐	☐	☐	☐
(10) Other: _____	☐	☐	☐	☐	☐	☐

The category "individuals" includes trusts, estates, 401(k) plans and IRAs of individuals and their family members, but does not include businesses organized as sole proprietorships.

Unless you provide advisory services pursuant to an investment advisory contract to an investment company registered under the Investment Company Act of 1940, check "None" in response to Item 5.D(4).

Compensation Arrangements

E. You are compensated for your investment advisory services by (check all that apply):
- ☐ (1) A percentage of assets under your management
- ☐ (2) Hourly charges
- ☐ (3) Subscription fees (for a newsletter or periodical)
- ☐ (4) Fixed fees (other than subscription fees)
- ☐ (5) Commissions
- ☐ (6) *Performance-based fees*
- ☐ (7) Other (specify): _____

Assets Under Management

F. (1) Do you provide continuous and regular supervisory or management services to securities portfolios?   ☐ Yes   ☐ No

(2) If yes, what is the amount of your assets under management and total number of accounts?

	U.S. Dollar Amount	Total Number of Accounts
Discretionary:	(a) $_____.00	(d) _____
Non-Discretionary:	(b) $_____.00	(e) _____
Total:	(c) $_____.00	(f) _____

Part 1A Instruction 5.b. explains how to calculate your assets under management. You must follow these instructions carefully when completing this Item.

Advisory Activities

G. What type(s) of advisory services do you provide? Check all that apply.
- ☐ (1) Financial planning services
- ☐ (2) Portfolio management for individuals and/or small businesses
- ☐ (3) Portfolio management for investment companies
- ☐ (4) Portfolio management for businesses or institutional *clients* (other than investment companies)
- ☐ (5) Pension consulting services
- ☐ (6) Selection of other advisers
- ☐ (7) Publication of periodicals or newsletters
- ☐ (8) Security ratings or pricing services
- ☐ (9) Market timing services
- ☐ (10) Other (specify): _____

Do not check Item 5.G(3) unless you provide advisory services pursuant to an investment advisory contract to an investment company registered under the Investment Company Act of 1940.

FORM ADV   Your Name: _____   *CRD* No.: _____

Part 1A   Date: _____   SEC 801-Number: _____

Page 9 of 16

H. If you provide financial planning services, to how many *clients* did you provide these services during your last fiscal year?

☐ 0   ☐ 1–10   ☐ 11–25   ☐ 26–50   ☐ 51–100   ☐ 101–250   ☐ 251–500

☐ More than 500

If more than 500, how many? _____ (round to the nearest 500)

I. If you participate in a *wrap fee program*, do you (check all that apply):

☐ (1) *sponsor* the *wrap fee program*?

☐ (2) act as a portfolio manager for the *wrap fee program*?

If you are a portfolio manager for a wrap fee program, list the names of the programs and their sponsors in Section 5.I(2) of Schedule D.

If your involvement in a wrap fee program is limited to recommending wrap fee programs to your clients, or you advise a mutual fund that is offered through a wrap fee program, do not check either Item 5.I(1) or 5.I(2).

Item 6 Other Business Activities

In this Item, we request information about your other business activities.

A. You are actively engaged in business as a (check all that apply):

☐ (1) Broker-dealer

☐ (2) Registered representative of a broker-dealer

☐ (3) Futures commission merchant, commodity pool operator, or commodity trading advisor

☐ (4) Real estate broker, dealer, or agent

☐ (5) Insurance broker or agent

☐ (6) Bank (including a separately identifiable department or division of a bank)

☐ (7) Other financial product salesperson (specify): _____

B. (1) Are you actively engaged in any other business not listed in Item 6.A. (other than giving investment advice)?   ☐ Yes   ☐ No

(2) If yes, is this other business your primary business?   ☐ Yes   ☐ No

If "yes," describe this other business on Section 6.B. of Schedule D.

(3) Do you sell products or provide services other than investment advice to your advisory *clients*?

☐ Yes   ☐ No

Item 7 Financial Industry Affiliations

In this Item, we request information about your financial industry affiliations and activities. This information identifies areas in which conflicts of interest may occur between you and your *clients*.

Item 7 requires you to provide information about you and your *related persons*. Your *related persons* are all of your *advisory affiliates* and any *person* that is under common *control* with you.

A. You have a *related person* that is a (check all that apply):

☐ (1) broker-dealer, municipal securities dealer, or government securities broker or dealer

☐ (2) investment company (including mutual funds)

☐ (3) other investment adviser (including financial planners)

☐ (4) futures commission merchant, commodity pool operator, or commodity trading advisor

☐ (5) banking or thrift institution

☐ (6) accountant or accounting firm

☐ (7) lawyer or law firm

☐ (8) insurance company or agency

☐ (9) pension consultant

☐ (10) real estate broker or dealer

☐ (11) sponsor or syndicator of limited partnerships

If you checked Item 7.A(3), you must list on Section 7.A. of Schedule D all your related persons that are invest-ment advisers. If you checked Item 7.A.(1), you may elect to list on Section 7.A. of Schedule D all your related persons that are broker-dealers. If you choose to list a related broker-dealer, the IARD will accept a single Form U-4 to register an investment adviser representative who also is a broker-dealer agent ("registered rep") of that related broker-dealer.

B. Are you or any *related person* a general partner in an *investment-related* limited partnership or manager of an *investment-related* limited liability company, or do you advise any other "private fund," as defined under SEC rule 203(b)(3)-1?   ☐ Yes   ☐ No

If "yes," for each limited partnership, limited liability company, or (if applicable) private fund, complete Section 7.B. of Schedule D. If, however, you are an SEC-registered adviser <u>and</u> you have related persons that are <u>SEC-registered</u> advisers who are the general partners of limited partnerships or the managers of limited liability com-panies, you do not have to complete Section 7.B. of Schedule D with respect to those related advisers' limited partnerships or limited liability companies.

To use this alternative procedure, you must state in the Miscellaneous Section of Schedule D: (1) that you have related SEC-registered investment advisers that manage limited partnerships or limited liability companies that are not listed in Section 7.B. of your Schedule D; (2) that complete and accurate information about those lim-ited partnerships or limited liability companies is available in Section 7.B. of Schedule D of the Form ADVs of your related SEC-registered advisers; and (3) whether your clients are solicited to invest in any of those limited partnerships or limited liability companies.

Item 8 Participation or Interest in *Client* Transactions

In this Item, we request information about your participation and interest in your *clients'* transactions. Like Item 7, this information identifies areas in which conflicts of interest may occur between you and your *clients*.

Like Item 7, Item 8 requires you to provide information about you and your *related persons*.

FORM ADV   Your Name: _____   *CRD* No.: _____
Part 1A   Date: _____   SEC 801-Number: _____
Page 11 of 16

Proprietary Interest in *Client* Transactions

	Yes	No

A. Do you or any *related person*:

(1) buy securities for yourself from advisory *clients*, or sell securities you own to advisory *clients* (principal transactions)? ☐ ☐

(2) buy or sell for yourself securities (other than shares of mutual funds) that you also recommend to advisory *clients*? ☐ ☐

(3) recommend securities (or other investment products) to advisory *clients* in which you or any *related person* has some other proprietary (ownership) interest (other than those mentioned in Items 8.A(1) or (2))? ☐ ☐

Sales Interest in *Client* Transactions

	Yes	No

B. Do you or any *related person*:

(1) as a broker-dealer or registered representative of a broker-dealer, execute securities trades for brokerage customers in which advisory *client* securities are sold to or bought from the brokerage customer (agency cross transactions)? ☐ ☐

(2) recommend purchase of securities to advisory *clients* for which you or any *related person* serves as underwriter, general or managing partner, or purchaser representative? ☐ ☐

(3) recommend purchase or sale of securities to advisory *clients* for which you or any *related person* has any other sales interest (other than the receipt of sales commissions as a broker or registered representative of a broker-dealer)? ☐ ☐

Investment or Brokerage Discretion

	Yes	No

C. Do you or any *related person* have *discretionary authority* to determine the:

(1) securities to be bought or sold for a *client's* account? ☐ ☐

(2) amount of securities to be bought or sold for a *client's* account? ☐ ☐

(3) broker or dealer to be used for a purchase or sale of securities for a *client's* account? ☐ ☐

(4) commission rates to be paid to a broker or dealer for a *client's* securities transactions? ☐ ☐

	Yes	No
D. Do you or any *related person* recommend brokers or dealers to *clients*?	☐	☐
E. Do you or any *related person* receive research or other products or services other than execution from a broker-dealer or a third party in connection with *client* securities transactions?	☐	☐
F. Do you or any *related person*, directly or indirectly, compensate any *person* for *client* referrals?	☐	☐

In responding to this Item 8.F., consider in your response all cash and non-cash compensation that you or a related person gave any person in exchange for client referrals, including any bonus that is based, at least in part, on the number or amount of client referrals.

Item 9 Custody

In this Item, we ask you whether you or a *related person* has *custody* of *client* assets. If you are registering or registered with the SEC and you deduct your advisory fees directly from your *clients'* accounts but you do not otherwise have *custody* of your *clients'* funds or securities, you may answer "no" to Item 9A.(1) and 9A.(2).

	Yes	No
A. Do you have *custody* of any advisory *clients'*:		
(1) cash or bank accounts?	☐	☐
(2) securities?	☐	☐
B. Do any of your *related persons* have *custody* of any of your advisory *clients'*:		
(1) cash or bank accounts?	☐	☐
(2) securities?	☐	☐
C. If you answered "yes" to either Item 9.B(1) or 9.B(2), is that *related person* a broker-dealer registered under Section 15 of the Securities Exchange Act of 1934?	☐	☐

Item 10 Control Persons

In this Item, we ask you to identify every *person* that, directly or indirectly, *controls* you.

If you are submitting an initial application, you must complete Schedule A and Schedule B. Schedule A asks for information about your direct owners and executive officers. Schedule B asks for information about your indirect owners. If this is an amendment and you are updating information you reported on either Schedule A or Schedule B (or both) that you filed with your initial application, you must complete Schedule C.

Does any *person* not named in Item 1.A. or Schedules A, B, or C, directly or indirectly, *control* your management or policies?   ☐ Yes ☐ No

If yes, complete Section 10 of Schedule D.

Item 11 Disclosure Information

In this Item, we ask for information about your disciplinary history and the disciplinary history of all your *advisory affiliates*. We use this information to determine whether to grant your application for registration, to decide whether to revoke your registration or to place limitations on your activities as an investment adviser, and to identify potential problem areas to focus on during our on-site examinations. One event may result in "yes" answers to more than one of the questions below.

Your *advisory affiliates* are: (1) all of your current *employees* (other than *employees* performing only clerical, administrative, support or similar functions); (2) all of your officers, partners, or directors (or any *person* performing similar functions); and (3) all *persons* directly or indirectly *controlling* you or *controlled* by you. If you are a "separately identifiable department or division" (SID) of a bank, see the Glossary of Terms to determine who your *advisory affiliates* are.

If you are registered or registering with the SEC, you may limit your disclosure of any event listed in Item 11 to ten years following the date of the event. If you are registered or registering with a state, you must respond to the questions as posed; you may, therefore, limit your disclosure to ten years following the date of an event only in responding to Items 11.A(1), 11.A(2), 11.B(1), 11.B(2), 11.D(4), and 11.H(1)(a). For purposes of calculating this ten-year period, the date of an event is the date the final order, judgment, or decree was entered, or the date any rights of appeal from preliminary orders, judgments, or decrees lapsed.

You must complete the appropriate Disclosure Reporting Page ("DRP") for "yes" answers to the questions in this Item 11.

For "yes" answers to the following questions, complete a Criminal Action DRP:

	Yes	No

A. In the past ten years, have you or any *advisory affiliate*:

(1) been convicted of or pled guilty or nolo contendere ("no contest") in a domestic, foreign, or military court to any *felony*?   ☐   ☐

(2) been *charged* with any *felony*?   ☐   ☐

If you are registered or registering with the SEC, you may limit your response to Item 11.A(2) to charges that are currently pending.

B. In the past ten years, have you or any *advisory affiliate*:

(1) been convicted of or pled guilty or nolo contendere ("no contest") in a domestic, foreign, or military court to a *misdemeanor* involving: investments or an *investment-related* business, or any fraud, false statements, or omissions, wrongful taking of property, bribery, perjury, forgery, counterfeiting, extortion, or a conspiracy to commit any of these offenses?   ☐   ☐

(2) been *charged* with a *misdemeanor* listed in Item 11.B(1)?   ☐   ☐

If you are registered or registering with the SEC, you may limit your response to Item 11.B(2) to charges that are currently pending.

FORM ADV   Your Name: _____   *CRD* No.: _____
Part 1A   Date: _____   SEC 801-Number: _____
Page 14 of 16

	Yes	No
For "yes" answers to the following questions, complete a Regulatory Action DRP:		

C. Has the SEC or the Commodity Futures Trading Commission (CFTC) ever:

   (1) *found* you or any *advisory affiliate* to have made a false statement or omission? ☐ ☐

   (2) found you or any *advisory affiliate* to have been *involved* in a violation of SEC or CFTC regulations or statutes? ☐ ☐

   (3) *found* you or any *advisory affiliate* to have been a cause of an *investment-related* business having its authorization to do business denied, suspended, revoked, or restricted? ☐ ☐

   (4) entered an *order* against you or any *advisory affiliate* in connection with *investment-related* activity? ☐ ☐

   (5) imposed a civil money penalty on you or any *advisory affiliate*, or *ordered* you or any *advisory affiliate* to cease and desist from any activity? ☐ ☐

D. Has any other federal regulatory agency, any state regulatory agency, or any *foreign financial regulatory authority*:

   (1) ever *found* you or any *advisory affiliate* to have made a false statement or omission, or been dishonest, unfair, or unethical? ☐ ☐

   (2) ever *found* you or any *advisory affiliate* to have been *involved* in a violation of investment-related regulations or statutes? ☐ ☐

   (3) ever *found* you or any *advisory affiliate* to have been a cause of an *investment-related* business having its authorization to do business denied, suspended, revoked, or restricted? ☐ ☐

   (4) in the past ten years, entered an *order* against you or any *advisory affiliate* in connection with an *investment-related* activity? ☐ ☐

   (5) ever denied, suspended, or revoked your or any *advisory affiliate's* registration or license, or otherwise prevented you or any *advisory affiliate*, by *order*, from associating with an *investment-related* business or restricted your or any *advisory affiliate's* activity? ☐ ☐

E. Has any *self-regulatory organization* or commodities exchange ever:

   (1) *found* you or any *advisory affiliate* to have made a false statement or omission? ☐ ☐

   (2) *found* you or any *advisory affiliate* to have been involved in a violation of its rules (other than a violation designated as a *"minor rule violation"* under a plan approved by the SEC)? ☐ ☐

FORM ADV   Your Name: _____   *CRD* No.: _____

Part 1A   Date: _____   SEC 801-Number: _____

Page 15 of 16

		Yes	No
(3)	*found* you or any *advisory affiliate* to have been the cause of an *investment-related* business having its authorization to do business denied, suspended, revoked, or restricted?	☐	☐
(4)	disciplined you or any *advisory affiliate* by expelling or suspending you or the *advisory affiliate* from membership, barring or suspending you or the *advisory affiliate* from association with other members, or otherwise restricting your or the *advisory affiliate's* activities?	☐	☐
F.	Has an authorization to act as an attorney, accountant, or federal contractor granted to you or any *advisory affiliate* ever been revoked or suspended?	☐	☐
G.	Are you or any *advisory affiliate* now the subject of any regulatory *proceeding* that could result in a "yes" answer to any part of Item 11.C., 11.D., or 11.E.?	☐	☐

For "yes" answers to the following questions, complete a Civil Judicial Action DRP:

		Yes	No
H. (1)	Has any domestic or foreign court:		
(a)	in the past ten years, *enjoined* you or any *advisory affiliate* in connection with any *investment-related* activity?	☐	☐
(b)	ever *found* that you or any *advisory affiliate* were *involved* in a violation of *investment-related* statutes or regulations?	☐	☐
(c)	ever dismissed, pursuant to a settlement agreement, an *investment-related* civil action brought against you or any *advisory affiliate* by a state or *foreign financial regulatory authority*?	☐	☐
(2)	Are you or any *advisory affiliate* now the subject of any civil *proceeding* that could result in a "yes" answer to any part of Item 11.H(1)?	☐	☐

Item 12 Small Businesses

The SEC is required by the Regulatory Flexibility Act to consider the effect of its regulations on small entities. In order to do this, we need to determine whether you meet the definition of "small business" or "small organization" under rule 0-7.

Answer this Item 12 only if you are registered or registering with the SEC and you indicated in response to Item 5.F(2)(c) that you have assets under management of less than $25 million. You are not required to answer this Item 12 if you are filing for initial registration as a state adviser, amending a current state registration, or switching from SEC to state registration.

For purposes of this Item 12 only:

• Total Assets refers to the total assets of a firm, rather than the assets managed on behalf of *clients*. In determining your or another *person's* total assets, you may use the total assets shown on a current balance sheet (but use total assets reported on a consolidated balance sheet with subsidiaries included, if that amount is larger).

• Control means the power to direct or cause the direction of the management or policies of a *person*, whether through ownership of securities, by contract, or otherwise. Any *person* that directly or indirectly has the right to vote 25 percent or more of the voting securities, or is entitled to 25 percent or more of the profits, of another *person* is presumed to control the other *person*.

	Yes	No
A. Did you have total assets of $5 million or more on the last day of your most recent fiscal year?	☐	☐

If "yes," you do not need to answer Items 12.B. and 12.C.

B. Do you:

    (1) *control* another investment adviser that had assets under management of $25 million or more on the last day of its most recent fiscal year? ☐ ☐

    (2) *control* another *person* (other than a natural person) that had total assets of $5 million or more on the last day of its most recent fiscal year? ☐ ☐

C. Are you:

    (1) *controlled* by or under common *control* with another investment adviser that had assets under management of $25 million or more on the last day of its most recent fiscal year? ☐ ☐

    (2) *controlled* by or under common *control* with another *person* (other than a natural person) that had total assets of $5 million or more on the last day of its most recent fiscal year? ☐ ☐

FORM ADV   Your Name: _____   SEC File No.: _____

Schedule A   Date: _____   CRD No.: _____

Direct Owners and Executive Officers

1. Complete Schedule A only if you are submitting an initial application. Schedule A asks for information about your direct owners and executive officers. Use Schedule C to amend this information.

2. Direct Owners and Executive Officers. List below the names of:

   (a) each Chief Executive Officer, Chief Financial Officer, Chief Operations Officer, Chief Legal Officer, Chief Compliance Officer (Chief Compliance Officer is required and cannot be more than one individual), director and any other individuals with similar status or functions;

   (b) if you are organized as a corporation, each shareholder that is a direct owner of 5% or more of a class of your voting securities, unless you are a public reporting company (a company subject to Section 12 or 15(d) of the Exchange Act);

   Direct owners include any *person* that owns, beneficially owns, has the right to vote, or has the power to sell or direct the sale of, 5% or more of a class of your voting securities. For purposes of this Schedule, a *person* beneficially owns any securities: (i) owned by his/her child, stepchild, grandchild, parent, stepparent, grandparent, spouse, sibling, mother-in-law, father-in-law, son-in-law, daughter-in-law, brother-in-law, or sister-in-law, sharing the same residence; or (ii) that he/she has the right to acquire, within 60 days, through the exercise of any option, warrant, or right to purchase the security.

   (c) if you are organized as a partnership, <u>all</u> general partners and those limited and special partners that have the right to receive upon dissolution, or have contributed, 5% or more of your capital;

   (d) in the case of a trust that directly owns 5% or more of a class of your voting securities, or that has the right to receive upon dissolution, or has contributed, 5% or more of your capital, the trust and each trustee; and

   (e) if you are organized as a limited liability company ("LLC"), (i) those members that have the right to receive upon dissolution, or have contributed, 5% or more of your capital, and (ii) if managed by elected managers, all elected managers.

3. Do you have any indirect owners to be reported on Schedule B?   ☐ Yes   ☐ No

4. In the DE/FE/I column below, enter "DE" if the owner is a domestic entity, "FE" if the owner is an entity incorporated or domiciled in a foreign country, or "I" if the owner or executive officer is an individual.

5. Complete the Title or Status column by entering board/management titles; status as partner, trustee, sole proprietor, elected manager, shareholder, or member; and for shareholders or members, the class of securities owned (if more than one is issued).

6. Ownership codes are: NA–less than 5%   B–10% but less than 25%   D–50% but less than 75%
   A–5% but less than 10%   C–25% but less than 50%   E–75% or more

7. (a) In the *Control Person* column, enter "Yes" if the *person* has *control* as defined in the Glossary of Terms to Form ADV, and enter "No" if the *person* does not have *control*. Note that under this definition, most executive officers and all 25% owners, general partners, elected managers, and trustees are *control persons*.

   (b) In the PR column, enter "PR" if the owner is a public reporting company under Sections 12 or 15(d) of the Exchange Act.

   (c) Complete each column.

FULL LEGAL NAME (Individuals: Last Name, First Name, Middle Name)	DE/FE/I	Title or Status	Date Title or Status Acquired MM YYYY	Owner-ship Code	Control Person		CRD No. If None: S.S. No. and Date of Birth, IRS Tax No., or Employer ID No.
						PR	

FORM ADV   Your Name: _____   *SEC File No.:* _____

Schedule B   Date: _____   *CRD No.:* _____

Indirect Owners

1. Complete Schedule B only if you are submitting an initial application. Schedule B asks for information about your indirect owners; you must first complete Schedule A, which asks for information about your direct owners. Use Schedule C to amend this information.

2. Indirect Owners. With respect to each owner listed on Schedule A (except individual owners), list below:

   (a) in the case of an owner that is a corporation, each of its shareholders that beneficially owns, has the right to vote, or has the power to sell or direct the sale of, 25% or more of a class of a voting security of that corporation;

   For purposes of this Schedule, a *person* beneficially owns any securities: (i) owned by his/her child, step-child, grandchild, parent, stepparent, grandparent, spouse, sibling, mother-in-law, father-in-law, son-in-law, daughter-in-law, brother-in-law, or sister-in-law, sharing the same residence; or (ii) that he/she has the right to acquire, within 60 days, through the exercise of any option, warrant, or right to purchase the security.

   (b) in the case of an owner that is a partnership, <u>all</u> general partners and those limited and special partners that have the right to receive upon dissolution, or have contributed, 25% or more of the partnership's capital;

   (c) in the case of an owner that is a trust, the trust and each trustee; and

   (d) in the case of an owner that is a limited liability company ("LLC"), (i) those members that have the right to receive upon dissolution, or have contributed, 25% or more of the LLC's capital, and (ii) if managed by elected managers, all elected managers.

3. Continue up the chain of ownership listing all 25% owners at each level. Once a public reporting company (a company subject to Sections 12 or 15(d) of the Exchange Act) is reached, no further ownership information need be given.

4. In the DE/FE/I column below, enter "DE" if the owner is a domestic entity, "FE" if the owner is an entity incorporated or domiciled in a foreign country, or "I" if the owner is an individual.

5. Complete the Status column by entering the owner's status as partner, trustee, elected manager, shareholder, or member; and for shareholders or members, the class of securities owned (if more than one is issued).

6. Ownership codes are: C–25% but less than 50%;   D–50% but less than 75%;
                      E–75% or more;   F–Other (general partner, trustee, or elected manager)

7. (a) In the *Control Person* column, enter "Yes" if the *person* has *control* as defined in the Glossary of Terms to Form ADV, and enter "No" if the *person* does not have *control*. Note that under this definition, most executive officers and all 25% owners, general partners, elected managers, and trustees are *control persons*.

   (b) In the PR column, enter "PR" if the owner is a public reporting company under Sections 12 or 15(d) of the Exchange Act.

   (c) Complete each column.

FULL LEGAL NAME (Individuals: Last Name, First Name, Middle Name)	DE/FE/I	Entity in Which Interest Is Owned	Status	Date Status Acquired MM YYYY	Owner-ship Code	*Control Person*	PR	*CRD* No. If None: S.S. No. and Date of Birth, IRS Tax No., or Employer ID No.

FORM ADV   Your Name: _____   SEC File No.: _____

Schedule C   Date: _____   *CRD* No.: _____

Amendments to Schedules A and B

1. Use Schedule C only to amend information requested on either Schedule A or Schedule B. Refer to Schedule A and Schedule B for specific instructions for completing this Schedule C. Complete each column.

2. In the Type of Amendment column, indicate "A" (addition), "D" (deletion), or "C" (change in information about the same person).

3. Ownership codes are: NA–less than 5%   C–25% but less than 50%   G–Other (general partner, or
    A–5% but less than 10%   D–50% but less than 75%   trustee, elected member)
    B–10% but less than 25%   E–75% or more

4. List below all changes to Schedule A (Direct Owners and Executive Officers):

FULL LEGAL NAME (Individuals: Last Name, First Name, Middle Name)	DE/FE/I	Type of Amend-ment	Title or Status	Date Title or Status Acquired MM YYYY	Owner-ship Code	*Control Person* PR	CRD No. If None: S.S. No. and Date of Birth, IRS Tax No., or Employer ID No.

5. List below all changes to Schedule B (Indirect Owners):

FULL LEGAL NAME (Individuals: Last Name, First Name, Middle Name)	DE/FE/I	Type of Amend-ment	Entity in Which Interest Is Owned	Status	Date Status Acquired MM YYYY	Owner-ship Code	*Control Person* PR	CRD No. If None: S.S. No. and Date of Birth, IRS Tax No., or Employer ID No.

FORM ADV   Your Name: _____   SEC File No.: _____
Schedule D   Date: _____   CRD No.: _____
Page 1 of 5

Certain items in Part 1A of Form ADV require additional information on Schedule D. Use this Schedule D Page 1 to report details for items listed below. Report only new information or changes/updates to previously submitted information. Do not repeat previously submitted information.

This is an ☐ INITIAL or ☐ AMENDED Schedule D Page 1.

SECTION 1.B. Other Business Names

List your other business names and the jurisdictions in which you use them. You must complete a separate Schedule D for each business name.

Check only one box: ☐ Add   ☐ Delete   ☐ Amend

Name _____ Jurisdictions _____

SECTION 1.F. Other Offices

Complete the following information for each office, other than your *principal office and place of business,* at which you conduct investment advisory business. You must complete a separate Schedule D Page 1 for each location. If you are applying for registration, or are registered, only with the SEC, list only the largest five (in terms of numbers of *employees*).

Check only one box: ☐ Add   ☐ Delete

_____
(number and street)

_____
(city)   (state/country)   (zip+4/postal code)

If this address is a private residence, check this box: ☐

_____
(area code)   (telephone number)   (area code)   (facsimile number)

SECTION 1.I. World Wide Web Site Addresses

List your World Wide Web site addresses. You must complete a separate Schedule D for each World Wide Web site address.

Check only one box: ☐ Add   ☐ Delete

World Wide Web Site Address: _____

SECTION 1.K. Location of Books and Records

Complete the following information for each location at which you keep your books and records, other than your *principal office and place of business.* You must complete a separate Schedule D Page 1 for each location.

Check only one box: ☐ Add   ☐ Delete   ☐ Amend

Name of entity where books and records are kept: _____

_____
(number and street)

_____
(city)   (state/country)   (zip+4/postal code)

If this address is a private residence, check this box: ☐

_____
(area code)   (telephone number)   (area code)   (facsimile number)

This is (check one):   ☐ one of your branch offices or affiliates.
                       ☐ a third-party unaffiliated recordkeeper.
                       ☐ other.

Briefly describe the books and records kept at this location. _____

FORM ADV   Your Name: _____   SEC File No.: _____

Schedule D   Date: _____   *CRD* No.: _____

Page 2 of 5

Use this Schedule D Page 2 to report details for items listed below. Report only new information or changes/updates to previously submitted information. Do not repeat previously submitted information.

This is an ☐ INITIAL or ☐ AMENDED Schedule D Page 2.

SECTION 1.L. Registration with *Foreign Financial Regulatory Authorities*

List the name, in English, of each *foreign financial regulatory authority* and country with which you are registered. You must complete a separate Schedule D Page 2 for each *foreign financial regulatory authority* with whom you are registered.

Check only one box: ☐ Add   ☐ Delete

English Name of *Foreign Financial Regulatory Authority* _____

Name of Country _____

SECTION 2.A(7) Affiliated Adviser

If you are relying on the exemption in rule 203A-2(c) from the prohibition on registration because you *control*, are *controlled* by, or are under common *control* with an investment adviser that is registered with the SEC and your *principal office* and *place of business* is the same as that of the registered adviser, provide the following information:

Name of Registered Investment Adviser _____

CRD Number of Registered Investment Adviser (if any) _____

SEC Number of Registered Investment Adviser 801-_____

SECTION 2.A(8) Newly Formed Adviser

If you are relying on rule 203A-2(d), the newly formed adviser exemption from the prohibition on registration, you are required to make certain representations about your eligibility for SEC registration. By checking the appropriate boxes, you will be deemed to have made the required representations. You must make both of these representations:

    ☐ I am not registered or required to be registered with the SEC or a *state securities authority* and I have a reasonable expectation that I will be eligible to register with the SEC within 120 days after the date my registration with the SEC becomes effective.

    ☐ I undertake to withdraw from SEC registration if, on the 120th day after my registration with the SEC becomes effective, I would be prohibited by Section 203A(a) of the Advisers Act from registering with the SEC.

SECTION 2.A(9) Multi-State Adviser

If you are relying on rule 203A-2(e), the multi-state adviser exemption from the prohibition on registration, you are required to make certain representations about your eligibility for SEC registration. By checking the appropriate boxes, you will be deemed to have made the required representations.

If you are applying for registration as an investment adviser with the SEC, you must make both of these representations:

    ☐ I have reviewed the applicable state and federal laws and have concluded that I am required by the laws of 30 or more states to register as an investment adviser with the securities authorities in those states.

    ☐ I undertake to withdraw from SEC registration if I file an amendment to this registration indicating that I would be required by the laws of fewer than 25 states to register as an investment adviser with the securities authorities of those states.

If you are submitting your *annual updating amendment*, you must make this representation:

    ☐ Within 90 days prior to the date of filing this amendment, I have reviewed the applicable state and federal laws and have concluded that I am required by the laws of at least 25 states to register as an investment adviser with the securities authorities in those states.

FORM ADV   Your Name: _____   SEC File No.: _____

Schedule D   Date: _____   *CRD* No.: _____

Page 3 of 5

Use this Schedule D Page 3 to report details for items listed below. Report only new information or changes/ updates to previously submitted information. Do not repeat previously submitted information.

This is an ☐ INITIAL or ☐ AMENDED Schedule D Page 3.

SECTION 2.A(11) SEC Exemptive *Order*

If you are relying upon an SEC *order* exempting you from the prohibition on registration, provide the following information:

Application Number: 803-_____ Date of *order*: _____
                                                                     (mm/dd/yyyy)

SECTION 4 Successions

Complete the following information if you are succeeding to the business of a currently registered investment adviser. If you acquired more than one firm in the succession you are reporting on this Form ADV, you must complete a separate Schedule D Page 3 for each acquired firm. See Part 1A Instruction 4.

Name of Acquired Firm _____

Acquired Firm's SEC File No. (if any) 801-_____ Acquired Firm's *CRD* Number (if any) _____

SECTION 5.I(2) *Wrap Fee Programs*

If you are a portfolio manager for one or more *wrap fee programs,* list the name of each program and its *sponsor.* You must complete a separate Schedule D Page 3 for each *wrap fee program* for which you are a portfolio manager.

Check only one box: ☐ Add   ☐ Delete   ☐ Amend

Name of *Wrap Fee Program* _____

Name of *Sponsor* _____

SECTION 6.B. Description of Primary Business

Describe your primary business (not your investment advisory business): _____

_____

_____

_____

_____

_____

SECTION 7.A. Affiliated Investment Advisers and Broker-Dealers

You MUST complete the following information for each investment adviser with whom you are affiliated. You MAY complete the following information for each broker-dealer with whom you are affiliated. You must complete a separate Schedule D Page 3 for each listed affiliate.

Check only one box: ☐ Add   ☐ Delete   ☐ Amend

Legal Name of Affiliate: _____

Primary Business Name of Affiliate: _____

Affiliated is (check only one box): ☐ Investment Adviser   ☐ Broker-Dealer
                                          ☐ Dual (Investment Adviser and Broker-Dealer)

Affiliated Adviser's SEC File No. (if any) 801-_____ Affiliate's *CRD* Number (if any) _____

FORM ADV   Your Name: _____   SEC File No.: _____

Schedule D   Date: _____   *CRD* No.: _____

Page 4 of 5

Use this Schedule D Page 4 to report details for items listed below. Report only new information or changes/updates to previously submitted information. Do not repeat previously submitted information.

This is an ☐ INITIAL or ☐ AMENDED Schedule D Page 4.

SECTION 7.B. Limited Partnership or Other Private Fund Participation

You must complete a separate Schedule D Page 4 for each limited partnership in which you or a *related person* is a general partner, each limited liability company for which you or a *related person* is a manager, and each other private fund that you advise.

Check only one box: ☐ Add   ☐ Delete   ☐ Amend

Name of Limited Partnership, Limited Liability Company, or other Private Fund: _____

Name of General Partner or Manager: _____

If you are registered or registering with the SEC, is this a "private fund" as defined under SEC rule 203(b)(3)-1?
☐ Yes   ☐ No

Are your *clients* solicited to invest in the limited partnership, limited liability company, or other private fund?
☐ Yes   ☐ No

Approximately what percentage of your *clients* have invested in this limited partnership, limited liability company, or other private fund? _____%

Minimum investment commitment required of a limited partner, member, or other investor: $_____

Current value of the total assets of the limited partnership, limited liability company, or other private fund:
$_____

SECTION 10 *Control Persons*

You must complete a separate Schedule D Page 4 for each *control person* not named in Item 1.A. or Schedules A, B, or C that directly or indirectly *controls* your management or policies.

Check only one box: ☐ Add   ☐ Delete   ☐ Amend

Firm or Organization Name _____

CRD Number (if any) _____ Effective Date _____ Termination Date _____
                                              (mm/dd/yyyy)   (mm/dd/yyyy)

Business Address:

_____
                         (number and street)

_____
    (city)   (state/country)   (zip+4/postal code)

If this address is a private residence, check this box: ☐

Individual Name (if applicable) (Last, First, Middle) _____

CRD Number (if any) _____ Effective Date _____ Termination Date _____
                                              (mm/dd/yyyy)   (mm/dd/yyyy)

Business Address:

_____
                         (number and street)

_____
    (city)   (state/country)   (zip+4/postal code)

If this address is a private residence, check this box: ☐

Briefly describe the nature of the *control*: _____

_____

FORM ADV   Your Name: _____   SEC File No.: _____

Schedule D   Date: _____   *CRD* No.: _____

Page 5 of 5

Use this Schedule D Page 5 to report details for items listed below. Report only new information or changes/ updates to previously submitted information. Do not repeat previously submitted information.

This is an ☐ INITIAL or ☐ AMENDED Schedule D Page 5.

Miscellaneous

You may use the space below to explain a response to an Item or to provide any other information.

_____

_____

_____

_____

_____

_____

_____

_____

_____

_____

CRIMINAL DISCLOSURE REPORTING PAGE (ADV)

GENERAL INSTRUCTIONS

This Disclosure Reporting Page (DRP ADV) is an ☐ INITIAL **OR** ☐ AMENDED response used to report details for affirmative responses to Items 11.A. or 11.B. of Form ADV.

Check item(s) being responded to: ☐ 11.A(1)   ☐ 11.A(2)   ☐ 11.B(1)   ☐ 11.B(2)

Use a separate DRP for each event or *proceeding*. The same event or *proceeding* may be reported for more than one *person* or entity using one DRP. File with a completed Execution Page.

Multiple counts of the same charge arising out of the same event(s) should be reported on the same DRP. Unrelated criminal actions, including separate cases arising out of the same event, must be reported on separate DRPs. Use this DRP to report all charges arising out of the same event. One event may result in more than one affirmative answer to the items listed above.

PART I

A. The *person(s)* or entity(ies) for whom this DRP is being filed is (are):

☐ You (the advisory firm)

☐ You and one or more of your *advisory affiliates*

☐ One or more of your *advisory affiliates*

If this DRP is being filed for an *advisory affiliate*, give the full name of the *advisory affiliate* below (for individuals, Last name, First name, Middle name).

If the *advisory affiliate* has a *CRD* number, provide that number. If not, indicate "non-registered" by checking the appropriate box.

Your Name _____ Your *CRD* Number _____

ADV DRP – *ADVISORY AFFILIATE*

CRD Number _____ This *advisory affiliate* is ☐ a firm   ☐ an individual

Registered: ☐ Yes   ☐ No

Name (For individuals, Last, First, Middle)_____

☐ This DRP should be removed from the ADV record because the *advisory affiliate(s)* is no longer associated with the adviser.

☐ This DRP should be removed from the ADV record because: (1) the event or *proceeding* occurred more than ten years ago or (2) the adviser is registered or applying for registration with the SEC and the event was resolved in the adviser's or *advisory affiliate's* favor.

B. If the *advisory affiliate* is registered through the IARD system or *CRD* system, has the *advisory affiliate* submitted a DRP (with Form ADV, BD or U-4) to the IARD or *CRD* for the event? If the answer is "Yes," no other information on this DRP must be provided.

☐ Yes   ☐ No

NOTE: The completion of this form does not relieve the *advisory affiliate* of its obligation to update its IARD or *CRD* records.

(continued)

CRIMINAL DISCLOSURE REPORTING PAGE (ADV)
(continuation)

PART II

1. If charge(s) were brought against an organization over which you or an *advisory affiliate* exercise(d) *control*: Enter organization name, whether or not the organization was an *investment-related* business and your or the *advisory affiliate's* position, title, or relationship.

_____

_____

2. Formal Charge(s) were brought in: (include name of Federal, Military, State or Foreign Court, Location of Court – City or County <u>and</u> State or Country, Docket/Case number).

_____

_____

3. Event Disclosure Detail (Use this for both organizational and individual charges.)

   A. Date First *Charged* (MM/DD/YYYY): _____ ☐ Exact ☐ Explanation

If not exact, provide explanation: _____

   B. Event Disclosure Detail (include Charge(s)/Charge Description(s), and for each charge provide: (1) number of counts, (2) *felony* or *misdemeanor,* (3) plea for each charge, and (4) product type if charge is *investment-related*).

_____

_____

_____

_____

   C. Did any of the Charge(s) within the Event involve a *felony*? ☐ Yes ☐ No

   D. Current status of the Event? ☐ Pending ☐ On Appeal ☐ Final

   E. Event Status Date (complete unless status is Pending) (MM/DD/YYYY): _____

      ☐ Exact ☐ Explanation

If not exact, provide explanation: _____

4. Disposition Disclosure Detail: Include for each charge (a) Disposition Type (e.g., convicted, acquitted, dismissed, pretrial, etc.), (b) Date, (c) Sentence/Penalty, (d) Duration (if sentence-suspension, probation, etc.), (e) Start Date of Penalty, (f) Penalty/Fine Amount, and (g) Date Paid.

_____

_____

_____

_____

_____

_____

(continued)

CRIMINAL DISCLOSURE REPORTING PAGE (ADV)
(continuation)

5. Provide a brief summary of circumstances leading to the charge(s) as well as the disposition. Include the relevant dates when the conduct which was the subject of the charge(s) occurred. (Your response must fit within the space provided.)

_____
_____
_____
_____
_____
_____
_____
_____
_____
_____
_____
_____
_____

REGULATORY ACTION DISCLOSURE REPORTING PAGE (ADV)

GENERAL INSTRUCTIONS

This Disclosure Reporting Page (DRP ADV) is an ☐ INITIAL **OR** ☐ AMENDED response used to report details for affirmative responses to Items 11.C., 11.D., 11.E., 11.F. or 11.G. of Form ADV.

Check item(s) being responded to: ☐ 11.C(1) ☐ 11.C(2) ☐ 11.C(3) ☐ 11.C(4) ☐ 11.C(5)
  ☐ 11.D(1) ☐ 11.D(2) ☐ 11.D(3) ☐ 11.D(4) ☐ 11.D(5)
  ☐ 11.E(1) ☐ 11.E(2) ☐ 11.E(3) ☐ 11.E(4)
  ☐ 11.F. ☐ 11.G.

Use a separate DRP for each event or *proceeding*. The same event or *proceeding* may be reported for more than one *person* or entity using one DRP. File with a completed Execution Page.

One event may result in more than one affirmative answer to Items 11.C., 11.D., 11.E., 11.F. or 11.G. Use only one DRP to report details related to the same event. If an event gives rise to actions by more than one regulator, provide details for each action on a separate DRP.

PART I

A. The *person(s)* or entity(ies) for whom this DRP is being filed is (are):

☐ You (the advisory firm)

☐ You and one or more of your *advisory affiliates*

☐ One or more of your *advisory affiliates*

If this DRP is being filed for an *advisory affiliate*, give the full name of the *advisory affiliate* below (for individuals, Last name, First name, Middle name).

If the *advisory affiliate* has a *CRD* number, provide that number. If not, indicate "non-registered" by checking the appropriate box.

Your Name _____ Your *CRD* Number _____

ADV DRP – *ADVISORY AFFILIATE*

CRD Number _____ This *advisory affiliate* is ☐ a firm ☐ an individual
  Registered: ☐ Yes ☐ No

Name (For individuals, Last, First, Middle)_____

☐ This DRP should be removed from the ADV record because the *advisory affiliate(s)* is no longer associated with the adviser.

☐ This DRP should be removed from the ADV record because: (1) the event or *proceeding* occurred more than ten years ago or (2) the adviser is registered or applying for registration with the SEC and the event was resolved in the adviser's or *advisory affiliate's* favor.

If you are registered or registering with a *state securities authority*, you may remove a DRP for an event you reported only in response to Item 11.D(4), and only if that event occurred more than ten years ago. If you are registered or registering with the SEC, you may remove a DRP for any event listed in Item 11 that occurred more than ten years ago.

B. If the *advisory affiliate* is registered through the IARD system or *CRD* system, has the *advisory affiliate* submitted a DRP (with Form ADV, BD or U-4) to the IARD or *CRD* for the event? If the answer is "Yes," no other information on this DRP must be provided.

☐ Yes ☐ No

NOTE: The completion of this form does not relieve the *advisory affiliate* of its obligation to update its IARD or *CRD* records.

(continued)

REGULATORY ACTION DISCLOSURE REPORTING PAGE (ADV)
(continuation)

PART II

1. Regulatory Action initiated by:
   ☐ SEC   ☐ Other Federal   ☐ State   ☐ *SRO*   ☐ Foreign
   (Full name of regulator, *foreign financial regulatory authority*, federal, state or *SRO*)

   _____

2. Principal Sanction (check appropriate item):
   ☐ Civil and Administrative Penalty(ies)/Fine(s)   ☐ Disgorgement   ☐ Restitution
   ☐ Bar   ☐ Expulsion   ☐ Revocation
   ☐ Cease and Desist   ☐ Injunction   ☐ Suspension
   ☐ Censure   ☐ Prohibition   ☐ Undertaking
   ☐ Denial   ☐ Reprimand   ☐ Other _____
   Other Sanctions:

   _____
   _____
   _____

3. Date Initiated (MM/DD/YYYY): _____ ☐ Exact   ☐ Explanation
   If not exact, provide explanation: _____

4. Docket/Case Number: _____

5. *Advisory Affiliate* Employing Firm when activity occurred which led to the regulatory action (if applicable):

   _____

6. Principal Product Type (check appropriate item):
   ☐ Annuity(ies) – Fixed   ☐ Derivative(s)   ☐ Investment Contract(s)
   ☐ Annuity(ies) – Variable   ☐ Direct Investment(s) – DPP & LP Interest(s) ☐ Money Market Fund(s)
   ☐ CD(s)   ☐ Equity – OTC   ☐ Mutual Fund(s)
   ☐ Commodity Option(s)   ☐ Equity Listed (Common & Preferred Stock)   ☐ No Product
   ☐ Debt – Asset Backed   ☐ Futures – Commodity   ☐ Options
   ☐ Debt – Corporate   ☐ Futures – Financial   ☐ Penny Stock(s)
   ☐ Debt – Government   ☐ Index Option(s)   ☐ Unit Investment Trust(s)
   ☐ Debt – Municipal   ☐ Insurance   ☐ Other _____
   Other Product Types:

   _____
   _____

(continued)

REGULATORY ACTION DISCLOSURE REPORTING PAGE (ADV)
(continuation)

7. Describe the allegations related to this regulatory action (your response must fit within the space provided):

_____

_____

_____

_____

_____

8. Current status?   ☐ Pending   ☐ On Appeal   ☐ Final

9. If on appeal, regulatory action appealed to (SEC, *SRO*, Federal or State Court) and Date Appeal Filed:

_____

_____

If Final or On Appeal, complete all items below. For Pending Actions, complete Item 13 only.

10. How was matter resolved (check appropriate item):

   ☐ Acceptance, Waiver & Consent (AWC)   ☐ Dismissed   ☐ Vacated

   ☐ Consent   ☐ *Order*   ☐ Withdrawn

   ☐ Decision   ☐ Settled   ☐ Other _____

   ☐ Decision & *Order* of Offer of Settlement   ☐ Stipulation and Consent

11. Resolution Date (MM/DD/YYYY):_____   ☐ Exact   ☐ Explanation

   If not exact, provide explanation:_____

12. Resolution Detail:

   A. Were any of the following Sanctions *Ordered* (check all appropriate items)?

      ☐ Monetary/Fine   ☐ Revocation/Expulsion/Denial   ☐ Disgorgement/Restitution

      Amount: $_____   ☐ Censure   ☐ Cease and Desist/Injunction   ☐ Bar   ☐ Suspension

   B. Other Sanctions *Ordered:*

_____

_____

_____

Sanction detail: if suspended, *enjoined* or barred, provide duration including start date and capacities affected (General Securities Principal, Financial Operations Principal, etc.). If requalification by exam/retraining was a condition of the sanction, provide length of time given to requalify/retrain, type of exam required and whether condition has been satisfied. If disposition resulted in a fine, penalty, restitution, disgorgement or monetary compensation, provide total amount, portion levied against you or an *advisory affiliate,* date paid and if any portion of penalty was waived:

_____

_____

_____

_____

_____

_____

(continued)

REGULATORY ACTION DISCLOSURE REPORTING PAGE (ADV)
(continuation)

13. Provide a brief summary of details related to the action status and (or) disposition and include relevant terms, conditions and dates (your response must fit within the space provided).

_____

_____

_____

_____

_____

_____

_____

_____

_____

_____

_____

_____

CIVIL JUDICIAL ACTION DISCLOSURE REPORTING PAGE (ADV)

GENERAL INSTRUCTIONS

This Disclosure Reporting Page (DRP ADV) is an ☐ INITIAL *OR* ☐ AMENDED response used to report details for affirmative responses to Item 11.H. of Part 1A and Item 2.F. of Part 1B of Form ADV.

Check Part 1A item(s) being responded to: ☐ 11.H(1)(a)   ☐ 11.H(1)(b)   ☐ 11.H(1)(c)   ☐ 11.H(2)

Check Part 1B item(s) being responded to: ☐ 2.F(1)   ☐ 2.F(2)   ☐ 2.F(3)   ☐ 2.F(4)   ☐ 2.F(5)

Use a separate DRP for each event or *proceeding*. The same event or *proceeding* may be reported for more than one *person* or entity using one DRP. File with a completed Execution Page.

One event may result in more than one affirmative answer to Item 11.H. of Part 1A or Item 2.F. of Part 1B. Use only one DRPto report details related to the same event. Unrelated civil judicial actions must be reported on separate DRPs.

PART I

A. The *person(s)* or entity(ies) for whom this DRP is being filed is (are):

☐ You (the advisory firm)

☐ You and one or more of your *advisory affiliates*

☐ One or more of your *advisory affiliates*

If this DRP is being filed for an *advisory affiliate,* give the full name of the *advisory affiliate* below (for individuals, Last name, First name, Middle name).

If the *advisory affiliate* has a *CRD* number, provide that number. If not, indicate "non-registered" by checking the appropriate box.

Your Name _____ Your *CRD* Number _____

ADV DRP – *ADVISORY AFFILIATE*

CRD Number _____ This *advisory affiliate* is ☐ a firm   ☐ an individual

Registered: ☐ Yes   ☐ No

Name (For individuals, Last, First, Middle)_____

☐ This DRP should be removed from the ADV record because the *advisory affiliate(s)* is no longer associated with the adviser.

☐ This DRP should be removed from the ADV record because: (1) the event or *proceeding* occurred more than ten years ago or (2) the adviser is registered or applying for registration with the SEC and the event was resolved in the adviser's or advisory affiliate's favor.

If you are registered or registering with a *state securities authority,* you may remove a DRP for an event you reported only in response to Item 11.H(1)(a), and only if that event occurred more than ten years ago. If you are registered or registering with the SEC, you may remove a DRP for any event listed in Item 11 that occurred more than ten years ago.

B. If the *advisory affiliate* is registered through the IARD system or *CRD* system, has the *advisory affiliate* submitted a DRP (with Form ADV, BD or U-4) to the IARD or *CRD* for the event? If the answer is "Yes," no other information on this DRP must be provided.

☐ Yes   ☐ No

NOTE: The completion of this form does not relieve the *advisory affiliate* of its obligation to update its IARD or *CRD* records.

(continued)

CIVIL JUDICIAL ACTION DISCLOSURE REPORTING PAGE (ADV)
(continuation)

PART II

1. Court Action initiated by: (Name of regulator, *foreign financial regulatory authority,* SRO, commodities exchange, agency, firm, private plaintiff, etc.)

_____

2. Principal Relief Sought (check appropriate item):

☐ Cease and Desist   ☐ Disgorgement   ☐ Money Damages (Private/Civil Complaint)

☐ Restraining Order   ☐ Civil Penalty(ies)/Fine(s)   ☐ Injunction

☐ Restitution   ☐ Other _____

Other Relief Sought:

_____

_____

3. Filing Date of Court Action (MM/DD/YYYY): _____ ☐ Exact   ☐ Explanation

   If not exact, provide explanation: _____

4. Principal Product Type (check appropriate item):

☐ Annuity(ies) – Fixed   ☐ Derivative(s)   ☐ Investment Contract(s)

☐ Annuity(ies) – Variable   ☐ Direct Investment(s) – DPP & LP Interest(s)   ☐ Money Market Fund(s)

☐ CD(s)   ☐ Equity - OTC   ☐ Mutual Fund(s)

☐ Commodity Option(s)   ☐ Equity Listed (Common & Preferred Stock)   ☐ No Product

☐ Debt – Asset Backed   ☐ Futures – Commodity   ☐ Options

☐ Debt – Corporate   ☐ Futures – Financial   ☐ Penny Stock(s)

☐ Debt – Government   ☐ Index Option(s)   ☐ Unit Investment Trust(s)

☐ Debt – Municipal   ☐ Insurance   ☐ Other _____

Other Product Types:

_____

5. Formal Action was brought in (include name of Federal, State or Foreign Court, Location of Court - City or County <u>and</u> State or Country, Docket/Case Number):

_____

6. *Advisory Affiliate* Employing Firm when activity occurred which led to the civil judicial action (if applicable):

_____

(continued)

CIVIL JUDICIAL ACTION DISCLOSURE REPORTING PAGE (ADV)
(continuation)

7. Describe the allegations related to this civil action (your response must fit within the space provided):

_____

_____

_____

_____

_____

8. Current status? ☐ Pending ☐ On Appeal ☐ Final

9. If on appeal, action appealed to (provide name of court) and Date Appeal Filed (MM/DD/YYYY):

_____

_____

10. *If pending, date notice/process was served (MM/DD/YYYY):*_____
   ☐ *Exact* ☐ *Explanation*
   If not exact, provide explanation: _____

If Final or On Appeal, complete all items below. For Pending Actions, complete Item 14 only.

11. How was matter resolved (check appropriate item):
   ☐ Consent   ☐ Judgment Rendered   ☐ Settled
   ☐ Dismissed   ☐ Opinion   ☐ Withdrawn   ☐ Other _____

12. Resolution Date (MM/DD/YYYY):_____ ☐ Exact ☐ Explanation
   If not exact, provide explanation: _____

13. Resolution Detail:
   A. Were any of the following Sanctions Ordered or Relief Granted (check appropriate items)?
   ☐ Monetary/Fine   ☐ Revocation/Expulsion/Denial   ☐ Disgorgement/Restitution
   Amount: $_____ ☐ Censure ☐ Cease and Desist/Injunction ☐ Bar   ☐ Suspension
   B. Other Sanctions:

_____

_____

_____

_____

(continued)

CIVIL JUDICIAL ACTION DISCLOSURE REPORTING PAGE (ADV)
(continuation)

C. Sanction detail: if suspended, *enjoined* or barred, provide duration including start date and capacities affected (General Securities Principal, Financial Operations Principal, etc.). If requalification by exam/ retraining was a condition of the sanction, provide length of time given to requalify/retrain, type of exam required and whether condition has been satisfied. If disposition resulted in a fine, penalty, restitution, disgorgement or monetary compensation, provide total amount, portion levied against you or an *advisory affiliate,* date paid and if any portion of penalty was waived:

_____

_____

_____

_____

14. Provide a brief summary of circumstances related to the action(s), allegation(s), disposition(s) and/or finding(s) disclosed above (your response must fit within the space provided).

_____

_____

_____

_____

_____

_____

_____

_____

_____

_____

_____

_____

Disclosure Document
SEC Form ADV, Part 2

All registered investment advisers are required to file Form ADV Part 1 with the Securities and Exchange Commission. Part 2 of Form ADV contains that information which the SEC requires each registered investment adviser to disclose to investors.

The purpose of this document is to inform clients of all material aspects of the organization, its fees and services, and key personnel. It is provided to new clients and also offered to all existing clients annually.

FORM ADV

Uniform Application for Investment Adviser Registration

Part 2 - Page 1

Name of Investment Adviser:

Address: (Number and Street)	(City)	(State)	(Zip Code)	Area Code: Telephone Number:

This part of Form ADV gives information about the investment adviser and its business for the use of clients. The information has not been approved or verified by any governmental authority.

Table of Contents

Item Number	Item	Page
1	Advisory Services and Fees	2
2	Types of Clients	2
3	Types of Investments	3
4	Methods of Analysis, Sources of Information and Investment Strategies	3
5	Education and Business Standards	4
6	Education and Business Background	4
7	Other Business Activities	4
8	Other Financial Industry Activities or Affiliations	4
9	Participation or Interest in Client Transactions	5
10	Conditions for Managing Accounts	5
11	Review of Accounts	5
12	Investment or Brokerage Discretion	6
13	Additional Compensation	6
14	Balance Sheet	6
	Continuation Sheet	Schedule F
	Balance Sheet, if required	Schedule G

(Schedules A, B, C, D, and E are included with Part 1 of this Form, for the use of regulatory bodies, and are not distributed to clients.)

FORM ADV	Applicant:	SEC File Number:	Date:
Part 2 - Page 2		801-	

1. A. Advisory Services and Fees. (check the applicable boxes)   For each type of service provided, state the
approximate % of total advisory billings
from that service. (See instruction below.)

Applicant:

- ☐ (1) Provides investment supervisory services _____ %
- ☐ (2) Manages investment advisory accounts not involving investment supervisory services _____ %
- ☐ (3) Furnishes investment advice through consultations not included in either service
  described above _____ %
- ☐ (4) Issues periodicals about securities by subscription _____ %
- ☐ (5) Issues special reports about securities not included in any service described above _____ %
- ☐ (6) Issues, not as part of any service described above, any charts, graphs, formulas, or
  other devices which clients may use to evaluate securities _____ %
- ☐ (7) On more than an occasional basis, furnishes advice to clients on matters not
  involving securities _____ %
- ☐ (8) Provides a timing service _____ %
- ☐ (9) Furnishes advice about securities in any manner not described above _____ %

(Percentages should be based on applicant's last fiscal year. If applicant has not completed its first fiscal year,
provide estimates of advisory billings for that year and state that the percentages are estimates.)

B. Does applicant call any of the services it checked above financial planning or some similar term?

☐ Yes   ☐ No

C. Applicant offers investment advisory services for: (check all that apply)

- ☐ (1) A percentage of assets under management   ☐ (4) Subscription fees
- ☐ (2) Hourly charges   ☐ (5) Commissions
- ☐ (3) Fixed fees (not including subscription fees) ☐ (6) Other

D. For each checked box in A above, describe on Schedule F:

- the services provided, including the name of any publication or report issued by the adviser on a
  subscription basis or for a fee
- applicant's basic fee schedule, how fees are charged, and whether its fees are negotiable
- when compensation is payable, and if compensation is payable before service is provided, how a
  client may get a refund or may terminate an investment advisory contract before its expiration date

2. Types of clients. Applicant generally provides investment advice to: (check those that apply)

- ☐ **A.** Individuals   ☐ **E.** Trusts, estates, or charitable organizations
- ☐ **B.** Banks or thrift institutions   ☐ **F.** Corporations or business entities other
- ☐ **C.** Investment companies   than those listed above
- ☐ **D.** Pension and profit sharing plans ☐ **G.** Other (describe on Schedule F)

Answer all items. Complete amended pages in full, circle amended items, and file with execution page (page 1).

FORM ADV **Part 2 - Page 3**	Applicant:	SEC File Number: 801-	Date:

3. Types of Investments. Applicant offers advice on the following: (check those that apply)

    A. Equity securities:
    ☐ (1) exchange-listed securities
    ☐ (2) securities traded over-the-counter
    ☐ (3) foreign issues

    ☐ **B.** Warrants

    ☐ **C.** Corporate debt securities
    (other than commercial paper)

    ☐ **D.** Commercial paper

    ☐ **E.** Certificates of deposit

    ☐ **F.** Municipal securities

    G. Investment company securities:
    ☐ (1) variable life insurance
    ☐ (2) variable annuities
    ☐ (3) mutual fund shares

☐ **H.** United States government securities

    I. Options contracts on:
    ☐ (1) securities
    ☐ (2) commodities

    J. Futures contracts on:
    ☐ (1) tangibles
    ☐ (2) intangibles

    K. Interests in partnerships investing in:
    ☐ (1) real estate
    ☐ (2) oil and gas interests
    ☐ (3) other (explain on Schedule F)

☐ **L.** Other (explain on Schedule F)

4. Methods of Analysis, Sources of Information, and Investment Strategies.

A. Applicant's security analysis methods include: (check those that apply)
☐ (1) Charting
☐ (2) Fundamental
☐ (3) Technical
☐ (4) Cyclical
☐ (5) Other (explain on Schedule F)

B. The main sources of information applicant uses include: (check those that apply)
☐ (1) Financial newspapers and magazines
☐ (2) Inspections of corporate activities
☐ (3) Research materials prepared by others
☐ (4) Corporate rating services
☐ (5) Timing services
☐ (6) Annual reports, prospectuses, filings with the Securities and Exchange Commission
☐ (7) Company press releases
☐ (8) Other (explain on Schedule F)

C. The investment strategies used to implement any investment advice given to clients include: (check those that apply)
☐ (1) Long-term purchases (securities held at least a year)
☐ (2) Short-term purchases
☐ (3) Trading (securities sold within 30 days)
☐ (4) Short sales
☐ (5) Margin transactions
☐ (6) Option writing, including covered options, uncovered (securities sold within a year) options, or spreading strategies
☐ (7) Other (explain on Schedule F)

Answer all items. Complete amended pages in full, circle amended items, and file with execution page (page 1).

FORM ADV **Part 2 - Page 4**	Applicant:	SEC File Number: 801-	Date:

5. Education and Business Standards.

Are there any general standards of education or business experience that applicant requires of those involved in determining or giving investment advice to clients? ☐ Yes ☐ No

(If yes, describe these standards on Schedule F.)

6. Education and Business Background.

For:

- each member of the investment committee or group that determines general investment advice to be given to clients, or
- if the applicant has no investment committee or group, each individual who determines general investment advice given to clients (if more than five, respond only for their supervisors)
- each principal executive officer of applicant or each person with similar status or performing similar functions.

On Schedule F, give the:

- name
- year of birth

- formal education after high school
- business background for the preceding five years

7. Other Business Activities. (check those that apply)

☐ **A.** Applicant is actively engaged in a business other than giving investment advice.

☐ **B.** Applicant sells products or services other than investment advice to clients.

☐ **C.** The principal business of applicant or its principal executive officers involves something other than providing investment advice.

(For each checked box describe the other activities, including the time spent on them, on Schedule F.)

8. Other Financial Industry Activities or Affiliations. (check those that apply)

☐ **A.** Applicant is registered (or has an application pending) as a securities broker-dealer.

☐ **B.** Applicant is registered (or has an application pending) as a futures commission merchant, commodity pool operator, or commodity trading adviser.

C. Applicant has arrangements that are material to its advisory business or its clients with a related person who is a:

☐ (1) broker-dealer

☐ (2) investment company

☐ (3) other investment adviser

☐ (4) financial planning firm

☐ (5) commodity pool operator, commodity trading adviser, or futures commission merchant

☐ (6) banking or thrift institution

☐ (7) accounting firm

☐ (8) law firm

☐ (9) insurance company or agency

☐ (10) pension consultant

☐ (11) real estate broker or dealer

☐ (12) entity that creates or packages limited partnerships

(For each checked box in C, on Schedule F identify the related person and describe the relationship and the arrangements.)

D. Is applicant or a related person a general partner in any partnership in which clients are solicited to invest? ☐ Yes ☐ No

(If yes, describe on Schedule F the partnerships and what they invest in.)

FORM ADV	Applicant:	SEC File Number:	Date:
Part 2 - Page 5		801-	

9. Participation or Interest in Client Transactions.

Applicant or a related person: (check those that apply)

☐ **A.** As principal, buys securities for itself from or sells securities it owns to any client.

☐ **B.** As broker or agent effects securities transactions for compensation for any client.

☐ **C.** As broker or agent for any person other than a client effects transactions in which client securities are sold to or bought from a brokerage customer.

☐ **D.** Recommends to clients that they buy or sell securities or investment products in which the applicant or a related person has some financial interest.

☐ **E.** Buys or sells for itself securities that it also recommends to clients.

(For each box checked, describe on Schedule F when the applicant or a related person engages in these transactions and what restrictions, internal procedures, or disclosures are used for conflicts of interest in those transactions.)

10. Conditions for Managing Accounts.

Does the applicant provide investment supervisory services, manage investment advisory accounts, or hold itself out as providing financial planning or some similarly termed services *and* impose a minimum dollar value of assets or other conditions for starting or maintaining an account?   ☐ Yes   ☐ No

(If yes, describe on Schedule F.)

11. Review of Accounts.

If applicant provides investment supervisory services, manages investment advisory accounts, or holds itself out as providing financial planning or some similarly termed services:

A. Describe below the reviews and reviewers of the accounts. **For reviews**, include their frequency, different levels, and triggering factors. **For reviewers**, include the number of reviewers, their titles and functions, instructions they receive from applicant on performing reviews, and number of accounts assigned each.

B. Describe below the nature and frequency of regular reports to clients on their accounts.

Answer all items. Complete amended pages in full, circle amended items, and file with execution page (page 1).

| **FORM ADV**
Part 2 - Page 6 | Applicant: | SEC File Number:
801- | Date: |

12. Investment or Brokerage Discretion.

A. Does applicant or any related person have authority to determine, without obtaining specific client consent, the:

(1) securities to be bought or sold?	☐ Yes	☐ No
(2) amount of the securities to be bought or sold ?	☐ Yes	☐ No
(3) broker or dealer to be used ?	☐ Yes	☐ No
(4) commission rates paid?	☐ Yes	☐ No

B. Does applicant or a related person suggest brokers to clients?   ☐ Yes   ☐ No

For each yes answer to A, describe on Schedule F any limitations on the authority. For each yes to A(3), A(4), or B, describe on Schedule F the factors considered in selecting brokers and determining the reasonableness of their commissions. If the value of products, research, and services given to the applicant or a related person is a factor, describe:

- the products, research, and services
- whether clients may pay commissions higher than those obtainable from other brokers in return for those products and services
- whether research is used to service all of applicant's accounts or just those accounts paying for it; and
- any procedures the applicant used during the last fiscal year to direct client transactions to a particular broker in return for products and research services received.

13. Additional Compensation.

Does the applicant or a related person have any arrangements, oral or in writing, where it:

A. is paid cash by or receives some economic benefit (including commissions, equipment, or non-research services) from a non-client in connection with giving advice to clients?   ☐ Yes   ☐ No

B. directly or indirectly compensates any person for client referrals?   ☐ Yes   ☐ No

(For each yes, describe the arrangements on Schedule F.)

14. Balance Sheet.

Applicant must provide a balance sheet for the most recent fiscal year on Schedule G if applicant:

- has custody of client funds or securities unless applicant is registered or registering only with the Securities and Exchange Commission; or
- requires prepayment of more than $500 in fees per client and 6 or more months in advance

Has applicant provided a Schedule G balance sheet?   ☐ Yes   ☐ No

---

Answer all items. Complete amended pages in full, circle amended items, and file with execution page (page 1).

Schedule F of **FORM ADV** **Continuation Sheet for** **Form ADV Part 2**	Applicant:	SEC File Number: 801-	Date:
Item of Form (identify)	Answer		

Schedule G of FORM ADV Balance Sheet	Applicant:	SEC File Number: 801-	Date:

(Answers in Response to Form ADV Part 2 Item 14.)

1. Full name of applicant exactly as stated in Item 1A of Part 1 of Form ADV: | IRS Empl. Ident. No.:

Instructions

1. The balance sheet must be:

    A. Prepared in accordance with generally accepted accounting principles

    B. Audited by an independent public accountant

    C. Accompanied by a note stating the principles used to prepare it, the basis of included securities, and any other explanations required for clarity.

2. Securities included at cost should show their market or fair value parenthetically.

3. Qualifications and any accompanying independent accountant's report must conform to Article 2 of Regulation S-X (17 CFR 210.2-01 et. seq.).

4. Sole proprietor investment advisers:

    A. Must show investment advisory business assets and liabilities separate from other business and personal assets and liabilities

    B. May aggregate other business and personal assets and liabilities unless there is an asset deficiency in the total financial position

Complete amended pages in full, circle amended items, and file with execution page (page 1).

APPENDIX C

Adviser Designation Requirements

Designation	Acronym	Organization Issuing Designation	Previous Experience/Educational Requirements
3 Dimensional Wealth Practitioner	C3DWP	3 Dimensional Wealth International	• AAMS AEP; CEP; CFA; CFP; ChFC; CIMA; CLU; CPA/PFS; EA; JD/LLB; LLM; MSFS; MSFM; RFC • Completion of 7 courses
Accredited Asset Management Specialist	AAMS	College for Financial Planning	An 11-module self-study course comprising 96–120 hours
Accredited Estate Planner	AEP	National Association of Estate Planners & Councils	• At least 5 years' experience in estate planning as an attorney, CPA, CLU/ChFC, CFP, or trust officer. • 2 graduate level courses at The American College
Accredited Financial Counselor	AFC	Association for Financial Counseling and Planning Education	• 2 years of financial counseling experience • 2 self-study courses of approximately 100–150 hours each
Accredited Investment Fiduciary	AIF	Center for Fiduciary Studies	• Investment fiduciary or adviser to investment fiduciaries • Completion of either: (1) 2.5-day classroom program; (2) 7-course web-based program; or (3) custom program
Accredited Investment Fiduciary Auditor	AIFA	Center for Fiduciary Studies	• Investment fiduciary or an adviser to investment fiduciaries • Must meet educational, credentialing, and professional experience prerequisites • Completion of either a classroom program or a supplemental program

Examinations	Website Information	Disciplinary/ Complaint Processes	Continuing Education or Other Ongoing Requirements
7 final examinations	www.3dwealth.org		One 200-series elective or 2 300-series electives biannually
Final certification exam	www.cffp.edu		
Final examinations in each course	www.naepc.org		30 hours every 24 months. Recertification every 5 years.
Final examination in each course	www.afcpe.org		30 hours biannually
Final certification exam	www.fi360.com	Investor complaint process and public disciplinary process	4 hours annually through 12/07 and 6 hours annually thereafter
Final certification exam	www.fi360.com	Investor complaint process and public disciplinary process	

Designation	Acronym	Organization Issuing Designation	Previous Experience/Educational Requirements
Board Certified in Asset Allocation	BCAA	Institute of Business & Finance	• 2 years' experience in financial services industry • 60-hour self-study course • 2 open-book case studies
Board Certified In Estate Planning	BCE	Institute of Business & Finance	• 60-hour self-study program
Board Certified in Securities	BCS	Institute of Business & Finance	• 60-hour self-study course
Certified Annuity Consultant	CAC	Annuity National Brokerage Co.	• Life insurance license • Seminar attendance
Certified Annuity Provider	CAA	Adviser Certification Services Inc.	• JD, CPA, CFP, or ChFC, or, professional involvement in financial services industry as a licensed insurance rep or registered investment adviser • CAA self-study or classroom course
Certified Annuity Specialist	CAS	Institute of Business & Finance	• CAS course of 6 modules totaling 60 hours
Certified Asset Protection Planner	CAPP	The Wealth Preservation Group	12-hour online or in-person course
Certified College Planning Specialist	CCPS	National Institute of Certified College Planners	• Professional financial certification/designation (CFP, RFC, ChFC, CLU, CEP, RIA, etc.), or • Professional financial licensing (securities, insurance, accounting, etc.), or • A combination of education and experience deemed satisfactory by the NICCP Advisory Council • Completion of 3 self-study modules
Certified Divorce Financial Analyst	CDFA	The Institute for Divorce Financial Analysts	• 2 years' experience in the financial-services field • 4-module self-study course

Examinations	Website Information	Disciplinary/ Complaint Processes	Continuing Education or Other Ongoing Requirements
Final examination for 3 courses	www.icfs.com		15 hours every 2 years
2 final examinations 2 open-book case studies	www.icfs.com		15 hours every 2 years
3 final examinations, plus 2 open-book case studies	www.icfs.com		15 hours every 2 years
Final examination	www.anbc.com		
Final examination	www.annuityadvisor.org		
Final exam and open-book case study	www.icfs.com		15 hours every 2 years
Final certification exam	www.thewpi.org		12 hours every 2 years, plus recertification exam every 3 years
3 final examinations for each module	http://www.niccp.com		12 hours annually
Computer exam for modules 1,2, 3; open-book case study for module 4	www.instituteEDFA.com	Investor complaint process	20 hours every 2 years

Designation	Acronym	Organization Issuing Designation	Previous Experience/Educational Requirements
Certified Employee Benefit Specialist	CEBS	International Foundation of Employee Benefit Plans and Wharton School of the University of Pennsylvania	• 6 required courses and 2 electives from CEBS curriculum
Certified Estate Adviser	CEA	National Association of Financial and Estate Planning	• CPA, CFP, RIA, or professional license (attorney, securities, insurance, real estate) • Self-study course
Certified Estate Planner	CEP	National Institute of Certified Estate Planners	• Classroom or self-study course of 8 modules
Certified Financial Educator	CFE	Heartland Institute of Financial Education	• 3 years' experience in financial services industry and teaching or training experience • Completion of instructor-led or self-study CFE course
Certified Financial Planner	CFP	Certified Financial Planner Board of Standards, Inc.	• 3 years' personal financial planning experience and a bachelor's degree • Completion of a CFP board registered program, or holding the following: CPA, ChFC, CLU, CFA, PhD in business or economics, Doctor of Business Administration, attorney's license
Certified Funds Specialist	CFS	Institute of Business & Finance	• CFS course of 6 modules totaling 60 hours
Certified Investment Management Analyst	CIMA	Investment Management Consultants Association	• 3 years' professional consulting experience • No answers to all Form U-4 disclosure questions, or satisfactory justification of "yes" answer • 4- to 6-month self-study program and 1-week on-site or online course
Certified Investment Management Consultant	CIMC	Investment Management Consultants Association	No longer accepting new designees, replaced by CIMA designation in 2004
Certified Retirement Administrator	CRA	International Foundation for Retirement Education	• 3 years' professional experience within previous 5 years • Successful completion of the Certified Retirement Counselor course • Self-study course

Examinations	Website Information	Disciplinary/ Complaint Processes	Continuing Education or Other Ongoing Requirements
Computer-based test for each course	www.ifebp.org		
Online certification exam	www.nafep.com	Investor complaint process	
2 exams	www.nicep.org	Investor complaint process	8 hours every 2 years
Certification exam	www.hife-usa.org		12 hours annually
Final certification exam	www.cfp.net	Investor complaint process and public disciplinary process	30 hours every 2 years
Final exam and open-book case study	www.icfs.com		15 hours every 2 years
2 final certification exams	www.imca.org/certify		40 hours every 2 years
1 final exam or 4 separate exams	www.infre.org		15 hours annually

Designation	Acronym	Organization Issuing Designation	Previous Experience/Educational Requirements
Certified Retirement Counselor	CRC	International Foundation for Retirement Education	• 2 years' professional experience within previous 5 years • Self-study course
Certified Retirement Financial Adviser	CRFA	Society of Certified Retirement Financial Advisors	• Classroom course or self-study course
Certified Senior Advisor	CSA	Society for Certified Senior Advisors	• Classroom study or self-study
Certified Senior Consultant	CSC	Institute of Business & Finance	• Self-study course of 5 modules totaling 30 hours
Certified Tax Specialist	CTS	Institute of Business & Finance	• 60-hour self-study course
Certified Trust and Estate Planner	CTEP	American Academy of Financial Management	• 3 years' experience in estate planning and trusts • Completion of either: (1) AAFM-approved degree in finance, tax, accounting, financial services, law, or a CPA, MBA, MS, PhD, or JD from an accredited school or organization; (2) 5 or more approved courses from an accredited business school or AAFM-sanctioned program; or (3) AAFM Executive Certification course
Certified Trust and Financial Advisor	CTFA	Institute of Certified Bankers	• Candidates must either: (1) have 3 years' personal trust experience plus ICB training program; (2) 5 years' personal trust experience and a bachelor's degree; or (3) 10 years' personal trust experience
Certified Wealth Consultant	CWC	The Heritage Institute	• Attend and complete Advanced Practice Academy • 1-day personal sabbatical • 6-book reading list • Mentor a provisional CWC member • Complete 2 Heritage Process Cases • Create personal catalogue of 4 stories

Examinations	Website Information	Disciplinary/ Complaint Processes	Continuing Education or Other Ongoing Requirements
1 final exam or 4 separate exams	www.infre.org		15 hours annually
Proctored exam	www.crfa.us/index.php	Online investor complaint process	15 hours annually
Final certification exam	www.csa-csa.com	Investor complaint process	18 SCSA credits every 3 years
3 course exams	www.icfs.com		15 hours annually
3 final examinations and an open-book case study	www.icfs.com		15 hours every 2 years
Varies	www.financialanalyst.org	Investor complaint process	15 hours annually
Final certification exam	www.aba.com		45 hours every 3 years with a minimum of 6 hours in each of 4 knowledge areas
	www.theheritageinstitute.com		Attend at least 1 Advanced Practice Academy annually

Designation	Acronym	Organization Issuing Designation	Previous Experience/Educational Requirements
Certified Wealth Preservation Planner	CWPP	The Wealth Preservation Group	• 24-hour online or in-person course
Chartered Alternative Investment Analyst	CAIA	Chartered Alternative Investment Analyst Association	• BA or equivalent and 1 year's experience in financial industry, or 4 years' experience in financial industry • Self-study certification program
Chartered Asset Manager	CAM	American Academy of Financial Management	• 3 years' financial-planning experience in asset management and financial planning • Completion of a finance degree or concentration from one of 435 AAFM board-registered and recognized AACSB business schools worldwide or an MBA, CPA, CFA, PhD, DBA, Masters degree, or law degree from an accredited university or college along with relevant experience. Managers or executives may take our 5-day on-site executive training courses with exit exams.
Chartered Estate Planning Practitioner	CEPP	Estate Planning Institute	• Professional license in securities, insurance, accounting, legal, banking, real estate, social work • Completion of a self-study program of 3 segments
Chartered Financial Analyst	CFA	CFA Institute	• Candidate must have an undergraduate degree and 3 years' professional experience (4 years of qualified work experience after 2007) • 3 levels of self-study program course work entailing 250 hours each
Chartered Financial Consultant	ChFC	The American College	• 3 years' full-time personal finance or insurance experience • 5 core and 3 elective American College courses
Chartered Financial Engineer	ChFE	The Financial Engineering Institute, LLC	• 10 years' financial advisory experience • Professional license • Financial Engineering Institute training course

Examinations	Website Information	Disciplinary/ Complaint Processes	Continuing Education or Other Ongoing Requirements
Final certification exam	www.thewpi.org		24 hours every 2 years, open-book recertification exam every 3 years
2 final examinations	www.caia.org		
Varies, depending on how educational requirements were completed	www.financialanalyst.org		15 hours annually
3 final examinations	www.cepp-epi.com		8 credits every 2 years
3 final examinations	www.cfainstitute.org	Investor complaint process	
Final exams for each course	www.theamericancollege.edu		30 continuing education credits every 2 years
Final certification exam	www.theFEI.com www.financialalliance.net		20 hours every 2 years

Designation	Acronym	Organization Issuing Designation	Previous Experience/Educational Requirements	
Chartered Investment Counselor	CIC	The Investment Counsel Association of America	• Employed by ICAA member firm for 1 year • 5 years' work experience in eligible occupational position • Complete CFA exams and have CFA designation	
Chartered Mutual Fund Counselor	CMFC	College for Financial Planning	• Self-study course of 9 modules totaling 72–90 hours	
Chartered Portfolio Manager	CPM	American Academy of Financial Management	• 3 years' experience actively managing investment portfolios • Successful completion of either: (1) AAFM-approved degree, or a CPA, MBA, MS, PhD, or JD from an accredited school; (2) 5 or more approved and related courses from an accredited business school or AAFM-sanctioned program; or (3) AAFM Executive Certification training course	
Chartered Retirement Planning Counselor	CRPC	College for Financial Planning	• Self-study course of 11 modules totaling 88–110 hours	
Chartered Retirement Plans Specialist	CRPS	College for Financial Planning	• Self-study course of 11 modules totaling 88–110 hours	
Chartered Senior Financial Planner	CSFP	Association of Chartered Senior Financial Planners	• Licensed insurance agent • 3-day classroom course	
Chartered Wealth Manager	CWM	American Academy of Financial Management	• Completion of either: (1) AAFM-approved degree in finance, tax, accounting, financial services, law, or a CPA, MBA, MS, PhD, or JD from an accredited school or organization; (2) 5 or more approved courses from an accredited business school or AAFM-sanctioned program; or (3) AAFM Executive Certification course	

Examinations	Website Information	Disciplinary/ Complaint Processes	Continuing Education or Other Ongoing Requirements
	www.icaa.org/html/cicp.html		Annually certify that employed by an ICAA member firm in an eligible occupational position, and not subject to disciplinary proceedings
Final exam	www.cffp.edu		
Varies	www.financialanalyst.org		15 hours annually
Final certification exam	www.cffp.edu		
Final certification exam	www.cffp.edu		
Open book certification exam	www.acsfp.com	Investor complaint process	
Varies	www.financialanalyst.org	Investor complaint process	15 hours annually

Designation	Acronym	Organization Issuing Designation	Previous Experience/Educational Requirements	
Christian Financial Professionals Network Certified Member	CFPN	Christian Financial Professionals Network	• CFP, ChFC, CPA, CPA/PFS, EA, CFA, CLU, or JD or 10 years' full-time financial experience • Candidates must adhere to Christian beliefs, must believe in Jesus Christ, and sign a "Statement of Faith" • Completion of 3 CFPN training sessions	
Financial Risk Manager	FRM	Global Association of Risk Professionals	• GARP membership • Self-study course	
Master Financial Manager	MFM	American Academy of Financial Management	• Management experience as a financial manager; or completed an accredited college degree in finance, tax, accounting, or financial management or financial services; or CPA, JD, MBA, PhD, or Masters or other relevant degree • 3 or more years of financial management experience	
Personal Financial Specialist	PFS	The American Institute of Certified Public Accountants	• AICPA members • State-issued CPA certificate • Must earn 100 points under PFS point system • Business experience in personal financial planning related services	
Professional Plan Consultant	PPC	Financial Service Standards, LLC	• 3 years' retirement plan industry experience • 16-hour program	
Qualified Financial Planner	QFP	International Association of Qualified Financial Planners	• Candidate must hold ChFC, CFP, PFS designation or have an MS in financial planning or financial services • Educational requirement which varies based on the above	
Registered Business Analyst	RBA	American Academy of Financial Management	• 3 or more years of financial management experience • Completion of a finance degree or concentration from one of 435 AAFM board-registered and recognized AACSB business schools worldwide or an MBA, CPA, CFA, PhD, DBA, Masters degree, or law degree from an accredited university or college along with relevant experience. Managers or executives may take our 5-day on-site executive training courses with exit exams.	

Examinations	Website Information	Disciplinary/ Complaint Processes	Continuing Education or Other Ongoing Requirements
Certification exam	http://www.cfpn.org		15 hours annually
Computer-based certification exam	www.garp.com		
	www.financialanaylyst.org		15 hours annually
Fina certification exam	www.aicpa.org		60 PFS points in personal financial planning business and qualified activities every 3 years
Final certification exam	www.financialservicestandards.com	Investor complaint process	4 hours annually
Varies	www.iaqfp.org	Investor complaint filing process and public disciplinary process	30 hours every 2 years or 15 hours annually
Varies	www.financialanalyst.org		15 hours annually

Designation	Acronym	Organization Issuing Designation	Previous Experience/Educational Requirements
Registered Financial Associate	RFA	International Association of Registered Financial Consultants	• Bachelor's or graduate degree in financial planning or related area
Registered Financial Consultant	RFC	International Association of Registered Financial Consultants	• Undergraduate or graduate degree in financial planning, or have one of the following designations: AAMS, AEP, CEP, CFA, CFP, ChFC, CLU, EA, LUTC, MS, MBA, JD, PhD or CFP equivalent • If operating on a commission basis, must meet licensing requirements for securities and life and health insurance • If operating on a fee-only basis, and not licensed, then must be a registered investment adviser • 4 years' full time experience as a financial planning practitioner. • Completion of approved college curriculum in personal financial planning or IARFC self-study course
Registered Financial Gerontologist	RFG	American Institute of Financial Gerontology	• Existing financial background designation, license, degree, or experience • Completion of 8 hours of community-based service learning within 1 year of passing certification exam • Self-study program of 6 courses totaling 24 hours
Registered Financial Planner	RFP	Registered Financial Planners Institute	• For 2-year designation, 2 years' financial-planning experience • For 5-year designation, 5 years' financial-planning experience • 4-module self-study course of 70 hours or RFPI-approved classroom course
Registered Financial Specialist	RFS	American Academy of Financial Management	• 3 years' financial planning in asset management and financial-planning experience • Either: (1) AAFM-approved degree in finance, tax, accounting, financial services, law; (2) 5 or more approved courses from an accredited business school or AAFM-sanctioned program; or (3) AAFM Executive Certification training course

Examinations	Website Information	Disciplinary/ Complaint Processes	Continuing Education or Other Ongoing Requirements
	www.iarfc.org		40 hours annually
Final certification exam for IARFC self-study course	www.iarfc.org		40 hours annually
Final certification exam	www.aifg.org		8 hours continuing education plus 8 hours service learning annually
	www.rfpi.com		
Varies	www.financialanalyst.org	Investor complaint process	15 hours per year

Designation	Acronym	Organization Issuing Designation	Previous Experience/Educational Requirements	
Retirement Plans Associate	RPA	International Foundation of Employee Benefit Plans and Wharton School of the University of Pennsylvania	• Self-study, online, or classroom completion of Certified Employee Benefit Specialist courses	
Wealth Management Specialist	WMS	Kaplan University	• High school diploma or GED • Self-study course	

Examinations	Website Information	Disciplinary/ Complaint Processes	Continuing Education or Other Ongoing Requirements
Computer-based exams	www.ifebp.org		
Certification exam	www.kaplan.edu/ms/wmb2b		

Continuing Education Exam

for CFP Continuing Education Credit
and PACE Recertification Credit

EARN TWENTY HOURS of continuing education credit by passing the following exam on our website, http://www.bloomberg.com/ce, and entering code **RIA927**. The material covered has been previewed by the CFP Board of Standards.

CHAPTER 1: Terms and Acronyms

1. Which of the following is an "investment adviser" as defined under the Investment Advisers Act of 1940?

a. An accountant with an accounting practice who also regularly provides investment advice to clients and receives a separate fee for doing so

b. A publisher of financial publications of general and regular circulation

c. Someone who only gives advice, analyses, or reports on securities that are direct obligations of the United States

d. A registered representative of a brokerage firm who provides advisory services only within the scope of her employment with the brokerage firm and who does not have a separate, independent financial-planning business

CHAPTER 2: Federal and State Laws and Other Regulations

2. Advisers who register with the SEC are totally exempt from all state laws regulating securities and investment advisers.

a. True
b. False

CHAPTER 3: RIA Registration: What It Means, How It's Done

3. Which of the following must register with the SEC?

a. A lawyer who gives investment advice solely incidental to her practice of law

b. Someone whose regular business is giving investment advice for a fee, and who has $50 million in assets under management

c. A broker whose provision of investment advice is solely incidental to his business and who receives no fee for doing so

d. Someone whose regular business is providing investment advice for a fee and who has $15 million in assets under management

4. Which of the following is not required to register with the SEC?

a. An adviser with less than $25 million of assets under management who has a national practice with clients in more than thirty states

b. An adviser with less than $25 million in assets under management who advises clients exclusively over the Internet

c. An adviser with more than $30 million in assets under management whose principal business is in one state and who provides no advice regarding securities listed on a national exchange

d. An adviser whose principal place of business is in a state that has no securities regulatory authority

5. An adviser whose principal place of business is in the state of Connecticut has less than $25 million in assets under management. Almost all of the adviser's clients reside in Connecticut, except for one couple who moved to New Hampshire and retained the adviser as their investment adviser. The adviser must register

a. only with Connecticut's state securities regulator

b. only with the SEC

c. with the state securities regulators in both New Hampshire and Connecticut

CHAPTER 4: The Nuts and Bolts of Form ADV

6. Once Form ADV is filed with the SEC, anyone who wants to can get a copy of it.
a. True
b. False

7. An adviser who changes the legal name of the firm can wait until the annual updating amendment is due before amending Form ADV Parts 1 and 2.
a. True
b. False

CHAPTER 5: How to Complete Form ADV Part 1

8. When determining the number of clients for filling out Form ADV Part 1, advisers must count clients who do not compensate the adviser.
a. True
b. False

CHAPTER 6: How to Complete Form ADV Part 2

9. Advisers can charge clients fees that are different from those described in Form ADV Part 2 as long as the fees are separately described in the advisory contract with a statement stating that the fees differ from those described in Form ADV.
a. True
b. False

CHAPTER 7: RIA Compliance Programs and Codes of Ethics

10. Advisers may divide chief compliance officer duties among two or more people in the firm.
a. True
b. False

11. Once compliance programs are in place, advisers need to review them at least annually.

a. True

b. False

12. Advisers who belong to professional associations that have codes of ethics do not have to draft and implement codes of ethics for their firms.

a. True

b. False

13. Advisers must

a. offer all new clients a copy of their code of ethics

b. describe their code of ethics on Form ADV Part 2

c. give all clients annually a copy of their code of ethics

14. Advisers must

a. give all the firm's employees a copy of the firm's code of ethics as soon as they are hired

b. give all firm-supervised persons a copy of the firm's code of ethics and obtain written acknowledgment of receipt

c. provide a posting in employee workrooms that the firm has a code of ethics and inform employees where they may view it

15. Advisers must provide ethics training annually for all firm employees.

a. True

b. False

CHAPTER 9: Advisory Contracts and Fees

16. Advisers may charge clients performance fees that are based on a share of capital gains or capital appreciation of client funds

a. never

b. only when the client has at least $750,000 in assets under the adviser's management or at least $1.5 million in net worth

c. only if the client is a foreign national

d. only if the client is either a foreign national or has at least $750,000 in assets under the adviser's management

17. Advisers who charge fees up front can keep those fees if the advisory contract is canceled by the client before it expires.

a. True

b. False

18. Advisory contracts may not be assigned at any time without the client's consent, and advisers may not impose penalties on clients for termination before the contract expires.

a. True

b. False

CHAPTER 10: Custody of Customer Accounts

19. Advisers who are authorized to deduct only their own advisory fees from client accounts are not subject to the custody rules of the Investment Advisers Act of 1940.

a. True

b. False

CHAPTER 11: Selecting Brokers and Executing Trades

20. Advisers can take into consideration factors beyond just lowest price when executing client trades and still meet the duty of best execution.

a. True

b. False

21. When advisers execute client trades, they

a. are not required to disclose to clients the factors they use in determining best execution

b. are required to provide clients with a statement that they execute trades and have a fiduciary duty to get the best execution

c. are required to disclose on Form ADV Part 2 the factors they use to determine best execution

CHAPTER 12: Personal Securities Trading and Reporting

22. Advisers are required to set up procedures

a. requiring all employees to get preclearance on all personal investments in any equity or fixed-income investment

b. requiring only access persons to get preclearance on all personal investments in any equity or fixed-income investment

c. requiring only access persons to get preclearance on initial public offerings and private placements

d. requiring only owners and directors to get preclearance on all personal investments in any equity or fixed-income investment

23. Advisers are required to have all access persons file holding and transaction reports.

a. True

b. False

24. If the adviser designates a third party to receive and review securities holding and transaction reports, the firm's chief compliance officer is relieved of the duty to review securities holding and transaction reports.

a. True

b. False

CHAPTER 13: Voting Client Proxies

25. Advisers who have the authority to vote client proxies must always vote those proxies.

a. True

b. False

26. Advisers must disclose to clients their proxy voting policies and procedures and tell clients how they can obtain information about how the adviser voted the proxies.

a. True

b. False

CHAPTER 14: Record-Keeping Requirements

27. Advisers can hire a third-party record keeper to maintain all the books and records required to be maintained under the Investment Advisers Act of 1940.
a. True
b. False

CHAPTER 15: Advertising and Client Communications

28. Sending a blast e-mail to clients must comply with the advertising rules under the Investment Advisers Act of 1940.
a. True
b. False

29. An adviser can place an advertisement in a newspaper with a statement from a local minister, who was never a client, attesting that the adviser "is a good Christian."
a. True
b. False

30. When registered investment advisers advertise, which of the following is not allowed?
a. Statements from current clients that they are satisfied with the adviser's services
b. A list of current clients
c. Third-party ratings of advisers
d. All of the above

31. SEC-registered investment advisers must file copies of their advertisements with the SEC.
a. True
b. False

CHAPTER 16: Referrals

32. If an adviser pays for referrals, the only requirement is that the arrangement be disclosed on Form ADV Part 2.

a. True
b. False

CHAPTER 17: ERISA Plans

33. Providing that the client is not an ERISA plan, advisers may enter into any kind of soft-dollar arrangement as long as the fiduciary duties of best execution and loyalty are met and the arrangement is fully disclosed to clients.

a. True
b. False

CHAPTER 19: Protecting Clients' Privacy

34. Advisers who never disclose client information to unaffiliated third parties do not have to provide clients with privacy notices.

a. True
b. False

35. The adviser has provided clients with a reasonable opportunity to opt out of disclosure of personal information if

a. the adviser includes an opt-out reply form with the privacy notice

b. the adviser has a toll-free number the client can call to opt out

c. the adviser instructs the client to write and mail a letter to the adviser but provides no other way to opt out

d. a and b but not c

e. none of the above

Index

access persons, 79–80
accountants, as investment advisers, 5, 32–33
account statements, custody rules and, 98–99
advertisements (advertising)
  brochures, 137
  defined, 130–131
  false or misleading statements in, 131
  fiduciary responsibilities, 137
  Internet and e-mail, 136, 137–138
  model portfolios, 133–134
  past recommendations in, 135
  performance results in, 132–134
  record-keeping requirements, 127
  RIA designation, use of, 132
  rules, 131
  state laws, 135–136
  testimonials, use of, 131–132
advice
  for compensation, 8
  solely incidental, 6
adviser(s)
  charged, 10–11
  defined, 4
  designation requirements, 262–279

laws governing, 20–25
Advisers Act. *See* Investment Advisers Act
advisory affiliates, 10
advisory contracts. *See* contracts
advisory representative, 112
aggregate orders, 104
amending contracts, 94
amending Form ADV, 44, 47–50
American College, 17
annual updating amendment, 10, 47–50
antifraud provisions, 21
arbitration claims, 60
asset-based fees, 91
assets under management, 31–32
audits, 157
    See also SEC examinations and enforcement actions
    money laundering activities and, 190
authority
    discretionary, 12
    foreign financial regulatory, 12
    state securities, 17

Bank Holding Company Act (1956), 7
banks
    defined, 8–9
    as investment advisers, 7

best execution, 102–103, 165
blogs, 136
blue sky laws, 20
bonding requirements, 96
brokerage services, safe harbor
    rules and, 163–165
brokers
    best execution, 102–103, 165
    conflicts of interest, 103
    as investment advisers, 6, 32–
        33
    selecting, 102–103
    violations by, 105

Canadian securities regulators,
    contacting, 213–215
CCO. *See* chief compliance officer
central registration depository
    (CRD) number, 40
certified financial planner (CFP),
    17
certified public accountant (CPA),
    18
CFA. *See* chartered financial
    analyst
CFA Institute, 17
CFP. *See* certified financial
    planner
charged, 10–11
chartered financial analyst (CFA),
    17
chartered financial consultant
    (ChFC), 17
chartered life underwriter (CLU),
    17
ChFC. *See* chartered financial
    consultant
chief compliance officer (CCO),
    17, 74–77
client(s)

base, 67
confidentiality rules and SEC
    examinations, 200
as consumers, 172
covered by privacy rules, 172
as customers, 173
defined, 11
minimums, 70
money laundering and high-
    risk, 187–188
privacy, 172–184
CLU. *See* chartered life under-
    writer
code of ethics, 74, 79–82
confidential treatment, 200–201
conflicts of interest
    disclosure of sales and, 105–106
    fiduciary, 86
    Form ADV, Part 1, noting, 58
    Form ADV, Part 2 (brochure),
        noting, 69
    selecting brokers and, 103
    voting client proxies and, 119
consumers, clients as, 172
continuous supervisory or man-
    agement services, 31–32
contracts
    administrative issues in, 93
    amending, 94
    dispute resolution policies, 93
    fee schedule in, 92
    liability limitations, 93–94
    services explained in, 92–93
    termination of, 94
    termination of, and fees, 91
control, 11
CPA. *See* certified public accoun-
    tant
custody
    account statements, 98–99

automatic fee deduction and, 97
defined, 11–12, 96–97
independent representative, 99
qualified custodian, 97–98
rules, 97
customers, clients as, 173

dealers, as investment advisers, 6, 32–33
disclosure of sales, conflicts of interest and, 105–106
Disclosure Reporting Pages (DRPs), 64
disclosure requirements, 21
discretionary authority, 12
dispute resolution policies, in contracts, 93
diversification rule, 157
due diligence, money laundering activities and, 190

electronic filing of Form ADV, 40
e-mail
    advertising using, 136, 137–138
    correspondence, keeping, 126–127
employee(s)
    compensation, 58–59
    defined, 12
    supervising, 192–194
Employee Retirement Income Security Act. *See* ERISA
employee trades, reporting of, 111–115
engineers, as investment advisers, 5, 32–33
enjoined, 12
ERISA (Employee Retirement Income Security Act), 18
    fiduciary responsibilities and, 86–87, 155–156
    investment advice defined, 153–154
    investment manager defined, 154
    prudent investments and, 87
    purpose of, 23
ERISA plans
    assets, 148–150
    audits, 157
    bonded, 158–159
    defined, 148
    diversify investments rule, 157
    exclusive benefit rule, 158
    indemnity, 156
    indicia of ownership rule, 158
    plan documents rule, 157
    plans not protected, 149
    prohibited transaction exemptions, 151–153
    prohibited transactions, 150–151
    prudence rule, 157
    soft dollars and, 168–169
    trust requirement rule, 157–158
ethics, code of, 74, 79–82
examinations. *See* SEC examinations and enforcement actions
exclusive benefit rule, 158

family limited partnerships, 57
family members
    as clients, 55
    holding and transaction reports, 115

fees
  adviser fees disclosed on Form
      ADV, Part 2, 67
  asset-based, 91
  automatic deduction of, 92, 97
  calculating, 90
  contract/client termination
      and, 91
  for filing Form ADV, 41, 50
  mutual funds and management,
      91
  performance-based, 15–16,
      90–91
  retirement plans and, 92
  schedule of, in contracts, 93
  solicitation and cash referral,
      141–143
  structuring, 90
  up-front, 91
  wealthy or foreign clients, 91
felony, 12
fidelity bond, 158–159
fiduciary
  conflicts of interest, 86
  defined, 84–85
fiduciary responsibilities, 84–86
  advertising and, 137
  ERISA and, 86–87, 155–156
  voting client proxies and, 120
foreign financial regulatory
      authority, 12
foreign nationals, 61, 63
  fees and, 91
Form ADV
  accessing past filings, 40–41
  amending, 44, 47–50
  cross-referenced questions, 38,
      49
  electronic filing, 40
  exemptions, 41–43

filing, 38–50
  filing fees, 41, 50
  notice filings, 47
  paper version example of, 216–
      261
  purpose of, 33, 38
  signing, 46–47
  terms used on, 10–17, 39
Form ADV, Part 1
  arbitration claims, 60
  business description, 54–55
  client transactions, 58
  conflicts of interest, 58
  custody of client assets, 59
  disciplinary history, 60
  Disclosure Reporting Pages,
      64, 242–253
  employee compensation, 58–59
  family limited partnerships, 57
  financial industry affiliations,
      disclosing, 55–56
  firms with multiple offices, 53
  foreign nationals, 61, 63
  general partners, 57–58
  legal name of firm, 53
  off-site location of records,
      54
  ownership questions, 53, 59–
      60, 61–62
  paper version example of, 218–
      233
  private funds, 56–57, 63
  related investment advisers,
      disclosing, 56
  Schedule A, 61–62, 234
  Schedule B, 62–63, 235
  Schedule C, 63, 236
  Schedule D, 63–64, 237–241
  Schedule G, 261
  schedules, types of, 60

services to relatives or friends, 55
state registration, 54
trusts, 62
websites, 53–54
wrap fee program clients, 55
Form ADV, Part 2 (brochure)
balance sheet, 72
client base, 67
client minimums, 70
conflicts of interest, 69
disclosure of brokerage discretion, 69
explanations, 71–72
fees charged, 67
investment recommendations, 67–68
investment supervisory services, 67
paper version example of, 253–260
purpose of, 43–46, 66
qualifications needed by employees, 68–69
relationships with other firms, 69
review of accounts, 70
soft-dollar practices, 70–71
Form ADV-NR (nonresident), 46
Form U-4, 24
found, 13
Freedom of Information Act, 200–201
friends, as clients, 55

government entity, 13
Gramm-Leach-Bliley Financial Services Modernization Act (1999), 172

hedge clauses, 93–94
high-net-worth individual, 13
holding and transaction reports, 112–115
home state, 13

IARD. *See* Investment Adviser Registration Depository
impersonal investment advice, 13
indemnity, 156
independent representative, 99
indicia of ownership, 158
indirect owners, 62
initial public offerings, allocations of, 107
insider trading, 104–105
inspections, 21
International Association for Financial Planning (IAFP), 140
Internet
advertising using the, 136, 137–138
registration requirements for advisers who use the, 30–31
investment adviser, defined, 4–8
Investment Adviser Registration Depository (IARD), 18, 40
Investment Advisers Act (1940)
bank, defined by, 8–9
investment adviser, defined by, 4–8
issues covered by, 20–21
Rule 204A-1 (code of ethics), 74, 79–82
Rule 206(4)-7 (policies and procedures), 74–79
security, defined by, 9
supervised person, defined by, 9

investment advice, defined, 153–
154
Investment Company Act (1940),
purpose of, 22
investment manager, defined, 154
investment related, 13–14
investment supervisory services,
67
involved, 14

joint ownership, 61

lawyers, as investment advisers, 5,
32–33
legal names, 53
liability limitations, in contracts,
93–94
limited partnerships
family, 57
quarterly account statements
and, 99

management fees, 91
management persons, 14
managing agent, 14
Mexican securities regulators,
contacting, 215
minor rule violation, 14
misdemeanor, 14–15
model portfolio, advertisements
and, 133–134
money laundering
anti-money laundering program, basics, 186–187
audits, 190
clients, high-risk, 187–188
clients, screening of, 187
compliance officers, 189
defined, 186
due diligence, 190

monitoring for suspicious activities, 188–189
training to detect, 189
multiple offices, 53
mutual funds, management fees
and, 91

NASAA. See North American
Securities Administrators
Association
NASD. See National Association
of Securities Dealers
NASD CRD, 15
National Association of Securities
Dealers (NASD), 18
New York Stock Exchange
(NYSE), 18
no-action letters, 203–204
nonresident, 15
North American Securities
Administrators Association
(NASAA), 18, 20
notice filing, 15
NYSE. See New York Stock
Exchange

Office of Compliance Inspections
and Examinations. See SEC
examinations and enforce-
ment actions
off-site location for records, 54
opt-out rules, 176–177, 179–184
order, 15

penalties, failure to register, 35
performance-based fee, 15–16,
90–91
performance results in advertisements, 132–134
person, 16

personal information
   nonpublic, 173
   publicly available, 174
personally identifiable financial
   information
   defined, 713
   examples of, 173–174
personal trading
   disclosure and consent, 110–
     111
   preclearance of employee
     investments, 111
   prohibited practices, 110
   reporting of employee trades,
     111–115
policies and procedures
   chief compliance officer, 74–77
   objectives, 77
   record keeping, 78–79
   review of, 78
   supervising employees and, 193
   topics covered in, 78
preclearance of employee investments, 111
preexecution consent, 106–107
privacy
   notices, 174–179
   opt-out rules, 176–177, 179–
     184
   policies and procedures, 174
   protecting client, 172–184
private funds, 56–57, 63
proceedings, 16
proxies, voting client
   conflicts of interest, 119
   fiduciary rules, 120
   policies and procedures, 118–
     121
   record-keeping requirements,
     120–121

retirement plans, 119–120
prudence rule, 157
Public Company Accounting
   Oversight Board (PCAOB),
   23
publishers, as investment advisers,
   7, 32–33

record keeping
   advertisements and, 127
   code of ethics and type of, 82
   e-mail correspondence, 126–
     127
   of employee trades, 111–115
   forms of, 125–126
   length of time to maintain, 125
   location of, 125
   off-site location of, 54
   of policies and procedures,
     78–79
   solicitation and, 145
   third party, 126
   types of information in, 124–
     125
   voting client proxies and, 120–
     121
referrals. See solicitation
registered financial consultant
   (RFC), 18
registered investment adviser
   (RIA), defined, 4, 18
registered representatives, as
   investment advisers, 6,
   32–33
registration
   exemptions, 32–33
   penalties, 35
   procedures and changes, 33–35
   requirements, 20
   SEC versus state, 28–31

related person, 16
reportable securities, 112–113
reporting
    of employee trades, 111–115
    violations, 194
research services, safe harbor rules
    and, 163–165
retirement plan assets, fees and,
    92
retirement plans
    See also ERISA plans
    soft dollars and, 168–169
    voting client proxies and, 119–
    120
RFC. *See* registered financial con-
    sultant
RIA. *See* registered investment
    adviser
riskless principal transactions,
    166–167
Rule 204A-1. *See* code of ethics
Rule 206(4)-7. *See* policies and
    procedures

safe harbor rules, 162–168
Sarbanes-Oxley Act (2002), pur-
    pose of, 23
SEC (Securities and Exchange
    Commission)
    contacting, 205–206
    defined, 4, 18
    investment advisers defined by,
    7
    registration, 28–35
    Regulation S-P, 172
SEC examinations and enforce-
    ment actions
    client confidentiality rules, 200
    common problems found, 198–
    199

confidential treatment, 200–
    201
disciplinary/enforcement
    actions, types of, 202–203
documents, books, and records
    examined, 199–200
no-action letters, 203–204
periodic, routine, 197
preparation for, 200
for suspected wrongdoing,
    197–198
sweep, 198
types of, 196–197
who conducts examinations,
    196
Securities and Exchange Act
    (1934), purpose of, 21–22
Securities Industry Association
    (SIA), 18
securities portfolio, accounts as,
    31
securities transactions
    aggregate orders, 104
    allocations of initial public
    offerings, 107
    buying and selling between
    clients, 104
    disclosure of sales and conflicts
    of interest, 105–106
    insider trading, 104–105
    preexecution consent, 106–107
security, defined, 9
self-regulatory organization
    (SRO), 16–17
SIA. *See* Securities Industry
    Association
soft dollars, 70–71
    agreements with brokers, 165
    brokerage and research services,
    163–165

categories of, 162
defined, 162
disclosure of, 167–168
retirement plans, 168–169
riskless principal transactions,
    166–167
safe harbor rules, 162–168
SEC enforcement actions, 168
transactions not covered by safe
    harbor, 166
solicitation
    cash referral fees, 141–143
    defined, 140
    disclosure for referrals, 144
    free research for, 144
    record-keeping requirements,
        145
    supervision of solicitors, 144
    written agreements, 143
solo practitioners, 34–35
sponsor, 17
state securities authority, 17
    contacting, 206–213
state securities laws
    advertising and, 135–136
    clients in several states, 30
    investment adviser defined by,
        8
    issues covered by, 23–25
    registration, 28–35, 54
supervised person, defined, 9, 79
supervising employees, 192–194
supervisor, defined, 192–193

teachers, as investment advisers,
    5–6, 32–33
termination
    contract, 94
    contract and fees, 91
trusts, 62, 157–158

U.S. government obligations,
    investment advisers and, 7

voting proxies. *See* proxies, voting
    client

wealthy clients, fees and, 91
websites
    disclosing, 53–54
    notices on, 178
wrap fee program, 17
    reporting number of clients, 55

About Bloomberg

Bloomberg L.P., founded in 1981, is a global information services, news, and media company. Headquartered in New York, the company has sales and news operations worldwide.

Bloomberg, serving customers on six continents, holds a unique position within the financial services industry by providing an unparalleled range of features in a single package known as the BLOOMBERG PROFESSIONAL® service. By addressing the demand for investment performance and efficiency through an exceptional combination of information, analytic, electronic trading, and Straight Through Processing tools, Bloomberg has built a worldwide customer base of corporations, issuers, financial intermediaries, and institutional investors.

BLOOMBERG NEWS®, founded in 1990, provides stories and columns on business, general news, politics, and sports to leading newspapers and magazines throughout the world. BLOOMBERG TELEVISION®, a 24-hour business and financial news network, is produced and distributed globally in seven languages. BLOOMBERG RADIO℠ is an international radio network anchored by flagship station BLOOMBERG® 1130 (WBBR-AM) in New York.

In addition to the BLOOMBERG PRESS® line of books, Bloomberg publishes *BLOOMBERG MARKETS®* magazine. To learn more about Bloomberg, call a sales representative at:

London:	+44-20-7330-7500
New York:	+1-212-318-2000
Tokyo:	+81-3-3201-8900

FOR IN-DEPTH MARKET INFORMATION and news, visit the Bloomberg website at **www.bloomberg.com**, which draws from the news and power of the BLOOMBERG PROFESSIONAL® service and Bloomberg's host of media products to provide high-quality news and information in multiple languages on stocks, bonds, currencies, and commodities.

About the Author

Elayne Robertson Demby, JD, is a nationally recognized journalist. Trained as an attorney, she is sought out for stories that break down complex legal material into simple, understandable English for the layman. Demby has worked in a number of prestigious New York law firms, including Proskauer Rose Goetz & Mendelsohn and Paul, Weiss, Rifkind, Wharton & Garrison.

In her work as a journalist, she specializes in business and legal issues such as securities law, tax law, finance, executive compensation, financial planning, human resources, retirement plans, health and welfare plans, corporate governance, nonprofits, collections and credit, and risk management. Demby's work has been published in numerous consumer and trade outlets, including the *New York Times*, WSJ.com, *Crain's New York Business, Bloomberg Wealth Manager* magazine, *Human Resource Executive, CFO* magazine, *Plansponsor* magazine, *Advisor Today* magazine, *Collections & Credit Risk* magazine, *Treasury & Risk Management* magazine, *Wealth Manager* magazine, and *Global Custodian.* After receiving her BA in economics from Boston University, magna cum laude, Demby received a JD from Fordham University's School of Law and an LLM in taxation law from New York University School of Law.